Money, Trade and Finance

Ioanna T. Kokores
Pantelis Pantelidis
Theodore Pelagidis • Demetrius Yannelis
Editors

Money, Trade and Finance

Recent Trends and Methodological Issues

palgrave
macmillan

Editors
Ioanna T. Kokores
Department of Economics
University of Piraeus
Piraeus, Greece

Pantelis Pantelidis
Department of Economics
University of Piraeus
Piraeus, Greece

Theodore Pelagidis
Bank of Greece, Athens, Greece

Department of Maritime Studies
University of Piraeus
Piraeus, Greece

Brookings Institution
Washington, DC, USA

Demetrius Yannelis
Department of Economics
University of Piraeus
Piraeus, Greece

ISBN 978-3-030-73218-9 ISBN 978-3-030-73219-6 (eBook)
https://doi.org/10.1007/978-3-030-73219-6

This Palgrave Macmillan imprint is published by the registered company Springer Nature Switzerland AG.
The registered company address is: Gewerbestrasse 11, 6330 Cham, Switzerland

Preface and Acknowledgements

The aim of this volume has been to honor *Professor Sophocles Brissimis*, a distinguished member of the Professors Emeriti of the Department of Economics, University of Piraeus, Greece, and former director-advisor of the Economic Research Department of the Bank of Greece. Prof. Brissimis graduated from the Athens School of Economics and Business Sciences (1971). He holds a Ph.D. in Economics from the University of Edinburgh (1976). He held an appointment as a professor in the Department of International and European Economic Studies of the Athens University of Economics and Business from 1993 to 2000. He then joined the Department of Economics of the University of Piraeus as a professor until 2015. In parallel with his academic journey, Prof. Brissimis has been with the Bank of Greece since 1976, where he was appointed as a director-advisor in the Economic Research Department for more than a decade. He has served on expert committees in Greece, the European Central Bank, and the European Union, and his research has been published in top-tier journals in the fields of international and monetary economics and banking.

While in academia and in the monetary authority, his twofold main contribution has been in terms of both high-quality research expertise and cordial professional comportment. His guidance to doctorate students, young academics, and researchers has been genuine, rigorous, attentive, and incessant. He combined a penetrating view on the specialized research advancements, the concurrent monetary policy agenda, and the unrelenting financial market practices, with a remarkable serenity and clarity in exposing his educated view. He, thus, provided a stimulus to many of us who, at all stages of scientific expertise, strive to acquire and maintain a more perceptive view of the complex mechanisms leading to a more efficient resource allocation.

Many thanks must go to all the scholars who contributed their research papers to the volume, both for their intellectually stimulating academic research and for their sincere effort to honor our fellow economist. We are also grateful to the two anonymous reviewers who provided helpful comments on the proposed volume along with their approval for publication. We are grateful to Taxiarchis Kokores (Ph.D. Econ) for his helpful suggestions and valuable comments throughout the undertaking of this project. We extent sincere thanks to the General Assembly members of the Department of Economics, University of Piraeus, under the chairmanship of Professor Demetrius Yannelis, for their applause and endorsement of the project at the initial stage. Finally, we owe a debt of gratitude to our publisher; Ruth Jenner, the commissioning editor, and Palgrave Macmillan's, and Springer Nature's editorial team, at all stages of publication, provided their ample, cordial support, and guidance.

The Editorial Committee

Editors: Ioanna T. Kokores,
Assistant Professor University of Piraeus, Greece
Pantelis Pantelidis,
Professor and Vice Rector University of Piraeus, Greece
Theodore Pelagidis,
Deputy Governor Bank of Greece, Greece; Professor University of Piraeus, Greece
Demetrius Yannelis
Professor University of Piraeus, Greece

Associate editors: Angelos Kanas
Professor University of Piraeus, Greece
Claire Economidou
Professor University of Piraeus, Greece
Konstantinos Eleftheriou
Associate Professor University of Piraeus, Greece

Contents

Notes on Contributors

Eleni Athanasiou Senior Analyst Alpha Bank Greece, Retail Banking Credit Risk Division, Greece

Zacharias G. Bragoudakis Senior Economist and Head of the Forecasting Section, Economic Analysis and Research Department, Bank of Greece, Greece; Visiting Professor Department of Economics, National and Kapodistrian University of Athens, Greece

Yannis Dendramis Assistant Professor Department of Economics, Athens University of Economics and Business, Greece

George S. Donatos Professor Emeritus, Department of Economics, University of Athens, Greece

Konstantinos Eleftheriou is an Associate Professor in the Department of Economics at the University of Piraeus, Greece

Dimitris A. Georgoutsos Professor Department of Accounting and Finance, Athens University of Economics and Business, Greece

Sarantis Kalyvitis Professor Department of International European and Economic Studies, Athens University of Economics and Business, Greece; Director Laboratory of International Economic Relations AUEB (LINER-AUEB)

Angelos Kanas Professor Department of Economics University of Piraeus, Greece; Scientific Committee, Parliamentary Budget Office, Hellenic Parliament, Athens, Greece

Margarita Katsimi Professor Department of International and European Economic Studies, Athens University of Economics and Business; Laboratory of International Economic Relations AUEB (LINER-AUEB), Athens, Greece; Research Fellow, CESifo

Ioanna T. Kokores Assistant Professor Department of Economics, University of Piraeus, Greece

Thomas I. Kounitis Data Scientist eBay Analytics, Zurich, Switzerland

Marina Kyriakou Ph.D. candidate Department of Business Administration, University of Piraeus, Greece

George C. Michailidis Professor and Director of the Informatics Institute at the University of Florida, USA

Michael Mitsopoulos Director of Business Environment and Regulatory Affairs, SEV Hellenic Federation of Enterprises, Greece

Stelios Th. Panagiotou Economist, Economic Analysis and Research Department, Bank of Greece, Greece; Department of Shipping, Trade and Transport, University of the Aegean, Chios, Greece

Pantelis Pantelidis Vice Rector and Professor Department of Economics, University of Piraeus, Greece

Sotiris K. Papaioannou Senior Research Fellow, Centre of Planning and Economic Research (KEPE), Athens, Greece

Theodore Pelagidis Deputy Governor Bank of Greece, Athens, Greece; Professor Department of Maritime Studies, University of Piraeus, Greece; NR Senior Fellow Brookings Institution, USA (ended 17/09/2020)

Michael L. Polemis Associate Professor Department of Economics, University of Piraeus, Greece; Hellenic Competition Commission, Athens, Greece

Helen A. Thanopoulou Professor Department of Shipping, Trade and Transport University of the Aegean, Greece; Honorary Visiting Professor Bayes Business School (formerly Cass), City, University of London, UK

Dikaios Tserkezos Professor Department of Economics and Business, Neapolis University Paphos, Cyprus; General Secretary Greek Econometric Institute

Markos Tsogas Assistant Professor Department of Business Administration, University of Piraeus, Greece

Elias Tzavalis Professor Department of Economics, Athens University of Economics and Business, Greece

Petros Varthalitis Assistant Professor Department of Economics, Athens University of Economics and Business, Greece

Demetrius Yannelis Professor Department of Economics, University of Piraeus, Greece

List of Figures

List of Tables

CHAPTER 1

Introduction

Ioanna T. Kokores and Konstantinos Eleftheriou

The law of business cycles dictates the inevitability of recessions. In terms of location, recessions can be either global, such as the financial crisis of 2007, or regional, such as Argentina's 2001 economic and financial crisis. Recessions can be triggered either by endogenous factors (e.g., European Periphery Debt Crisis) or by exogenous factors (e.g., the current COVID-19 pandemic). The high level of global economic integration leads to the fast transmission of local economic crises, yet also to the enhanced stimulus of efficient resource allocation in terms of both relative price changes and effective value chain advancements. The main channels of these spillovers are financial and trade linkages. Specifically, according to the seminal account of Frankel and Rose (1998) trade partners with more intense trade flows have correlated business cycles, whereas, for example, Kodres and Pritsker (2002) highlight in a prime attempt of a now-vast and growing literature, the role of investors' adjustment of

I. T. Kokores (✉)
Department of Economics, University of Piraeus, Piraeus, Greece
e-mail: ikokores@unipi.gr

K. Eleftheriou
Department of Economics, University of Piraeus, Piraeus, Greece

I. T. Kokores et al. (eds.), *Money, Trade and Finance*,
https://doi.org/10.1007/978-3-030-73219-6_1

portfolios' exposures in the transmission of idiosyncratic shocks. Within the above context, understanding how international trade is affected by the characteristics of the labor market and the expansion strategies of firms and how financial markets impact the macroeconomic environment (indisputably, the function of financial markets is vital for the development of international trade) is of crucial importance for policymakers. Moreover, the role of the environment in ensuring sustainable growth and the characteristics of the corporate landscape should also be considered. Of equal importance is the examination of the effectiveness of fiscal and monetary policy in smoothing the intensity of business cycles.

The present volume, titled *Money, Trade and Finance: Recent Trends and Methodological Issues*, attempts to shed some light on the above issues by presenting a collection of chapters divided into the following six parts: (1) liquidity, trade flows and international factor mobility, (2) corporate landscape advancement, (3) trends in policy analysis, (4) financial markets and the macroeconomy, (5) trends in econometric methodology and (6) international business—expansion and environmental issues.

In the first chapter in Part I, Chapter 2, Kokores, Pantelidis and Yannelis investigate the evolution of investment funding practices in the European Common Currency Area in the aftermath of the Global Financial Crisis and the European Sovereign Debt Crisis. They examine the effect on bilateral Intra-Eurozone (EZ) foreign direct investment (FDI) posed by the evolving regulation on financial integration in the Eurozone and the resurgent shift in bank competition. They disentangle the impact of regional asymmetries among EZ member countries by estimating treatment effects of macroprudential and monetary policy interventions on Intra-EZ FDI in both an unmatched and a matched sample of 12 EZ member countries using standard bipartite matching methods, namely matching by propensity score estimation and the Mahalanobis distance metric. Kokores, Pantelidis and Yannelis find that lower bank competition has a significant positive impact on Intra-EZ FDI. Furthermore, they assess whether a complementarity exists between financial integration, measured by a proxy reflecting the cost of interbank funds denominated in the same (common) currency, and bank competition, proxied by the Lerner index. Their results report a significant level of reverse causation between treatments, yet at a varied degree among core and periphery EZ countries.

The second chapter in Part I, Chapter 3, by Kalyvitis and Katsimi, presents a set of empirical regularities that characterize the activity of Greek exporters. Kalyvitis and Katsimi decompose firm-level exports by their margins (numbers of products and destinations, export values, quantities, prices) and relate them to skilled relative to unskilled employment and wages, and financial conditions. Their findings corroborate main motivating facts from existing studies on the role of quality for firm heterogeneity in international trade.

Part II also consists of two chapters. In the first chapter, Chapter 4, Mitsopoulos and Pelagidis focus on the deficiency of Greece regarding its manufacturing base and its relation with a series of facts that show how in a changing world a balanced corporate landscape is directly related with key dimensions of governance and institutional quality, as well as the efficiency of public policies like education. They argue that only with the establishment of a balanced corporate landscape Greece will be able to prosper, and this can only be achieved with progress on all fronts. A more prominent role for those "making things" is strongly correlated with the creation of such a balanced landscape, as they are more strongly affected by the strengths of weaknesses of the institutions and regulatory quality of a country. An attempt to move Greece in such direction will, in turn, require a close cooperation between the public and private sector. Getting all these issues right needs to happen at the same time. Piecemeal advances will not suffice to ensure the desired results.

In the second chapter of Part II, Chapter 5, Bragoudakis, Panagiotou and Thanopoulou focus on the receipts from shipping services as a vital resource for the Greek economy in covering a perennial trade deficit. The downward adjustment in freight rates, following the Lehman brothers collapse, was swift impacting severely on Greek shipping inflows into the country. Almost two years later, Greece, facing a debt crisis, had to agree to an economic adjustment program with its institutional lenders. In the process, country risk rose to record levels, peaking around the two successive national elections of 2012. The banking sector survived minimum confidence only through the increase of central bank financing; this included emergency liquidity assistance of about €140 billion. Against this backdrop, concerns were voiced about the sustainability of Greek shipping inflows. Bragoudakis, Panagiotou and Thanopoulou investigate both the long- and short-term determinants of shipping inflows in the Greek balance of payments throughout this turbulent period marked by high freight market volatility by using an error correction framework (ECM). They next assess the impact of the country-specific risk on monthly shipping inflows.

The third part deals with fiscal and monetary policy issues in two distinct chapters. Specifically, in Chapter 6, Papaioannou analyzes if the growth influence of fiscal policy can be affected by business cycle conditions. Markov Switching regression results are reported on quarterly data for five peripheral EU countries (Spain, Italy, Portugal, Ireland and Cyprus) and show us that the effects of public spending on growth are asymmetric over the business cycle. The highest influence on growth is observed when the output gap is low or negative. On the contrary, in periods of high and positive output gaps, the impact of public spending remains weak or even becomes negative.

On the other hand, in Chapter 7, Kokores and Kanas assess whether monetary policymakers follow systemic risk in adjusting monetary policy for the United States over a period spanning from 1960 to 2011. They evaluate the reactions of monetary policy variables during the corresponding periods of high and low systemic risk. The authors estimate a threshold Vector Autoregressive (VAR) model and provide evidence that U.S. monetary policy is affected by systemic risk measured by CATFIN, proposed by Allen et al. (2012). This effect is asymmetric between periods of high systemic risk and periods of low systemic risk. The threshold value of CATFIN is in the area of 0.048–0.054. Their results support the monitoring of CATFIN by the monetary authorities, as an effective proxy of financial fragility to be included in the monetary policy strategy.

In the first chapter of Part IV, Chapter 8, Dendramis, Tzavalis, Varthalitis and Athanasiou investigate the ability of loan-specific and macroeconomic covariates to predict the probability of default (PD) using a large micro data set of loan accounts consisting of restructured and non-restructured loans. They seek to investigate whether differences in the PD between the two categories of loans can be attributed to moral hazard effects. The authors provide clear-cut evidence that the PD of consumer loans and expected default rates are higher for the restructured than the nonrestructured loans. They also show that loan-specific covariates, reflecting behavioral attitudes of borrowers in consumer loan markets, constitutes relatively more important determinants of the PD changes than the macro-economic covariates. This result is more striking for the restructured loans. They find that the ratio of delinquent amount of a loan over its total balance constitutes the most influential factor of the PD. This result is more intense on the restructured loans category. Dendramis, Tzavalis, Varthalitis and Athanasiou argue that the latter can be mostly attributed to moral hazard incentives of borrowers. On the other hand, they show that the ratio of a loan's payments to the personal income of its obligor can signal reductions in the PD. Finally, they argue that this ratio signals the commitment of borrowers without moral hazard incentives to service their debt.

In the second chapter of Part IV, Chapter 9, Georgoutsos and Kounitis deal with the dynamic relationship between term and credit spreads within a framework that incorporates regime shifts. Through the estimation of an asymmetric Markov-Switching Vector Equilibrium Correction Model (MS-VECM), comprising the short- and long-term risk-free rate and the Moody's Baa-rated bond rate, they arrive at three basic results. First, the short-run relationship between credit and term spreads is regime dependent, being negative and significant during low volatility periods only and in the presence of an inverted yield curve. Second, through an impulse response analysis, it is established that the response of credit spreads to a given change in the term spread depends on the rate, short or long-term, that has caused this change. Third, a probit analysis reveals that the credit spread is a useful predictor of future economic recessions, both at a six-month and a one-year-ahead horizon, and that this result is valid even in the presence of the term spread variable.

Part V covers econometric methodological issues. In particular, in Chapter 10, Donatos and Michailidis study the sample properties of the least squares (LS) and ridge estimators (and predictors) for alternative models of heteroscedasticity at various levels of multicollinearity, under normal and nonnormal disturbances with small and large variances. Their simulation study shows that when the regression coefficient vector β is aligned to the normalized eigenvector corresponding to the largest eigenvalue of the $X'X$ matrix, the GCV estimator in almost all cases is superior to the other estimators examined in their study; on the other hand, when β is aligned to the normalized eigenvector corresponding to the smallest eigenvalue of the $X'X$ matrix, the ranking of the estimators does not follow a clear pattern for all the examined specifications. They also "confirm" that the LS estimator exhibits a poor performance independent of the level of multicollinearity for all the examined criteria with the notable exception of that multiple correlation coefficient. Finally, the authors note that the behavior of the estimators considered in their study is very sensitive to the choice of both the disturbance distribution and the functional distribution from heteroscedasticity.

Tserkezos, in Chapter 11, focuses on the stationarity properties of a time series as a crucial aspect of empirical research. Specifically, he examines the effects of temporal aggregation on the power properties of the

Augmented Dickey Fuller t-test (ADF) stationarity test developed by Dickey and Fuller (1979). The conducted Monte Carlo simulation experiments show that the use of temporally aggregated data seriously affects the power of the ADF t-test to detect stationarity.

Finally, in Part VI, Chapter 12, Polemis reexamines the Environmental Kuznets Curve Hypothesis using a balanced panel of pollutants (CO_2, SO_2 and NOx emissions per capita) drawn from the electricity sector of 51 U.S. regions covering the period 1990–2012. The empirical findings indicate a strong evidence of nonlinear cointegrated relationships between local (SO_2 and NO_X) and global (CO_2) emissions generated in the electricity sector with the level of economic growth. The dynamic Panel-VAR results using impulse response functions and variance decomposition support the validity of these findings further. These results call for the need to strengthen the effectiveness of environmental degradation policies by ensuring sustainability of the electricity sector in order to drastically reduce global and local pollutants.

In the last chapter of Part VI, Chapter 13, Kyriakou and Tsogas attempt to define a typology of international expansion strategies accounting for antecedents (potentially conscious or subconscious) that influence exports marketing managers' decisions, thereby formulating a new theoretical framework to bridge the current theory—practice gap in international expansion. Based on the dimensions of the internationalization path, their study defines a typology of strategic alternatives which depicts how a firm's expansion to international markets relates to the number of markets and to the time frame of internationalization. The authors postulate a typology of firms' strategic expansion and approach to international markets that is influenced by product's factors, firm's dynamism and innovativeness, firm's approach to markets, firm's strength of dominance and level of foreign market development.

The views expressed in each chapter are only of the contributing authors' and should not be associated with the official views of their affiliated institutions.

References

Allen, L., T. G. Bali, and Y. Tang (2012). Does Systemic Risk in the Financial Sector Predict Future Economic Downturns?, *Review of Financial Studies*, 25(10), 3000–3036.

Dickey, D. A. and W. A. Fuller (1979). Distribution of the Estimators for Autoregressive Time-series with a Unit Root. *Journal of the American Statistical Association,* 74, 427–431.

Frankel, J.A., Rose, A.K. (1998). The Endogeneity of the Optimum Currency Area Criteria. *Economic Journal* 108(449), 1009–1025.

Kodres, L. E., Pritsker, M. (2002). A Rational Expectations Model of Financial Contagion. *Journal of Finance* 57, 769–799.

PART I

Liquidity, Trade Flows and International Factor Mobility

CHAPTER 2

Financial Integration, Bank Competition and Intra-Eurozone Foreign Direct Investment

Ioanna T. Kokores, Pantelis Pantelidis, and Demetrius Yannelis

1 Introduction and Overview

Corporate investment can be financed through equity, bank/financial intermediaries' capital, or direct investment, and is affected by the level of economy-wide liquidity provision, business potential and macroeconomic prospects. In this analysis, we investigate the evolution of investment funding practices in the European Common Currency Area (Eurozone) in the aftermath of the Global Financial Crisis and the European Sovereign Debt Crisis. We examine the effect on bilateral Intra-Eurozone foreign direct investment (FDI) posed by the evolving regulatory stance on financial integration in the Eurozone (EZ) and the resurgent shift in bank competition.

I. T. Kokores (✉) • P. Pantelidis • D. Yannelis
Department of Economics, University of Piraeus, Piraeus, Greece
e-mail: ikokores@unipi.gr

I. T. Kokores et al. (eds.), *Money, Trade and Finance*,
https://doi.org/10.1007/978-3-030-73219-6_2

FDI by a legal entity (corporate or physical) is the acquisition of a (minority)[1] fraction of the physical assets of a company that resides in a foreign country with operating control residing with the parent corporation. Being distinct from portfolio investment in a foreign entity, FDI is justified in obtaining a 'lasting interest' in a company resident in another country (IMF 2008a).[2] In fact, FDI levels, in the EZ and globally, have been the first indicators of economic recovery to bounce back after the global financial crisis and the Eurozone sovereign debt crisis. According to the European Union (EU) statistical service Eurostat, during 2009–2012, inward and outward EU member country FDI rose by about 40%, apparently justifying European Commission's "Call for immediate action for a 'European Industrial Renaissance'" at the time (European Commission 2014).

Investment funding is primarily driven by current practices and economic potential[3] of both the investment initiating and the investment acquiring entity, as well as the underlying macroeconomic context and competing funding practices. Since our aim is to analyse the flow of FDI inside the EZ, we need to investigate the extent that euro financial market practices and context affect FDI among EZ member countries.

The extant literature on FDI determinants gives ample evidence on the effects of a common currency union formation (see, for example, De Sousa and Lochard 2011; Pantelidis et al. 2014) and of varied overall institutional arrangements (see, for example, Walsh and Yu 2010). However—to our knowledge—it does not address the effect posed by the prevailing financial market structure and regulatory context as confounding factors. Di Giovanni (2005) points towards the importance of the prevailing financial structure in the choice of FDI by multinational enterprises, estimating a 'gravity type' model, yet not in the context of a currency union. The analysis yields a positive but not significant effect of credit to GDP on the choice of FDI. Therefore, in our analysis we address

[1] According to International Monetary Fund (IMF) definition, a direct investment relationship is created when an enterprise resident in one economy owns *10%* or more of the *ordinary shares* or *voting power* for an incorporated enterprise that is resident in another economy. For a foreign unincorporated enterprise, the fraction of operating control is estimated accordingly (IMF 2008b: 4).

[2] In this manner, 'Direct investment' comprises both the initial transaction that establishes the relationship between the investor and the enterprise and, in addition, all subsequent transactions between them and among affiliated enterprises, incorporated and/or unincorporated (IMF BPM5, par. 359: 86).

[3] Preferably over a long-term horizon, see, for example, McKinsey & Co (2020).

the effect on FDI in the European common currency area posed by both the main competing form of investment (namely channelled through the banking sector) and by the regulatory context that affects the latter, that is, the degree and distinct features of financial market integration.

In particular, we analyse bilateral FDI flows among EZ countries in an effort to grasp a clearer view on prevailing EZ financial imbalances. In the era antecedent to the global financial crisis, the EZ *as a whole* ran a current account balance with the rest of the world however (as became apparent in the brink of the crisis) with prominent internal financial imbalances.[4] In their early influential account, Blanchard and Giavazzi (2002) argued on how increased financial integration caused savings investments correlations to fall at the outset of the monetary union. In the years that followed, capital flows seemed to have been stirring those internal EZ imbalances driven by domestic distortions and capital misallocation (see, for example, Lane 2006; Zemenek et al. 2009; Berger and Nitsch 2010).

Portes (2014) notably remarks that the so-called EZ periphery countries (namely Greece, Ireland, Portugal, Spain—GIPS) had sound fiscal positions but were running large current account deficits *within* the monetary union, which were financed by equally large capital flows from the surplus countries. He further notes: "Unlike the United States, however, the GIPS were not 'free spenders'—Ireland and Spain had housing booms, but they and Greece all saw a fall in consumption as a share of GDP and a rise in the investment share during 2000–2007 (the investment share fell slightly in Portugal). And unlike China, the capital flows from Germany and some other countries, like France, came primarily from banks—they were private, not official, flows" (Portes 2014: 425).

Furthermore, under frictionless market integration, there should be no relation between domestic saving and investment. Flows of domestic saving would depend on worldwide (or to the greatest extent, Intra-EZ) saving opportunities, and domestic investment would be financed by the worldwide (or, equivalently, Intra-EZ) pool of savings. However, if domestic saving is to a greater extent reinvested in the country of origin, then differences among countries in saving rates should correspond to differences in investment rates. This phenomenon is referred to as the so-called 'home bias', which has been rather projected in post–global financial crisis private and sovereign debt markets, particularly in the periphery

[4] See, for example, Chen, Milesi-Ferretti and Tressel (2012).

countries severely affected by the crisis (see, for example, Battistini et al. 2013; Hobza and Zeugner 2014).

However, as Vivar et al. (2020) demonstrate, among EZ countries the home bias in investment fund holdings is to a great extent lower than suggested in the pertinent literature, due to a misspecification in the way to address (and, eventually, measure) the investment origin. They suggest that investment origin is defined by the fund's domicile rather than the fund holder's country of residence. They highlight that euro area investors put the majority of their assets in funds domiciled in euro area financial centres, and these funds invest in more diversified portfolios than funds domiciled in other euro area countries, contributing to a lower home bias across euro area investors, yet, to our conjecture, giving an impetus to further stir the aforementioned asymmetries.

Therefore, in an attempt to analyse investment flows across the EZ, we consider it imperative to make an account of the inherent euro area regional asymmetries. We, thus, disentangle the impact of regional asymmetries among EZ member countries by attempting to estimate *implicit* treatment effects of macroprudential and monetary policy interventions on Intra-EZ FDI. We observe both an unmatched and a matched sample of 12 EZ member countries using standard bipartite matching methods, namely matching by propensity score estimation and the Mahalanobis distance metric. To our knowledge, our analysis, using a method commonly employed in evaluation research, makes a contribution to the extant pertinent literature on both Intra-EZ FDI determinants and on the euro area–wide economic effects posed by bank competition and financial (fragmentation or) integration[5] in the EZ financial sector.

In a similar fashion, Zhou (2020) uses multiple treatment propensity score matching to estimate the concurrent effect of outward FDI and export levels on the productivity of manufacturing firms using data from the Chinese market. For the pivotal role of propensity score estimation in observational studies for causal effects, see, for example, Rosenbaum and Rubin (1983). Abadie and Imbens (2016) derive the large sample distribution of propensity score matching estimators, while, for an exposition of the common method of multivariate matching based on the Mahalanobis distance, see, for example, Cohran and Rubin (1973) and Rubin (1980). For a combination of the two methods, so as to ripe the benefits provided

[5]The concept of financial fragmentation as opposed to financial integration is not always addressed in a mutually exclusive manner.

by each (i.e. minimizing both the discrepancy along the propensity scores and minimizing the distance between the individual coordinates of the observable covariates), see, for example, Rosenbaum and Rubin (1985).

Our results demonstrate that lower bank competition in the euro area has a significant positive impact on Intra-EZ FDI. Furthermore, we assess whether a complementarity exists between financial integration, measured by a proxy reflecting the cost of interbank funds denominated in the same (common) currency, and bank competition, proxied by the Lerner index. Our results report a significant level of reverse causation between treatments, yet at a varied degree among core and periphery EZ countries. The analysis proceeds as follows. Section 2 describes the analytical method exploited, and Sect. 3 provides details on the data used. Section 4 is an exposition and discussion of the results of our analysis, and Sect. 5 concludes.

2 Methodology

We empirically address the effects on Intra-EZ FDI posed by the common EZ monetary and macroprudential policy interventions in the manner of *implicit* 'treatment' assignments to 'treated' and 'non-treated' or 'control' groups that may have large differences in their observed covariates. These differences may lead to biased estimates of the 'treatment' or policy intervention effects.

Monetary and macroprudential policy interventions are addressed in an implicit manner, that is, in terms of the *liquidity provision* in the EZ through the actions of both the monetary authority and the workings of financial intermediaries (domestic and cross-border). At normal times, money created by the central bank and the banking system are perfect substitutes, while at times of financial crisis doubts arise about the 'liquidity' of money created through credit provision by financial intermediaries, which does not constitute legal tender (and thus can be refused in the settlement of debt). Therefore, at times of financial crises, payments settlement breaks down calling for an ad hoc monetary authority intervention to facilitate liquidity provision. In this manner, financial sector practices and the corresponding monetary authority reaction alter both the concurrent investment sentiment and financial market expectations of economic prospects, eventually affecting both financial intermediaries' corporate strategies and the monetary authority's stance in the conduct of monetary policy.[6] In an effort to eventuate in more muted (less destabilizing) reactions by both the financial sector and the monetary authority, policymakers point towards the establishment of more efficient financial market practices. Therefore, instead of addressing macroprudential and monetary policy interventions per se, we view the combined effects posed by the evolving regulatory stance on financial integration in the Eurozone EZ and the resurgent shift in bank competition.

We attempt to address financial integration through balances in TARGET2, the Eurosystem's real-time gross settlement system for euro-denominated large value payments in central bank money. Financial integration in our analysis is, thus, proxied in terms of the quantity-based indicators that tend to be constructed from data on cross-border stock and flows of financial investments (see, for example, Baltzer et al. 2008). Such measures are based on the premise that an efficient interbank money market is essential for the stability of the financial system, as a whole, and plays a critical role in the transmission of monetary policy. Additionally, since our proxy of financial integration, namely the accumulation of TARGET2 claims or liabilities, is interest bearing (see, for example, Sinn and Wollmershäuser 2012: 470), it also tends to reflect fluctuations in the *cost* of interbank funds denominated in the same (common) currency; the latter being a (price-based) measure of financial integration as, for example, in Laeven and Tressel (2014: 52, 63).

TARGET2 balances constitute Intra-Eurosystem claims and liabilities of Euro Area National Central Banks (vis-à-vis the ECB) that arise from net cross-border payment flows in the form of central bank reserves, which are executed through TARGET2. In the Eurosystem's real-time gross settlement system, payments are settled individually and with instant finality (irrevocably) in real time.

[6] Similar results, also, arise by private and public payment-system competition with respect to collateralized intraday (and overnight) overdrafts to wholesale money market participants. Even at normal times, the cost of collateral requirements, both within individual national payment systems and through the use of securities of foreign governments as collateral (subject to pertinent central bank regulatory requirements), may alter the portfolio allocation of financial intermediaries participating in the payment system (see, for example, Kahn 2013). Equivalently, the resulting Financial Collateral Arrangements Directive issued by the European Parliament and Council (2002/47/EC June 6, and further amended) contains further provisions on the enforceability of collateral arrangements (as regards linked systems and credit claims) in order to limit contagion effects in the event of default by a participant in the Financial Market Infrastructures.

Prevailing imbalances in TARGET2 net transactions started to rise in the outset of the global financial crisis, during the European debt crisis, and as a result of the ECB's launch of the asset purchase programme in 2015 (which provided additional monetary accommodation at times when interest rates have been at levels too low to be exploited as a tool for the conduct of monetary policy). TARGET2 imbalances are indicative of the levels of excess liquidity at the Eurosystem level. Even though they are not a direct measure of stress in the financial system and, thus, should not be a call for concern (per se),[7] we contend that they may reflect the level of financial integration and the presence of (inherent and, at times, prevailing) arbitrage opportunities among EZ goods, services and financial asset markets. Such imbalances may not exist, unless due to differences reflecting net (EZ) cross-border trade not matched by investment flows in the opposite direction. For example, according to the exposition and theoretical construct of Steinkamp et al. (2018), an increase in bad loan rollover (an effect known as 'evergreening') should be correlated with an increase of monetary refinancing operations and TARGET2 liabilities. In view of the above argumentation and subject to data availability, we use TARGET2 balances of Eurosystem participating National Central Banks as a proxy of financial integration.

Our proxy of the second 'treatment' indicator, namely bank competition, is the Lerner index, which is a direct measure of market power in the banking market. It is based on the 'new empirical industrial organization' literature (see, for example, Appelbaum 1982; Roberts 1984; Alexander 1988), which contrasts the Structure-Conduct-Performance paradigm, and takes account of the concept of market contestability (for seminal contributions see Baumol et al. 1982; Baumol and Willig 1986; Brock 1983), that is prevalent in contemporary banking sectors. In contestable markets, bank behaviour is determined by the threat of entry and exit. Hence, irrespective of even high levels of market concentration, banks are urged to adhere to projected competition in an industry facing low entry

[7] In October 2008, as a response to the collapse of interbank markets (after the Lehman failure), the Eurosystem launched the introduction of fixed rate full allotment tender procedures in all refinancing operations, thus abandoning central bank reserve provision quantity controls. Due to the underlying tension in terms of banks' access to market funding across the euro area, the Eurosystem fully accommodated the resurgent banks' aggregate demand for reserves, subject to (*sufficient*) *eligible* collateral availability (see, for example, ECB 2013). Increased intermediation of the Eurosystem in bank funding so as to maintain price stability in the medium term thus gave rise to large TARGET balances.

restrictions on new banks and easy exit conditions for unprofitable institutions.

The Lerner index is a bank-level non-structural indicator of bank competition, defined as the difference between output prices and marginal costs (relative to prices). Prices are calculated as total bank revenue over assets, while marginal costs are obtained from an estimated translog cost function with respect to output. Higher values of the Lerner index indicate less bank competition (for the Index estimation's methodology see Demirgüç-Kunt and Martínez Pería 2010).

The proxies of EZ financial integration and of Intra-EZ bank competition are, thus, addressed in our analysis as 'treatment' assignments, implicit of macroprudential and monetary policy interventions. 'Periphery' EZ economies are viewed as the 'treatment' group, while the remaining 'core' EZ countries are considered as the 'control' group. Common EZ monetary and macroprudential policy interventions are addressed to all EZ member countries. However, inherent regional asymmetries hamper the efficient transmission of policy, thus resulting in varied ultimate policy effects. This discrepancy justifies our distinction of a 'treatment' and 'control' group of EZ member countries.

We use standard bipartite matching methods for the estimation of causal effects on Intra-EZ FDI individually generated by multiple treatments. In particular, so as to eliminate observable differences between treated and untreated country pairs, we use the generalized propensity score (GPS) and the Mahalanobis distance metric in the double (individual) treatment setting, as in Lechner (2001), Scotina and Gutman (2019) and Zhou (2020). In this manner, we identify the causal effects on Intra-EZ FDI without strong assumptions on functional forms about the selection on observables, while, however, ensuring a high degree of comparability of matched units. The de facto clustering of the sample, in treatment and control groups, is by geographic context and overall country economic performance of the sample 'individuals' (i.e. EZ member countries), which coincides with (rather homogeneous) cluster-specific common patterns in each group (i.e. EZ 'core' and 'periphery' countries). For example, EZ periphery countries have—each one individually—recently experienced an era of a country 'tailor-made' austerity programme. Similarly, EZ core countries are the domicile of euro-area financial centres and tend to be dominant EZ providers mainly in the manufacturing and services sectors.

The two matching methods employed are widely used to address selection bias (caused by the 'treatment status' being determined by the individual behaviour that depends on the potential outcomes). The methods employed are the propensity score matching and matching based on the Mahalanobis[8] distance metric, since it performs adequately in contexts similar to our analysis, namely with less than eight covariates and for continuous covariates following a near normal distribution (see, for example, Gu and Rosenbaum 1993). In our analysis that seeks to evaluate how macroprudential and monetary policy interventions in the EZ affect, through their impact on the levels of EZ member countries' financial integration and bank competition, the EZ-based firms' choice of FDI among EZ member countries, selection bias applies to the firm's decision on which country to place a (potentially) long-lasting investment. EZ member countries form economies that operate in a unified framework, but are inherently asymmetric with respect to infrastructure, factor endowments and economic precedence and potential. Investment decisions are, thus, concurrently affected by both policy interventions.

A fundamental problem of causal inference applies, in that one cannot observe an individual (EZ member country economy) under *each* of the multiple treatments being compared, but observe *only* what happens to an individual (EZ member country economy) under the treatment (policy intervention) condition they *actually* received. Hence our choice of method, in that propensity score and Mahalanobis metric matching controls for the selection on both observables and unobservables.

The propensity score (PS) is a conditional probability of being treated given the covariates and is used to balance the covariates in the treatment and control groups, so as to reduce bias. In a random sample, as in our analysis, the PS assignment mechanism is the probability for each unit to

[8]The Mahalanobis distance metric has been commonly used as it mitigates the obvious limitation of the Euclidean distance (used as a matching metric) in terms of the latter's sensitivity to the correlation structure of the covariates (see, for example, Krzanowski 2000), also giving credence to the varied scientific contribution of Pransanta Chandra Mahalanobis (1893–1972), Officer of the Order of the British Empire, Fellow of the Royal Society (UK), Fellow of the Indian Academy of Sciences, Fellow of the Econometric Society (US), Fellow of the American Statistical Association (US), Weldon memorial prize winner University of Oxford, Honorary Fellow Cambridge University, Foreign member of the Academy of Sciences (USSR) (among other).

receive one treatment. Following standard notation,[9] let $W_i \in \mathfrak{M} = \{1,\ldots,Z\}$ denote the treatment group identification for unit $i = \{1, \ldots, n\}$ for Z possible treatment groups (with Z=2 in our analysis, separately addressed), where n_w denotes the size of the treatment group w, such that $\sum_{w=1}^{Z} n_w = n$, and T_{iw} is the treatment indicator function, which—for binary treatment variables (as in our analysis)—equals to one when the individual unit i participates to treatment, that is, $W_i = w$, and is equal to zero otherwise. Furthermore, let $\mathfrak{Y}_i = \{Y_i(1),\ldots,Y_i(Z)\}$ be the set of potential outcomes for unit i, where $Y_i(w)$ is the potential outcome for unit i, if it were exposed to treatment w. In practice, only the potential outcome corresponding to the intervention that affected unit i is observed. Under the stable unit treatment value assumption (that there is no interference between units and no different versions of a treatment, Rubin 1980a), the observed outcome for unit i (outward bilateral FDI levels for a country pair) is $Y_i^{obs} = T_{i1} Y_i(w)$.[10]

In order to make causal inference, we use variables that are not per se affected by the treatment; these are the covariates X_i. Then, under the unconfoundness assumption,[11] the assignment mechanism, namely the probability of each unit to receive one of the treatments, is defined as follows:

$$P(W_i = w \mid X_i, \mathfrak{Y}_i, \phi) = P(W_i = w \mid X_i, \phi) \equiv r(w, X_i), \text{for all } i = 1,\ldots,n,$$

where $r(w, X_i)$ is the propensity score of unit i for treatment w, and ϕ is a vector parameter governing the PS distribution and is probabilistic subject to the (sufficient) overlap[12] condition

$$0 < P(W = w \mid X_i, \mathfrak{Y}) < 1, \text{ for all } w$$

[9] Notation is, for example, as in Scotina and Gutman (2019) [setting the treatment (status) variable, D, equal with the treatment instrument, Z].

[10] Under outcome estimation in the concurrent treatment context, the observed outcome is affected by each individual unit's exposure to *each* treatment, namely $Y_i^{obs} = T_{i1} Y_i(1) + \ldots + T_{iZ} Y_i(Z)$.

[11] The 'unconfoundness' assumption states that there is no unmeasured confounding and is a *weak* conditional independence assumption (in fact, it is a conditional mean independence assumption), and that each potential outcome is independent of the treatment conditional on the covariates, yet only in the control group. The former assumption suffices for the estimation of the Average Treatment Effects on the Treated (ATT).

[12] The sufficient overlap assumption implies that no values of pretreatment covariates exist, which could occur only among units receiving one of the treatments.

A linear generalized PS distance measure is used in our treatment setting (comparing only one component at a time) defined, in terms of a multinomial logit estimation of the generalized PS, as follows:

$$\left|\text{logit}\left[r\left(w,\mathrm{X}_i\right)\right]-\text{logit}\left[r\left(w,\mathrm{X}_j\right)\right]\right|,\ i\neq j\in\{1,\ldots,n\},\ \text{and}\ w\in\{1,\ldots,Z\}.$$

Additionally, the Mahalanobis distance metric used in our analysis is the distance between two vector $\mathrm{V}_i = (v_{i1}, \ldots, v_{iP})$ and $\mathrm{V}_j = (v_{j1}, \ldots, v_{jP})$ of the vector of original covariates (and, equivalently, the untransformed estimated PS vector), and is of the form

$$\left\{\left(\mathrm{V}_i-\mathrm{V}_j\right)^{\mathrm{T}}\overset{-1}{\Sigma}\left(\mathrm{V}_i-\mathrm{V}_j\right)\right\}^{\frac{1}{2}},$$

where we use an estimate of the unknown Σ, the covariance matrix of V_i.

We may individually extract causal effect estimands as functions of the unit (EZ member country)-level potential outcome (on Intra-EZ FDI) on a common set of units. The estimands under consideration are pairwise average treatment effects between each treatment, that is, lower degree of bank competition (a higher level for the Lerner index) *or* a lower degree of financial integration (the accumulation of EZ country national central bank liabilities with the ECB). we address both treatment variables as binary (please refer to Table 2.1 for details on our construction of each binary treatment variable).

We estimate the population average treatment effects (ATE) and population average treatment effects of the treated (ATT) after balancing our original sample with the matched sample under *each* of the dual treatments of financial integration and bank competition separately. In this manner, in the original (unmatched) sample we account for the existence of regional asymmetries in the Eurozone clustered among a group of 'core' versus a group of 'periphery' countries. In the matched sample, and upon assessment of the balance effected in the sample, the inherent asymmetries (generating the confounding variables data generating processes) remain with respect to the covariates in total. ATT finds the effect of treatment of interest only on those units that received that treatment. To compute ATT one needs an estimate of the counterfactual outcome of the treated individual units under no treatment. As the latter outcome is not

Table 2.1 Variable definitions and sources

Variable	*Definition*	*Data Sources*
Outcome variable		
Intra Eurozone foreign direct investment (FDI)	Bilateral (outward) FDI measured in stocks	OECD (BMD3, and BMD4)
Covariates: Independent variables outcome model specification		
GDP (home)	FDI-*home* country real gross domestic product	European Central Bank, statistical data warehouse and AMECO annual macro-economic database, European Commission directorate general of economic and financial affairs
GDP (host)	FDI-*host* country real gross domestic product	European Central Bank, statistical data warehouse and AMECO
Openness to trade (host)	Indicator constructed by the sum of intra–European Union trade flows (exports plus imports) over host country GDP	European Central Bank, statistical data warehouse and AMECO
Instrumental variables outcome model specification		
Leverage ratio (LR) (home) and (host)	Ratio depicting how much money a bank can lend relative to how much capital it devotes to its assets. Consolidated banking data per EZ member country comprising data from domestic banking groups and stand-alone banks, foreign- (EU and non-EU) controlled subsidiaries and foreign- (EU and non-EU) controlled branches. Full sample reporting framework.	European Central Bank, statistical data warehouse

Table 2.1 (continued)

Variable	*Definition*	*Data Sources*
OIS rate [three-month]	Rate on three-month Overnight Indexed Swap (OIS) contracts; over-the-counter trade derivatives where each counterparty exchanges floating and fixed interest rate payments, the former being the overnight interbank rate, a measure of actual (de facto) monetary policy stance. OIS rates are considered to reflect monetary policy expectations (see, for example, Christensen and Rudebusch, 2012).	European money markets institute
Treatments		
TARGET balances	Intra-Eurosystem claims and liabilities of euro area National Central Banks (NCBs) [Vis-à-Vis the ECB] that arise from net cross-border payment flows in the form of central bank reserves, which are executed through TARGET2, the Eurosystem's real-time gross settlement system. Binary treatment variable constructed by assigning the value 1 *below* an (arbitrary) threshold value of—€78 billion, and zero otherwise (following Sinn and Wollmershäuser (2012) seminal account, p. 485) to account for the accumulation of TARGET2 liabilities.	European Central Bank, statistical data warehouse
Lerner index	Bank-level non-structural indicator of bank competition, defined as the difference between output prices and marginal costs (relative to prices). Prices are calculated as total bank revenue over assets, while marginal costs are obtained from an estimated translog cost function with respect to output. Higher values of the Lerner index indicate less bank competition. Index estimation methodology as in Demirgüç-Kunt and Martínez Pería (2010). Binary treatment variable constructed by assigning value 1 *above* an (arbitrary) threshold value of 0.15, and zero otherwise.	Bankscope and Orbis Bank focus, bureau van Dijk

observable, the PS method matches treated group individual units ('periphery' EZ countries) with control group individual units ('core' EZ countries) with similar propensity scores conditional on the covariates.

The ATE of treatment t relative to no treatment is the comparison of mean outcomes had the entire population been observed under the (respective) treatment, versus had the entire population been observed under no treatment. ATEs are estimated following $\tau \equiv E[\Upsilon(t) - \Upsilon(0)]$, where expectation is taken over the entire population. Equivalently, ATTs are defined as $\tau^t \equiv E[(\Upsilon(t)|T = 1) - (\Upsilon(t)|T = 0)]$, where expectation is taken over the treated group.

To implement the above methodological approach, we estimate a log-linear model of the outcomes, namely bilateral FDI among EZ countries, in a standard manner as in the pertinent literature; for a review on FDI determinants, see Bloningen (2005). For expositional ease, we address outward FDI (stocks) from EZ core countries to both EZ core and periphery countries. The explanatory variables in the multinomial logit regression that estimates the propensity score include the following, other than bilateral outward Intra-EZ FDI: the logarithm of FDI home-country real GDP, the logarithm of FDI host country real GDP, host country openness to trade, the three-month Overnight Indexed Swap rate, and a (representative) (bank) leverage ratio.

In particular, since our aim is to decipher trends in investment funding practices in the European common currency area, we add a common determinant, namely the logarithm of FDI home- (and host-) country real GDP to account for the size of the economy in the country that generates (receives) the investment. The effect of trade on FDI is uncontested and evidenced by the fact that FDI host country 'openness to trade', measured as the ratio of international trade (both exports and imports) to (nominal) gross domestic product (GDP) of the FDI host country, is widely used in the empirical literature on FDI determinants. Trade openness of an economy demonstrates that a country's integration to the world market is associated with both export orientation and a liberal attitude towards imports. Bloningen and Piger (2014), using a Bayesian Model Averaging selection method among several FDI determinants, find little support for the inclusion of multilateral trade openness in an FDI estimation. However, Kokores et al. (2017) find strong support of the latter using both single-equation estimation methods and Structural Equation Model estimation. We, therefore, include a term of trade openness in the FDI equation used in our method.

We also address shifts in macroprudential regulation (reflected in bank leverage ratios reached in response to Capital Requirements Regulations and amendments) and monetary policy interventions (conventional and unconventional). They are viewed through the very short end of the monetary transmission mechanism instead of the policy intervention per se, to account for the inherent inefficiencies in the channels of the common monetary policy transmission in the EZ due to both financial fragmentation spanning the EZ as a whole and the presence of inherent regional asymmetries. We, therefore, add as *instruments* to our FDI model two variables related to macroprudential regulation and monetary policy (ad hoc and rule-based) interventions. The instruments themselves do not belong in the 'structural' explanatory equation (hence—to our knowledge—the extant literature refrains from such a model estimation), but are correlated with the explanatory variables, conditionally on the value of other covariates. We use the three-month Overnight Indexed Swap (OIS) rate as a financial-market-based indicator of monetary policy expectations (as, for example, in Christensen and Rudebusch 2012, for the unconventional monetary policy stance) and a leverage ratio as the instrument on shifts in macroprudential regulation. The FDI instrument inclusion in our model to an extent follows Di Giovanni (2005), and it estimates an FDI model while incorporating the determinants of domestic credit provided by the banking sector in the FDI host country (as % of GDP), [in addition to host country (stock) market capitalization, namely market capitalization of listed companies (as % of GDP)].

3 Data

We use an unbalanced dataset of 12 EZ countries spanning from 2008 to 2015, with ultimately monthly frequency, subject to data availability. We define (de facto) groups of EZ 'core' and 'periphery' countries for the 12 EZ member countries in our sample. The latter are selected in that they participated in the EZ as 'initial' members since 2002. The group of EZ 'periphery' countries consists of the countries of the 'European South' that went under austerity programmes at varied stages of the Eurozone sovereign debt crisis, namely Greece, Ireland, Portugal and Spain, also including Italy. The group of EZ 'core' countries comprises of the rest of the pool of initial EZ members, that is, Austria, Belgium, Finland, France, Germany, Luxembourg and the Netherlands. Table 2.2 reports the descriptive statistics for each variable with respect to EZ periphery country ('treatment') group and the EZ core country ('control') group.

The dataset comprises of annual bilateral outward FDI (stocks by 11 partner EZ countries) (directional principle) that spans from May 2008 to December 2015 included. The sample potentially contains 11.132 observations, that is, from 121 FDI EZ country pairs spanning over 7.5 years

Table 2.2 Descriptive statistics

Variable	*Eurozone periphery countries*					*Eurozone core countries*				
	Obs.	*Mean*	*Std.dev.*	*Min*	*Max*	*Obs.*	*Mean*	*Std.dev.*	*Min*	*Max*
Intra-Eurozone foreign direct investment (outward, home)	–	–	–	–	–	3125	2407.592	6638.753	-14,574	61,644.7
Intra-Eurozone foreign direct investment (outward, host)	1780	1178.08	3247.926	-7517	16,075	1345	4034.752	9155.792	-14,574	61,644.7
GDP (home)	–	–	–	–	–	5152	999.357	942.57	36.268	3025.9
GDP (host)	2944	406.399	381.382	166.1575	1116.21	5152	999.357	942.57	36.268	3025.9
Openness to trade (host)	2944	0.3443	0.12	0.17	0.499	1932	0.729	0.359	0.296	1.323
Leverage ratio (home)	–	–	–	–	–	4144	0.1474	0.0798	-0.067	0.288
Leverage ratio (host)	2852	16.762	5.843	7.8237	50.46	4144	0.1474	0.0798	-0.067	0.288
OIS rate (three-month)	2944	0.6162	1.033	-0.2354	4.329	2944	0.6162	1.033	-0.2354	4.329
TARGET2 balances	2949	-86,543.3	79,530.89	-434,428	-429.25	5152	43,538.26	173,586.6	-411,595	843,439.2
Lerner index	1616	0.2324	0.107	-0.0136	0.3904	4144	0.1474	0.0798	-0.067	0.288
TARGET2 balances (binary)	2944	0.375	0.4842	0	1	5152	0.1046	0.306	0	1
Lerner index (binary)	2944	0.4294	0.4950	0	1	5152	0.3804	0.486	0	1

Notes: Each variable in the full (unmatched) sample potentially contains 8096 observations clustered in 88 country groups (i=8, j=11), each of which contains 92 monthly observations for each year from 2008 (May) to 2015 inclusive. Values in FDI, GDP and TARGET2 balances reported in million euros (overall 92 months). FDI data from 2008 to 2015 are extracted from the OECD benchmark definition third and fourth edition (OECD 2016). Annual data on per country GDP and Trade openness are provided by the ECB's Statistical Data Warehouse and the Annual Macro-Economic database of the European Commission's Directorate General for Economic and Financial Affairs (AMECO). Monthly data on the three-month OIS are extracted by the European Money Markets Institute, and values of a representative leverage ratio are provided on a quarterly frequency by ECB's Statistical Data Warehouse from 2007 to 2015 [since 2013, under European Banking Authority's technical standards on reporting and information disclosure (Capital Requirements Regulation No. 575/2013 and further amendments, as regards the leverage ratio)]. Monthly data on TARGET balances (per country of analysis), since May 2008, are extracted from ECB's Statistical Data Warehouse, and the data used to estimate annual levels of the Lerner Index for each country in our analysis are provided by Bureau van Dijk (Bankscope and Orbis Bank Focus) from 2008 to 2014.

4 Empirical Results

Our results are reported in Table 2.3. The causal estimands of our model are (population) ATE and ATET for each treatment individually, using respectively a propensity score matching estimator and a nearest-neighbour matching estimator. The latter uses the Mahalanobis distance metric (see Sect. 2) to match each treatment group participant with the *single* closest possible control group participant.

In the propensity score matching model, on average core country outward FDI is higher by approximately €813 million in EZ countries with more concentrated banking sectors. ATE is statistically significant at the 5% statistical significance level (s.s.l.). Additionally, on average core country outward FDI is higher by about €1050 million in EZ periphery countries with more concentrated banking sectors; ATET is statistically significant at 10% s.s.l. Addressing the accumulation of TARGET2 liabilities as the treatment indicator variable, by the estimated (population) ATE we may deduce that on average core country outward FDI is higher by approximately €993 million in EZ countries with higher accumulation of TARGET2 liabilities. ATE is statistically significant at 10% s.s.l. Furthermore, on average core country outward FDI is higher by about

Table 2.3 Causal estimands: Population average treatment effects (ATE) and average treatment effects on the treated (ATT)

	Propensity score matching		*Nearest neighbour matching (by Mahalanobis distance metric)*	
	ATE	*ATT*	*ATE*	*ATT*
Treatment				
Financial integration: TARGET2 liability accumulation	992.2198* (538.0984)	145.7027 (305.1145)	-562.9754*** (168.3281)	475.9671** (170.4213)
Bank competition: Lerner index	812.9672** (300.9825)	1049.946* (551.729)	638.3486*** (146.1622)	2270.573*** (249.8564)

Notes: Robust Standard Errors reported in parentheses, (* denotes $p<0.10$, ** denotes p<0.05, *** denotes p<0.01)

€146 million in EZ periphery countries with higher accumulation of TARGET2 liabilities. ATET statistically insignificant.

In the nearest neighbour matching (by the Mahalanobis distance metric) model, our results, when 'lower bank competition' is the treatment indicator, demonstrate that on average core country outward FDI is higher by approximately €638 million in EZ countries with more concentrated banking sectors; ATE is statistically significant at 1% s.s.l. On average, core country outward FDI is higher by €2270 million in EZ periphery countries with more concentrated banking sectors. ATET is statistically significant at 1% s.s.l. Finally, viewing the 'accumulation of TARGET2 liabilities' as the treatment indicator, we report that on average core country outward FDI is *lower* by €563 million in EZ countries with higher accumulation of TARGET2 liabilities. The estimated ATE is statistically significant at 1% s.s.l. However, in a contradicting manner, according to the estimated ATET in this case, on average core country outward FDI is higher by approximately €476 million in EZ periphery countries with higher accumulation of TARGET2 liabilities; ATET is statistically significant at the 5% s.s.l.

A summary assessing the covariates balance is provided in Tables 2.4a and 2.4b. A near balance is reported for the 'Lower bank competition' treatment in Table 2.4a, since a *perfectly* balanced covariate yields a standardized difference of zero and a variance ratio of one. Table 2.4a reports covariate balance assessments for the model of propensity score matching

Table 2.4a Balance assessment: Propensity score matching

	Propensity score matching							
			Observations		*Standardized differences*		*Variance ratio*	
			Raw	*Matched*	*Raw*	*Matched*	*Raw*	*Matched*
Treatment								
Financial integration: TARGET2 liability accumulation								
		No. of obs	3032	1250				
		Treated obs	625	625				
		Control obs	2407	625				
	Covariates							
	Lerner index				-0.2316115	0.0208241	0.8790165	1.017747
	GDP (home)				0.109404	-0.141066	1.043791	0.9926004
	GDP (host)				0.6609399	-0.2502948	2.925996	0.8124352
	Trade (host)				-0.6852394	0.0099389	0.6066577	1.642728
	OIS_3m				-0.2276818	-0.4545335	0.3275302	0.4149869
	LR (host)				0.2326602	0.3489386	3.127025	6.611622
	LR (home)				-0.0345884	-0.3640331	0.8184678	0.6464034
Bank competition: Lerner index								
		No. of obs	3032	6064				
		Treated obs	1208	3032				
		Control obs	1824	3032				
	Covariates							
	TARGET2				-0.1905971	0.2106553	0.7472202	1.293013
	GDP (home)				-0.1131809	-0.1031169	0.869059	0.9026045

Propensity score matching						
	Observations		*Standardized differences*		*Variance ratio*	
	Raw	*Matched*	*Raw*	*Matched*	*Raw*	*Matched*
GDP (host)			0.2500256	0.1243825	2.241342	1.877658
Trade (host)			0.3674576	-0.0274494	1.398995	0.8356855
OIS_3m			0.1078844	-0.0247907	0.8528899	0.569303
LR (host)			0.1276335	-0.0733227	0.2550535	0.3378808
LR (home)			-0.0525156	-0.0126482	1.002777	0.9614866

Table 2.4b Balance assessment: Nearest neighbour matching (by Mahalanobis distance metric)

	Nearest neighbour matching (by Mahalanobis distance metric)							
			Observations		*Standardized differences*		*Variance ratio*	
			Raw	*Matched*	*Raw*	*Matched*	*Raw*	*Matched*
Treatment								
Financial integration: TARGET2 liability accumulation								
		No. of obs	3124	1364				
		Treated obs	682	682				
		Control obs	2442	682				
	Covariates							
	Lerner index				-0.162688	-0.0608933	0.9299444	0.9664102
	GDP (home)				0.0357337	-0.0124158	1.043327	1.012507
	GDP (host)				0.7370817	-0.0144916	2.715454	0.9431496
	Trade (host)				0.7011737	0.0291592	0.5607194	1.108742
	OIS_3m				0.2685365	-0.1983314	0.3068503	0.9680612
	LR (home)				-0.0150338	-0.1203605	0.7674756	0.8818131
Bank competition: Lerner index								
		No. of obs	3124	2576				
		Treated obs	1288	1288				
		Control obs	1836	1288				
	Covariates							
	TARGET2				-0.1362812	-0.0489607	0.8257201	0.9274052
	GDP (home)				-0.1643178	-0.1451035	0.8618391	0.8794437
	GDP (host)				0.357207	-0.0100878	2.483915	1.04482
	Trade (host)				0.3108204	0.0671668	1.387055	1.155986
	OIS_3m				0.1143068	0.1092717	0.8637218	0.9168469
	LR (home)				0.0029786	-0.0566359	1.017258	0.95113

for the 'TARGET2 liability accumulation' treatment, also showing a near balance; yet to a smaller extent than the previous model (potentially justifying the insignificance of the reported ATET in this model). The less-balanced covariates in this model are GDP of the corresponding FDI host country and the banking sector's leverage ratio in the corresponding FDI host country. This result is warranted by the presence of the aforementioned EZ regional asymmetries. The latter hamper an obvious identification of a concretely estimated model. Additionally, we consider as imperative the presence of these two covariates in our model (as argued in Sect. 2), and, thus, refrain from omitting and substituting them with other contestant covariates. Product transformations of combinations of these two covariates do not yield a desired balance. Therefore, future research warrants a more precise definition of the set of covariates, or potentially an estimation of endogenous treatment effects where the treatment model is per se estimated. Finally, Table 2.4b reports assessment of balance gained by the nearest neighbour matching method using the Mahalanobis distance metric. In this case, near balance is also achieved to a greater extent than both parts in Table 2.4a.

In an attempt to assess a possible complementarity between treatments, we explicitly estimate endogenous treatment effects, setting each treatment,

Table 2.5 Treatment complementarity (endogenous treatment estimation)

	Eurozone periphery countries		*Eurozone core countries*	
	Financial integration: TARGET2 liability accumulation	*Bank competition: Lerner index*	*Financial integration: TARGET2 liability accumulation*	*Bank competition: Lerner index*
Treatment				
Financial integration: TARGET2 liability accumulation	–	-0.16956*** (0.044842)	–	-6.3022*** (0.23794)
Chi-squared 2(1)		466.96		48.60
Bank competition: Lerner index	-0.21909*** (0.06557)	–	-2.6051*** (0.40893)	–
Chi-squared 2(1)	25.77		181.71	

Notes: Robust Standard Errors reported in parentheses (* denotes p<0.10, ** denotes p<0.05, *** denotes p<0.01)

respectively, as a covariate in the other treatment's equation. Table 2.5 reports significant results for each treatment supporting a reverse causation in both EZ core and periphery countries. The results are more projected in the EZ core country group. Therefore, higher bank competition (lower values of the Lerner index) is related to higher TARGET2 liability accumulation. A further (to our knowledge) more valid assessment of complementarity among treatments may be reached by a comparison of ATTs estimated in a multiple (and concurrent) treatment setting which, however, warrants further research. In particular, following the notation as in Sect. 2, between treatments j and k, where $(j,k) \in \mathfrak{Y}^2$ and $j \neq k$, the population ATT contrasts treatments among a subset of units in the population (the treated group) receiving one of the two treatments and is defined as

$$\tau_{jk}^{t} \equiv E\left[Y(j) - Y(k) \mid W = t\right],$$

for a reference treatment group t. Under multiple treatments, the ATT of j *relative* to k, which is the ATT of treatment k among those treated with treatment j, presents, for the 'individual units' that we treated with k, a comparison of their mean outcome when treated with k, as they were, with the mean outcome they would have had if they had instead been treated with treatment j. In this manner, upon estimation one may assess a potential degree of complementarity among treatments j and k.

Our results demonstrate the asymmetric response of EZ periphery countries to the progressing liquidity provision in the EZ (by the monetary authority and the financial sector), in terms of FDI attraction by EZ core countries. Our analysis, thus, further justifies the merits of effective monetary and macroprudential policy coordination (for an early thorough account, see Kokores 1989). Openness of an economy warrants policy coordination, as the former imposes constraints on domestic macroeconomic policy reflected either in a reduced ability to control the instruments of policy (like the nominal money supply under fixed exchange rates), or in a reduced ability to influence the targets of policy (like the level of real output) or in increased uncertainty regarding the link between instruments and targets due to the effects on expectations. Under effective EZ member country cooperation, dependence and interdependence would further be overcome, and policy could be determined as in the closed economy. Irrespective of the adversities in the implementation of common policy structures, the potential benefit from coordination remains in recovering greater control over the domestic economies in terms of macroeconomic stability and economic efficiency (Kokores 1989:31).

5 Conclusions

We attempt to investigate the evolution of investment funding practices in the European Common Currency Area in the aftermath of the Global Financial Crisis and the European Sovereign Debt Crisis. We examine the effect on bilateral Intra-Eurozone foreign direct investment (FDI) posed by the evolving regulation on financial integration in the Eurozone (EZ) and the resurgent shift in bank competition. In our analysis we attempt to disentangle the impact of regional asymmetries among EZ member countries by estimating treatment effects of macroprudential and monetary policy interventions on Intra-EZ FDI in both an unmatched and a matched sample of 12 EZ member countries using standard bipartite matching methods, namely matching by propensity score estimation and nearest neighbour matching using the Mahalanobis distance metric.

Our results demonstrate that lower bank competition in the euro area has a significant positive impact on Intra-EZ FDI. Finally, we assess whether a complementarity exists between financial integration, measured by a proxy reflecting the cost of interbank funds denominated in the same (common) currency, and bank competition, proxied by the Lerner index. Our results report a significant level of reverse causation between treatments, yet at a varied degree among core and periphery EZ countries, being more projected in the former.

References

Abadie, A and Imbens, G. (2016). Notes and Comments: Matching on the Estimated Propensity Score. *Econometrica*, 84(2), 781–807.

Alexander, D. L. (1988). The Oligopoly Solution Tested. *Economics Letters*, 28, 361–364.

Appelbaum, E. (1982). The Estimation of the Degree of Oligopoly. *Journal of Econometrics*, 19, 287–299.

Baltzer, M., L. Cappiello, R.A. De Santis, and S. Manganelli (2008). Measuring Financial Integration in New EU Member States. *European Central Bank Occasional Paper Series* No 81 (March).

Battistini, N., M. Pagano, and S. Simonelli (2013). Systemic Risk and Home Bias in the Euro Area. *European Economy*, Economic Papers 494.

Baumol, W.J., J.C. Panzar and R.D. Willig (1982). *Contestable Markets and the Theory of Industry Structure*. New York: Harcourt Brace Jovanovich, Inc. 1982.

Baumol, W.J. and R.D. Willig (1986). Contestability: developments since the book. *Oxford Economic Papers* 38 Supplement November, 9–36.

Berger, H. and V. Nitsch (2010). The Euro's Effect on Trade Imbalances. IMF Working Paper, No 10/226.

Blanchard, O. and F. Giavazzi (2002). Current Account Deficits in the Euro Area: The End of the Feldestein-Horika Puzzle? *Brookings Papers on Economic Activity*, 33(2), 147–86.

Bloningen, B. A. (2005). A Review of the Empirical Literature on FDI Determinants. *Atlantic Economic Journal*, 33(4), 383–403.

Bloningen, B.A. and J. Piger (2014). Determinants of Foreign Direct Investment. *Canadian Journal of Economics*, 47(3), 775–812, August.

Brock, W. A. (1983). Contestable Markets and the Theory of Industry Structure: A Review Article. *Journal of Political Economy* 91(6), 1055–64.

Chen, R., G. M. Milesi-Ferretti, and T. Tressel (2012). External Imbalances in the Euro Area. IMF Working Paper 12/236, International Monetary Fund, Washington.

Christensen, J. H. E. and G. D. Rudebusch (2012). The Response of Interest Rates to US and UK Quantitative Easing. *Economic Journal*, 122, F385–F414.

Cohran, W.G. and Rubin, D.B. (1973). Controlling Bias in Observational Studies: A Review. *Sankhya A*, 35, 417–446.

Demirgüç-Kunt, A. and Martínez Pería, M.S. (2010). A Framework for Analysing Competition in the Banking Sector: An Application to the Case of Jordan. Policy Research Working Paper 5499, Development Research Group, World Bank, Washington, DC.

de Sousa, J. and J. Lochard (2011). Does the Single Currency Affect Foreign Direct Investment? *Scandinavian Journal of Economics* 113(3), 553–578.

di Giovanni, J. (2005). What Drives Capital Flows? The case of cross-border M&A activity and financial deepening. *Journal of International Economics* 65, 127–149.

European Commission (2014). Commission Calls for Immediate Action for a European Industrial Renaissance. *Press release*, 22nd January. European Commission, Brussels.

European Central Bank (2013). TARGET Balances and Monetary Policy Operations. *ECB Monthly Bulletin*, May, 103–114.

Gu X.S., and P.R. Rosenbaum (1993). Comparison of Multivariate Matching Methods: Structures, Distances, and Algorithms. *Journal of Computational Graphical Statistics* 2(4), 405–420.

Hobza, A. and S. Zeugner (2014). Current Accounts and Financial Flows in the Euro Area. *Journal of International Money and Finance*, 48: 291–313.

IMF (2008a). *Balance of Payments Manual.* 5th edition. International Monetary Fund, Washington D.C. Available online at: https://www.imf.org/external/np/sta/bop/BOPman.pdf

IMF (2008b). 'Glossary of Foreign Direct Investment Terms'. In IMF (ed.) *Balance of Payments Manual.* 5th edition. International Monetary Fund, Washington. Available online at: https://www.imf.org/external/np/sta/di/glossary.pdf

Kahn, C. M. (2013). Private Payment Systems, Collateral, and Interest Rates. *Annals of Finance* 9: 83–114.

Kokores, I.T., C. Kottaridi, and P. Pantelidis (2017). Intra-Eurozone Foreign Direct Investment and Deflation. *International Advances in Economic Research* 23, 217–229.

Kokores, T. (1989). *Euro-banking Innovations and EEC Monetary Coordination (Studies 4),* Institute of European Civilization, Brussels, Athens: Papazisis.

Krzanowski, W.J. (2000). *Principles of Multivariate Analysis: A User's Perspective.* New York: Oxford University Press.

Laeven, L. and T. Tressel (2014). European Union Financial Integration Before the Crisis. In Enoch, C., L. Evaraert, T. Tressel, and J. Zhou (eds.), *From Fragmentation to Financial Integration in Europe.* Washington D.C.: International Monetary Fund.

Lane, P.R. (2006). The Real Effects of European Monetary Union. *Journal of Economic Perspectives*, 20(4), 47–66.

Lechner, M. (2001). Identification and Estimation of Causal Effects of Multiple Treatments under the Conditional Independence Assumption. In M. Lechner and F. Pfeiffer (eds.), *Econometric Evaluation of Active Labour Market Policies* (pp. 43–58). Heidelberg: Physica.

McKinsey & Co. (2020). From There to Here: 50 years of Thinking on the Social Responsibility of Business (Reflecting on Milton Friedman's 1970 pathbreaking essay), *Article*, Sept. 11. Available online at: https://www.mckinsey.com/featured-insights/corporate-purpose/from-there-to-here-50-years-of-thinking-on-the-social-responsibility-of-business?cid=other-eml-alt-mip-mck&hlkid=67a9b344939b483393e9a620f9221aee&hctky=11922066&hdpid=80e1385d-2ce3-493f-88a5-ee124a8b8058

OECD (2016). Foreign Direct Investment: positions by partner country (Edition 2016). OECD International Direct Investment Statistics, Benchmark definition, 4th edition (BMD4). Available online at: https://doi.org/10.1787/idi-data-en

Pantelidis, P., D. Kyrkilis and E. Nikolopoulos (2014). Effects of European Monetary Integration on Intra-EMU Foreign Direct Investment. *SPOUDAI Journal of Economics and Business*, 64(4), 67–74.

Portes, R. (2014). The Eurozone Crisis. In D.D. Evanoff, C. Holthausen, G.G. Kaufman and M. Kremer (Eds.), *The Role of Central Banks in Financial*

Stability: How has it changed? (pp. 423–432). 30th World Scientific Studies in International Economics. Singapore: World Scientific Publishing Co. Pte. Ltd.

Roberts, M. (1984). Testing Oligopolistic Behaviour. *International Journal of Industrial Organization*, 2, 367–383.

Rosenbaum, P. R., and Rubin, D. B. (1983). The Central Role of the Propensity Score in Observational Studies for Causal Effects. *Biometrika*, *70*(1), 41–55.

Rosenbaum, P. R., and Rubin, D. B. (1985). Constructing a Control Group using Multivariate Matched Sampling Methods that Incorporate the Propensity Score. *The American Statistician*, 39(1), 33–38.

Rubin, D.B. (1980). Bias Reduction Using Mahalanobis-Metric Matching. *Biometrics*, 36(2), 293–298.

Rubin, D.B. (1980a). Randomization Analysis of Experimental Data: the Fisher Randomization Test Comment. *Journal of the American Statistical Association* 75, 591–593.

Scotina, A.D. and R. Gutman (2019). Matching Algorithms for Causal Inference with Multiple Treatments. *Statistics in Medicine* 38, 3139–3167.

Sinn, H., and T. Wollmershäuser (2012). Target Loans, Current Account Balances and Capital Flows: the ECB's rescue facility. *International Tax and Public Finance* 19, 468–508.

Steinkamp, S., A. Tornell and F. Westermann (2018). Evergreening in the Euro Area: Facts and Explanation. Working Paper, No 113, Institute of Empirical Economic Research, Osnabrück University, Germany.

Vivar, M.L., Lambert, C., M. Wedow, M. Giuzio (2020). Is the Home Bias Biased? New Evidence from the Investment Fund Sector. In ECB (ed.) *Financial Integration and Structure in the Euro Area*. Frankfurt: ECB.

Walsh, J.P. and J. Yu (2010). Determinants of Foreign Direct Investment: A Sectoral and Institutional Approach. IMF working paper No 187, July.

Zemenek, H., A. Belke and G. Schnabl (2009). Current Account Imbalances and Structural Adjustment in the Euro Area: How to Rebalance Competitiveness. *IZA Policy Paper*, No 7, IZA Institute of Labour Economics, Deutsche Post Foundation and University of Bonn, Germany.

Zhou, C. (2020). The Effects of Outward FDI and Export on Firm Productivity in Emerging Markets: Evidence from Matching Approach. *Economics Letters*, 195, doi:https://doi.org/10.1016/j.econlet.2020.109462.

CHAPTER 3

Export Margins, Employment Skills and Financial Conditions: Stylized Facts from Greek Exporters

Sarantis Kalyvitis and Margarita Katsimi

1 Introduction

An extensive theoretical and empirical literature has shown that heterogeneity in trade has important implications for aggregate economic outcomes, like productivity and welfare. An important question that remains

We thank R. Calmuc for excellent research assistance and participants of the CESifo–Delphi Conference 2015 for comments and suggestions on a preliminary draft. We also thank A. Crespo and E. Dinopoulos for many helpful discussions. Financial support through the project Aristeia II Action of the Operational Programme Education and Lifelong Learning (No. 3879), co-funded by the European Social Fund (ESF) and national resources, is acknowledged.

S. Kalyvitis (✉)
Department of International European and Economic Studies, Athens University of Economics and Business, Athens, Greece

Laboratory of International Economic Relations AUEB (LINER-AUEB), Athens, Greece
e-mail: skalyvitis@aueb.gr

I. T. Kokores et al. (eds.), *Money, Trade and Finance*,
https://doi.org/10.1007/978-3-030-73219-6_3

open involves the underlying linkages with various sources of heterogeneity on the margins of exporters, given by the numbers of products and destinations, and the value, price and quantity of exports at the firm level. In this short chapter, we use a newly developed dataset from Greek exporters, and we present a number of stylized facts that aim at addressing empirically the following questions: How are (i) the number of products exported per destination ('exporter scope at the destination') and the number of destinations per product to which a firm exports ('exporter scope of the product'), (ii) the value, quantity and price of exports, related at the firm level to the allocation between skilled and unskilled employment and wages, and the financial conditions proxied by cash flows and credit scores?

While it has already been established that exporters outperform non-exporters (they are larger, pay higher wages and are more productive), the association between the various margins of exporting with factor inputs goes beyond the traditional theories of international trade, in which unskilled-intensive production is carried out by combining labor, capital, and a technology. Several models, including those by Yeaple (2005), Verhoogen (2008), Arkolakis (2010), and Brambilla et al. (2012), have internalized some of the complexities of modern production processes in trade by assuming that the production of goods comprises the combination of marketing, distribution, foreign trade activities, and exporting services. These extra fixed and variable costs typically need to be paid up front due to long time lags between production and sales, whereas the realization of revenues is uncertain and typically involves more complex, riskier, and less enforceable contracts between the lender and the borrower. As a result, potential exporters must have enough liquidity at hand, and, not

---

M. Katsimi
Department of International European and Economic Studies, Athens University of Economics and Business, Athens, Greece

Laboratory of International Economic Relations AUEB (LINER-AUEB), Athens, Greece

CESifo, Munich, Germany

surprisingly, there is empirical evidence that financial constraints affect exporting decisions (see e.g. Bellone et al. 2010; Berman and Héricourt 2010; Chaney 2016; Feenstra et al. 2014; Greenaway et al. 2007; Manova 2013; Manova et al. 2015; Minetti and Zhu 2011; Muûls 2015).

Keeping these considerations in mind, in this chapter we attempt to provide an empirical assessment of the questions posed in the beginning of the chapter using a newly developed dataset on Greek exporting firms, described in more detail in Sect. 2. In Sect. 3, we present the three main empirical findings. First, the proportional allocation of skilled to unskilled labor and the wage skill premium are positively associated with the number of products sold at a given destination ('exporter scope at the destination'), but not with the number of destinations to which a product is exported ('exporter scope of the product'). Second, firms with higher export sales and quantities have lower-skilled to unskilled wage bill ratios, an effect that is driven by lower-skilled to unskilled employment ratios across firms rather than differences in the wage skill premia. Third, there is some evidence, albeit weak, that financial restrictions are adversely related to the 'exporter scope at the destination' and the 'exporter scope of the product', as well as revenues and quantities. The latter effect however should be interpreted with caution, as virtually all Greek exporters faced substantial financial restrictions in our sample year (2014). In the conclusion, we discuss what we consider to be the main implications of these findings for related theoretical and empirical work on Greek exporters.

2 Data

Our focus lies on patterns of export sales of individual products and destinations across Greek firms. Given the questions at hand, we cover various margins of export activity at the firm level, given by the 'exporter scope at the destination', the 'exporter scope of the product', and sales and quantities per product at the destination. Export values and quantities are of special interest as they yield unit values (export prices). In this section, we briefly describe our data sources and provide some descriptive statistics for the data at hand.

2.1 Data Sources

We use a newly compiled dataset on Greek exporting firms that merges data from three main sources for 2014. Trade data at the firm–product–destination level are obtained from the Intrastat databank, and firm-level variables are obtained from the Annual Manufacturing Survey (AMS), both available via the Greek Statistical Agency (ELSTAT). Financial variables are obtained from the ICAP database, which collects balance sheet and financial information on Greek firms. Below we give a brief description of our main sources.

The Intrastat databank collects information and produces statistics on dispatches and arrivals of goods and replaced customs declarations as the source of trade statistics. In particular, the national authorities collect data on the identification number allocated to the party responsible for providing information, the reference period, the flow (arrival, dispatch), the value and quantity of the goods in net mass (weight excluding packaging), and the supplementary unit (liter, m^2, number of items, etc.) if relevant, and their destination. Firms whose annual trade amount is above a certain value are responsible for providing information, and this threshold value is redefined so that a minimum amount of data is collected for each trade flow. Each year, national authorities define their thresholds, set in such a way so as to collect data relating to at least 97% of all dispatches with approximately 4600 firms recorded as exporters for 2014. The classification of all reported exported goods (approximately 2500 products) follows the Standard International Trade Classification (SITC) system. Our dataset consists of manufacturing products in the following sectors: *chemicals* (Sector 5), *machinery and transport equipment* (Sector 7), *other manufactured goods* (Sectors 6 and 8). We calculate unit prices using our export revenue and quantity data as follows: firm *f*'s average export price for product *p* in destination *d* is given by the $price_{fpd} = \frac{revenue_{fpd}}{quantity_{fpd}}$.

To obtain data on employment at the firm level, we use survey data from the AMS, which is carried out annually and contains data related to economic activity of medium-scale and large-scale manufacturing firms. The survey provides figures on labor force variables (number of employees and remuneration per type of worker).[1] The firm survey is collected at the

[1] For a more detailed description of the external sector statistics and the Annual Industrial Survey, see Theofilakou and Stournaras (2013) and Tsakanikas and Vassiliadis (2013).

plant level, but export and financial information is recorded at the firm level. A key limitation of these data is therefore sample size in some regressions, with roughly 400 (manufacturing) firms in our cross-section for 2014 when employment data are considered.

We match the data on exports by ELSTAT with financial sheet data from database supplied by ICAP, which is the largest Greek firm that supplies business information. ICAP provides information on financial variables. In total, roughly 35,000 firms are included in the ICAP database. The ICAP database also contains credit scores for selected firms, which express firm-specific multivariate estimates of credit quality with respect to the probability of default and/or bankruptcy, thus controlling for insolvency, excessive and/or bad debts, overdue accounts, and other typical commercial risks in a single indicator.[2] Given that high cash flow is considered to be indicator of good financial health and low credit risk, it is also mirrored in a higher credit score. Both measures typically capture the access of firms to financial markets and indicate lower credit rationing. We therefore use them interchangeably as firm-level measures of credit rationing for Greek exporters.[3]

To avoid misreporting by some firms, we follow Feenstra et al. (2014), and we clean the sample for mismeasurement and for very small firms by checking that key financial variables, such as total assets and sales are not missing. We also confirm that total assets exceed liquid assets and fixed assets and that exports do not exceed total sales. Finally, we impose the restriction that export revenue should exceed €10,000 in total, €1000 for each destination, and €100 for each product-destination pair.

2.2 *Descriptive Statistics*

Table 3.1 reports some key statistics for our full sample of exporting firms. In the first column, we present for comparison purposes the statistics for the full coverage of exporters across all sectors, whereas in the second

[2] In the micro-exporting literature, Muûls (2015) uses a similar credit score to explore empirically its effects on firm sales and the numbers of products exported and destinations served. The author reports that a higher credit score is associated with higher growth rates in all the aforementioned margins.

[3] Notice that, as pointed out by Minetti and Zhu (2011), it is possible that, for instance, a firm that faces financial constraints hoards cash or suffers from credit rationing due to high existing debt.

column we report the same statistics for manufacturing firms.[4] Approximately 2500 products are exported with the average number of products per firm amounting to 7.5 for all exporters and 7.2 for manufacturers, whereas the average number of destinations per firm is 7.3 and 8.1, respectively.[5]

In the theoretical literature of microexporting it is common to model firm heterogeneity along the dimension of productivity (Melitz 2003). One of the most robust predictions in these models is that higher-productivity firms will be larger in equilibrium. Motivated by this argument, in Table 3.2 we focus on how key firm characteristics relate to export size. To this end, we decompose exporters in 'high exports' and 'low exports' with the cutoff point given by the median of the distribution of export sales. As can be readily seen, the differences between all exporters (first and second columns) and manufacturing firms (third and fourth columns) are not qualitatively essential. Turning to manufacturing firms, for which employment data from AMS are available, we observe that larger exporters have, as expected, substantially higher total sales and gross profits, but of similar magnitude as percentage of their assets. Larger firms pay less for skilled relative to unskilled employment, as indicated by the wage bill ratios for the two groups, with the difference stemming from the relative number of employees rather than the skill premium through the wage rate. To assess their financial status of exporting firms, we also report their cash flows and credit rating from the ICAP database. In manufacturing, larger exporters have higher cash flows and higher credit rating, a finding that is consistent with the hypothesis that larger firms are less credit rationed.

In the next section, we attempt to explore in more detail the implications of these differences across the dimensions of the export margins.

3 Export Margins and Factor Inputs

We begin the analysis of export margins by reporting in Table 3.3 some simple correlations between firm revenues, quantities, and prices, with the number of products and destinations per firm in the form of OLS

[4] In empirical specifications related to labor variables, only a subset of these firms (matched with AMS) are due to data availability.

[5] See Arkolakis and Muendler (2013) on the similarities of the Greek dataset with datasets that have been used in the related empirical literature.

regressions including. We stress that in Table 3.3 and in all subsequent tables, the estimated coefficients reflect correlations, rather than causal effects. Product fixed effects are included to control for systematic differences across goods in consumer appeal, comparative advantage, transportation costs, units of measure (kilos vs. units), and other product-specific characteristics. We also include destination fixed effects to account for destination-specific characteristics, such as consumer income, general demand conditions, transportation costs, as well as inflation and exchange rates.

Panel A of Table 3.3 reports the results on export revenues. Columns (1) and (2) show that higher revenues are correlated positively with quantities and negatively with prices, a finding that is consistent with similar correlations for the US (Gervais 2015). Columns (3) and (4) report that exporters with higher revenues sell less products to more destinations. The same patterns are confirmed in columns (5) and (6) of Panel A, where the numbers of products and destinations are used jointly with quantities and prices respectively as r.h.s. variables. Panels B and C report the corresponding regressions with the components of revenues, namely quantity and price as l.h.s. variables respectively, and show that the estimated relationships in revenues, reported in Panel A, are mainly driven by changes in quantities rather than prices. Specifically, Panel B confirms that higher quantities are associated with higher export revenues and, in addition, with lower prices. Also, higher quantities are associated with less products sold to more destinations. In columns (1) and (2) of Panel C, we establish that higher prices are associated with lower revenues and quantities, whereas columns (3) and (4) report that higher prices are associated with more products exported to a smaller number of destinations. However, in columns (5) and (6), which estimate the relationships jointly, we find that the correlations do not always retain their signs and significance. In short, we find that the correlations between the components of the export margins, given by the 'exporter scope at the destination' and the 'exporter scope of the product', revenues and quantities-prices, are sufficiently worthy of further investigation.

3.1 Employment Skills

Table 3.4 presents regressions that relate the numbers of products and destinations to the structure of employment at the firm level. All employment variables are reported as ratios of skilled to unskilled labor. Column (1) in Panel A shows that the firms in which the aggregate wage bill for skilled relative to unskilled labor is higher export more products in each destination. In columns (2) and (3), the total wage costs are decomposed in the number of employees and the wage rate. We find that firms with relatively more skilled employees and higher wage skill premia export more products, a finding that is confirmed in column (4) in which the two variables are used jointly.[6] In Panel B of Table 3.4, we perform the same exercise using the number of destinations for each product as an l.h.s. variable and find that it is not affected by the relative wage bill or its components. An important point to notice therefore from this evidence is that both the proportional allocation of skilled to unskilled labor and the skill premium are positively associated with the exporter scope at the destination, but not with the exporter scope of the product. We consider this set of facts to be the first main finding of this chapter.

We next turn into the analysis of export sales (Panel C of Table 3.4). Column (1) shows that firms with higher export sales have lower-skilled to unskilled wage bill ratios. When the wage bill variable is decomposed into employment and wages in columns (2) and (3), we find that firms with higher sales have lower-skilled to unskilled employment ratio, but no differences in their wage skill premia. This implies that the linkage with the aggregate wage bill stems from lower-skilled to unskilled employment, rather than lower skill premia. These individual effects persist, if we include both the employment ratio and the skill premium in a single specification in column (4). To shed some further light in these effects, in Panels D and E we use as dependent variables the quantity and price variables, respectively. The association of export sales with the wage bill ratio and its components is driven by its quantity component: all coefficients in Panel D have the same magnitude and statistical significance with those reported in Panel C. In contrast, when prices are used as the l.h.s. variable, the correlation evaporates (with the exception of a weak negative association with the skill premium). These correlations suggest that changes in quantities are the driving force of the negative association between revenues and the

[6]The wage rate for skilled and unskilled workers is calculated by dividing the wage bill to the number of employees. Denoting the wage bill, employment, and the wage rate by *wb*, *n*, and *w* respectively, we get that $\frac{w^s}{w^u} ? \left(\frac{wb^s}{n^s}\right) / \left(\frac{wb^u}{n^u}\right) = \left(\frac{wb^s}{wb^u}\right)\left(\frac{n^u}{n^s}\right)$, where *s* and *u* denote skilled and unskilled labor.

ratio of skilled to unskilled employment across exporting firms, and we consider them to be our second main finding.

3.2 *Financial Conditions*

The financial conditions of firms, through their cash flows and credit scores, are the main points of interest in this subsection. In columns (1) and (2) of Panels A and B in Table 3.5, we relate the 'exporter scope at the destination' and the 'exporter scope of the product' with these financial measures. Specifically, columns (1) in Panels A and B show that cash flow is positively associated with the 'exporter scope of the product', but not the 'exporter scope at the destination'. In columns (2) in Panels A and B, we use as r.h.s. variable the lagged credit score of the firm (which is based on information available at the end of each year). We find that it is positively, but weakly, associated with the 'exporter scope at the destination', but not the 'exporter scope of the product'.

In Panels C, D, and E of Table 3.5, we regress export revenues and their components on financial conditions. Column (2) in Panel C shows that firms with higher export sales have higher credit scores but their sales are not related to their cash flow in column (1). In turn, in Panel D we use quantities as l.h.s. variable. Again, cash flow is not significantly associated with the quantities exported, whereas the credit score in column (2) is weakly significant with a positive sign. When we look at prices (Panel E), we find that they both are not associated with cash flow and credit ratings. The evidence, albeit weak, that financial restrictions are adversely related to the 'exporter scope at the destination' and the 'exporter scope of the product', as well as revenues and quantities, is the third finding of the chapter.

4 Suggestive Theories on the Role of Quality for Greek Exporters

What lies behind these correlations of export margins with employment skills and financial conditions? In this section, we set out to uncover some of the channels behind our results. Casual empiricism suggests that the quality channel is the most obvious candidate that explains this type of association. That is, the correlations could be largely explained by unobservable differences in the quality of inputs reflecting differences in average input costs, which are in turn reflected in output quality (Kugler and Verhoogen 2012). In an empirical context, Manova and Zhang (2012) establish that Chinese export prices are higher in richer, larger, and more distant destinations and support the empirical relevance of trade models with endogenous product quality. Consistent with the quality interpretation, Atkin et al. (2015) point out that larger firms have greater costs primarily because they use higher-quality, more costly inputs, and Gervais (2015) finds that export demand is positively correlated with advertising expenditures, wage rates, and material costs. Indeed, some papers have highlighted the role of quality in models where consumers value quality, but quality is expensive to produce (Harrigan et al. 2015). Baldwin and Harrigan (2011) develop a heterogeneous firms trade model in which consumers appreciate quality. Higher quality is associated with higher marginal cost, which however is more than offset by the advantage of high quality.

There are various reasons why quality in exporting may demand relatively more skilled employment along with a higher skill premium. For instance, international marketing and commercialization, transportation and distribution, and advertising require expertise in international businesses, languages, foreign technologies, and the social idiosyncrasies of foreign markets. Verhoogen (2008) develops a model where exporting allows for quality upgrading and skill-intensive services, a channel that might be particularly relevant if it involves accessing high-income destinations with higher valuation for quality (Brambilla et al. 2012). In a related vein, exporting may require varying levels of skills due to 'skilled-bias globalization', in which international trade activities use skill-intensive resources (Matsuyama 2007).

Regarding financial conditions, how do our empirical findings relate to the margins of Greek exporters? The main issue that Greek exporting firms faced during the global financial crisis and, even more intensely, during the Greek crisis was the lack of access to credit, which particularly affected their expansion to new market. According to the European Central Bank (ECB 2017), while in the Eurozone the terms of financing have become more favorable over the last years, in Greece 23% of Greek SMEs declare that the lack of access to credit is the most acute problem faced. Not surprisingly, around 70% of Greek exporters are ranked between 1 and 4 on the 10-scale credit rating by ICAP.

In the exporting market, credit can be used to finance marketing, advertising, price-based promotions and create brand loyalty through artificial product differentiation, and hence affect the exporter scope at the destination. In a related vein, Arkolakis (2010) has put forward the idea that marketing expenditures affect trade at the firm level, which is corroborated by the evidence reported in Atkin et al. (2015). This channel of credit constraints is particularly relevant for the exporter scope of the product, as exporters face extra costs due to information gathering, building distribution and sales systems, offering additional customer services and warranties, as well as adjusting products to local legislation and tastes. As pointed out by Arkolakis et al. (2019), the first exported item to a particular destination may face higher importer costs than a subsequent item, due to, for example, the financial cost and time required for both paperwork and border compliance, sanitary and phytosanitary as well as other technical regulations that can affect approval of a first export product differently from subsequent products, and price or quantity control measures with differential importance.

5 Conclusions

In this chapter, we have documented a number of facts about the margins of exports across Greek exporters. Although focused on a specific country, our results have the advantage that they are based on empirical regularities and do not require the strong assumptions of structural approaches. What are the implications of our findings for the heterogeneous firms literature and, more specifically, for Greek exporters? In relation to the existing literature on export margins, perhaps our most interesting finding is that other exporting margins, and not just export sales, are systematically related to employment skills and financial conditions. It will be important to investigate whether these patterns hold, or are more intense, in other destination characteristics like income, size, and distance. But assuming that these patterns prove to be general, they suggest that the theoretical literature should focus on models that can rationalize, or at least verify, consistent strong relationships between export margins and quality.

We believe that our findings point to several potentially fruitful directions for future work. However, caution is warranted in interpreting these correlations. It may be that quality is part of what is typically thought of as managerial ability, which may matter more for high-quality products, or the firms that face financial constraints have suffered from adverse world demand shocks. In short, there may be complicated interactions between quality, employment skills, and financial constraints. The correlations reported in the chapter suggest that export margins are sufficiently worthy of further investigation.

Appendix

Table 3.1 Greek exporters, exporting characteristics

	All exporters	*Manufacturers*
Number of exporting firms	4216	3159
Value of exports	5002	3942
Number of products	2460	1938
Number of destinations	186	182
Average number of products per firm	7.5	7.2
Average number of destinations per firm	7.3	8.1
Average number of destinations per product	4.1	3.7
Number of observations	79,076	60,607

Notes: Value of exports is reported in thousand Euros

Table 3.2 Greek exporters, firm characteristics

	A. All exporters		*B. Manufacturers*	
	High exports	*Low exports*	*High exports*	*Low exports*
Total sales	39,300	6336	29,200	5014
Gross profits	7540	1440	7638	1407
Total assets	51,444	7531	43,400	7410
Fixed assets	30,933	3005	25,342	3075
Employment	n.a.	n.a.	56	32
Wage bill (skilled/unskilled)	n.a.	n.a.	1.65	1.90
Employment (skilled/unskilled)	n.a.	n.a.	1.02	1.37
Skill premium (wage rate)	n.a.	n.a.	1.58	1.49
Cash flow	0.074	0.090	0.084	0.075
Credit score	4.0	3.4	4.0	3.4

Notes: *Total assets*, *fixed assets*, *gross profits*, and *operating costs* are reported in thousand Euros. *Cash flow* is calculated as profits net of tax expenditures plus depreciation and is normalized by *total assets*. Splitting in high and low exports is done at the median of the distribution

Table 3.3 Export performance and export margins

	(1)	*(2)*	*(3)*	*(4)*	*(5)*	*(6)*
A. Dependent variable: Revenues						
Quantity	0.711***				0.702***	
	(104.83)				(100.34)	
Price		-0.123***				-0.083***
		(-5.40)				(-4.14)
# of products			-0.219***		-0.009	-0.170***
			(-11.48)		(-1.08)	(-10.94)
# of destinations				0.581***	0.098***	0.552***
				(20.55)	(7.70)	(21.27)
R-sq	0.810	0.261	0.268	0.306	0.811	0.315
B. Dependent variable: Quantity						
Revenues	1.046***				1.034***	
	(127.44)				(130.00)	
Price		-1.123***				-1.083***
		(-49.42)				(-53.94)
# of products			-0.289***		-0.055***	-0.170***
			(-11.15)		(-4.95)	(-10.94)
# of destinations				0.687***	0.079***	0.552***
				(18.60)	(4.82)	(21.27)
R-sq	0.859	0.628	0.459	0.484	0.860	0.655
C. Dependent variable: Price						
Revenues	-0.046***				-0.034***	
	(-5.65)				(-4.24)	
Quantity		-0.289***				-0.298***
		(-42.57)				(-42.67)
# of products			0.069***		0.055***	-0.009
			(5.68)		(4.95)	(-1.08)
# of destinations				-0.106***	-0.079***	0.098***
				(-6.41)	(-4.82)	(7.70)
R-sq	0.627	0.747	0.627	0.627	0.630	0.749

Notes: All variables are in logs. The regressions include a constant term, and t statistics (in parentheses) are based on robust standard errors clustered at product level (* denotes $p<0.10$, ** denotes $p<0.05$, *** denotes $p<0.01$). *# of products* and *# of destinations* denote the 'exporter scope at the destination' and the 'exporter scope of the product' respectively (see text for definitions. All regressions include product and destination fixed effects. In all regressions the number of observations is 60,607 and the number of clusters (products) is 2264

Table 3.4 Export margins and labor variables (skilled/unskilled ratios)

	(1)	*(2)*	*(3)*	*(4)*
A. Dependent variable: Number of products per destination				
Wage bill ratio	0.299***			
	(6.82)			
Employment ratio		0.315***		0.309***
		(6.97)		(6.94)
Skill premium			0.285***	0.238***
			(4.87)	(4.18)
N	5745	5745	5745	5745
R-sq	0.345	0.336	0.231	0.346
B. Dependent variable: Number of destinations per product				
Wage bill ratio	-0.019			
	(-0.44)			
Employment ratio		-0.014		-0.016
		(-0.30)		(-0.34)
Skill premium			-0.035	-0.039
			(-0.26)	(-0.28)
N	5745	5745	5745	5745
R-sq	0.741	0.741	0.741	0.741
C. Dependent variable: Revenues				
Wage bill ratio	-0.325***			
	(-5.91)			
Employment ratio		-0.345***		-0.352***
		(-6.11)		(-6.25)
Skill premium			-0.072	-0.150
			(-0.49)	(-0.95)
N	5745	5745	5745	5745
R-sq	0.474	0.474	0.464	0.474
D. Dependent variable: Quantity				
Wage bill ratio	-0.317***			
	(-3.64)			
Employment ratio		-0.372***		-0.371***
		(-4.23)		(-4.17)
Skill premium			0.124	0.042
			(0.59)	(0.19)
N	5745	5745	5745	5745
R-sq	0.630	0.631	0.625	0.631
E. Dependent variable: Price				
Wage bill ratio	-0.008			
	(-0.14)			
Employment ratio		0.027		0.019
		(0.44)		(0.32)
Skill premium			-0.196*	-0.191*
			(-1.85)	(-1.78)
N	5745	5745	5745	5745
R-sq	0.789	0.789	0.789	0.790

Notes: All variables are in logs. The regressions include a constant term and *t* statistics are in parentheses (* denotes $p<0.10$, ** denotes $p<0.05$, *** denotes $p<0.01$). All r.h.s. variables are expressed as ratios of skilled to unskilled labor. Regressions in Panel A include destination fixed effects, in Panel B product fixed effects, and in Panels C-E product and destination fixed effects. Standard errors in Panel A are clustered at destination level whereas in Panels B-E are clustered at product level

Table 3.5 Export margins and financial variables

	(1)	*(2)*
A. Dependent variable: Number of products per destination		
Cash flow	0.012	
	(0.24)	
Credit score		0.153*
		(1.82)
N	3432	5640
R-sq	0.314	0.227
B. Dependent variable:Number of destinations per product		
Cash flow	0.158**	
	(2.14)	
Credit score		0.077
		(0.87)
N	3432	5640
R-sq	0.814	0.753
C. Dependent variable: Revenues		
Cash flow	0.104	
	(1.05)	
Credit score		0.317**
		(2.24)
N	3432	5640
R-sq	0.522	0.466
D. Dependent variable: Quantity		
Cash flow	0.106	
	(0.77)	
Credit score		0.334*
		(1.73)
N	3432	5640
R-sq	0.652	0.620
E. Dependent variable: Price		
Cash flow	-0.003	
	(-0.03)	
Credit score		-0.017
		(-0.17)
N	3432	5640
R-sq	0.819	0.789

Notes: All variables are in logs. The regressions include a constant term and *t* statistics are in parentheses (* denotes $p<0.10$, ** denotes $p<0.05$, *** denotes $p<0.01$). Credit score is the 20,013 score. Regressions in Panel A include destination fixed effects, in Panel B product fixed effects, and in Panels C–E product and destination fixed effects. Standard errors in Panel A are clustered at destination level, whereas in Panels B–E they are clustered at product level

References

Atkin D., A. Chaudhry, S. Chaudry, A. K. Khandelwal and E. Verhoogen (2015). Mark-Up and Cost Dispersion Across Firms: Direct Evidence from Producer Surveys in Pakistan. *American Economic Review*, 105(5), 537–544.

Arkolakis C. (2010). Market Penetration Costs and the New Consumers Margin in International Trade. *Journal of Political Economy*, 118(6), 1151–1199.

Arkolakis C. and M.A. Muendler (2013). Exporters and Their Products: A Collection of Empirical Regularities. *CESifo Economic Studies*, 59(2), 223–248.

Arkolakis C., S. Ganapati and M.A. Muendler (2019). The Extensive Margin of Exporting Products: A Firm-level Analysis. Working Paper.

Baldwin R. and J. Harrigan (2011). Zeros, Quality, and Space: Trade Theory and Trade Evidence. *American Economic Journal: Microeconomics*, 3(2), 60–88.

Bellone F., P. Musso, L. Nesta and S. Schiavo (2010). Financial Constraints and Firm Export Behaviour. *World Economy*, 33(3), 347–373.

Berman N. and J. Héricourt (2010). Financial Factors and the Margins of Trade: Evidence from Cross-Country Firm-level Data. *Journal of Development Economics*, 93(2), 206–217.

Brambilla I., D. Lederman, and G. Porto (2012). Exports, Export Destinations, and Skills. *American Economic Review*, 102(7), 3406–3438.

Chaney T. (2016). Liquidity Constrained Exporters. *Journal of Economic Dynamics and Control*, 72, 141–154.

ECB (2017). Survey on the Access to Finance of Enterprises in the Euro Area. Available online at: https://www.ecb.europa.eu/pub/pdf/other/ecb.accesstofinancesmallmediumsizedenterprises201711.en.pdf

Feenstra R.C., Z. Li, and M. Yu (2014). Exports and Credit Constraints under Incomplete Information: Theory and Evidence from China. *Review of Economic and Statistics*, 96(4), 729–744.

Gervais A. (2015). Product Quality and Firm Feterogeneity in International Trade. *Canadian Journal of Economics*, 48(3), 1152–1174.

Greenaway D., A. Guariglia and R. Kneller (2007). Financial Factors and Exporting Decisions. *Journal of International Economics*, 73(2), 377–395.

Harrigan J., X. Ma and V. Shlychkov (2015). Export prices of U.S. Firms. *Journal of International Economics*, 97(1), 100–111.

Kugler M. and E. Verhoogen (2012). Prices, Plant Size, and Product Quality. *Review of Economic Studies*, 79(1), 307–339.

Matsuyama K. (2007). Beyond Icebergs: Towards a tTheory of Biased Globalization. *The Review of Economic Studies*, 74(1), 237–253.

Manova K. (2013). Credit Constraints, Heterogeneous Firms and International Trade. *Review of Economic Studies*, 80(2), 711–744.

Manova K. and Z. Zhang (2012). Export Prices Across Firms and Destinations. *Quarterly Journal of Economics*, 127(1), 379–436.

Manova K., S. Wei and Z. Zhang (2015). Firm Exports and Multinational Activity under Credit Constraints. *Review of Economics and Statistics*, forthcoming.

Melitz M.J. (2003). The Impact of Trade on Intra-Industry Reallocations and Aggregate Industry Productivity. *Econometrica*, 71(6), 1695–1725.

Minetti R. and S. C. Zhu (2011). Credit Constraints and Firm Export: Microeconomic Evidence from Italy. *Journal of International Economics*, 83(2), 109–125.

Muûls M. (2015). Exporters, Importers and Credit Constraints. *Journal of International Economics*, 95(2), 333–343.

Theofilakou N.K. and Y. Stournaras (2013). An analysis of Greek External Sector Statistics and Their Application in Academic Research and Economic Policy Making. *Journal of Economic and Social Measurement*, 38(1), 41–56.

Tsakanikas A. and M. Vassiliadis (2013). A Methodological Review of the Greek Annual Industrial Survey. *Journal of Economic and Social Measurement*, 38(1), 57–77.

Verhoogen E.A. (2008). Trade, Quality Upgrading, and Wage Inequality in the Mexican Manufacturing Sector. *Quarterly Journal of Economics*, 123(2), 489–530.

Yeaple S.R. (2005). A Simple Model of Firm Heterogeneity, International Trade, and Wages. *Journal of International Economics*, 65(1), 1–20.

PART II

Corporate Landscape Advancement

CHAPTER 4

Why a Revival of Greek Manufacturing Is a Prerequisite to Ensure a Prosperous Future for the Country and How to Achieve It

Michael Mitsopoulos and Theodore Pelagidis

1 Introduction

As Greece develops its post-program and post-pandemic growth strategy, the debate regarding the most attractive growth drivers for the country is receiving increased attention. While it is true that this time, for the first time since the 1950s and 1960s (when strong incentives counterbalanced the always-present weaknesses of the country), manufacturing does receive credit and attention in the related debate, it is not always obvious that this reference is based on a solid understanding of the role that manufacturing does actually play in a modern economy. Especially during an age when

M. Mitsopoulos
SEV Hellenic Federation of Enterprises, Athens, Greece

T. Pelagidis (✉)
Bank of Greece, Athens, Greece

Department of Maritime Studies, University of Piraeus, Piraeus, Greece

Brookings Institution, Washington, DC, USA
e-mail: pelagidi@unipi.gr

I. T. Kokores et al. (eds.), *Money, Trade and Finance*,
https://doi.org/10.1007/978-3-030-73219-6_4

the value created in services and manufacturing often is merged, in a way that is difficult to disentangle, manufacturing takes on a new role that is quite different from the role it had during the previous century. Thus, its main contribution is found less in the value added from actually making things, and more as a key part, but certainly a necessary part even if not always quantitatively representing a majority in statistics, of a fluid process that integrates services and production along complex value chains. In such a setting, the sector of activity becomes less decisive than the existence of a balanced, according to size but also activity, corporate landscape.

A difficulty to document the constantly changing, but always crucial, role of the sector in a modern economy that ensures prosperity for its citizens is also the result of the collection of statistics according to the realities formed over decades during previous years. In spite of this, a detailed breakdown of data, and a focus on company size data, allows us to describe aspects of this role, and to document its correlation with key aspects that, overall, describe the institutional maturity of a country. While this chapter does not attempt to investigate the direction of causality, which is in itself a vibrant research topic, the presented evidence suffices to document the need to ensure advancement on all fronts that signal the institutional maturity of a country, and the attractiveness of an environment shaped by taxation, the services rendered in return, regulations and public policies if one wants to support an revival of the productive base of the country. That is because such an improved environment stands to benefit disproportionally those that endeavor "to make things" along more elaborate and complex value chains.

In the end, the challenges posed by the modern, fast-changing world suggest that if a close collaboration between the private and the public sector was needed in the past to establish that the policies applied manage to satisfy the needs of both the public interest and the private sector, this is true today to an even larger extent. Only through a framework that encourages such a relationship to be deep and constructive, for both parties, can a country hope to manage the challenges of the modern age, it is argued in the final part of this chapter. This is even more the case for a country that has, along the way, to cover significant deficiencies in many dimensions of policy design and implementation as well as to create a strong productive base and seize the employment opportunities that can be created along such a path.

2 The Link Between Manufacturing and the Path to Prosperity for European Countries

Visiting a topic that receives lately extensive coverage, and that regards the usefulness of manufacturing (e.g. IMF 2018), we turn to detailed data regarding the sample of EU countries, of which Greece is a member. In this data we observe that the EU member countries that have a strong manufacturing base can produce goods that are internationally in demand (Fig. 4.1), a fact well established in the literature that links positively the contribution of manufacturing to GDP with exports. They also create more jobs, not only in the manufacturing sector but also in all of the economy (Fig. 4.2). In addition, they appear to encourage a closer cooperation between business and research centers as they strive to increase value added, something that is compatible with a higher business expenditure on R&D (Fig. 4.3).

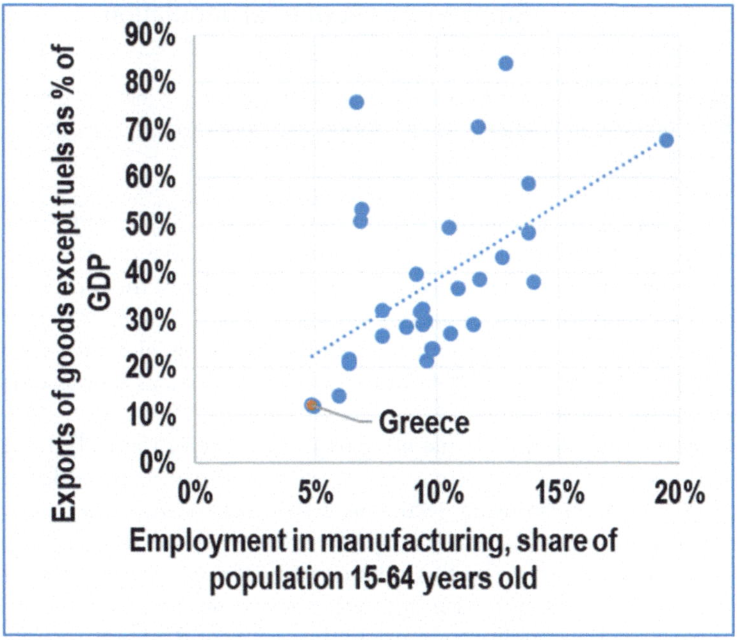

Fig. 4.1 Exports of goods (except fuels) and employment in Manufacturing (*Eurostat, 2015*)

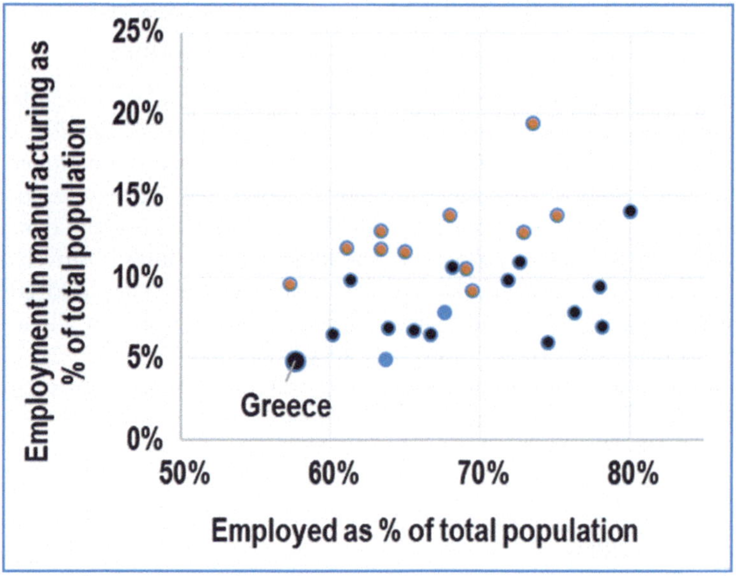

Fig. 4.2 Employment in the economy as an aggregate and in manufacturing as a % of total population (*Eurostat, 2015, Orange color former socialist countries, blue Cyprus and Malta*)

Per capita GDP, on the other hand, has a more complicated relationship with manufacturing. There are countries with a manufacturing base linked to lower value-added activities, mainly countries of the former communist bloc, and for these countries a reduction of the share of manufacturing in total value added (and thus GDP) often coincides with the fast growth of value added produced in the services sectors, as their economy grows fast and modernizes.

For developed countries, that are part of the core of the EU, the relationship becomes visibly positive and an increase of the value added produced by the manufacturing sector, as a share of the total, is positively linked with an increase in prosperity (Fig. 4.4). Related research argues that in developed countries this relationship reflects a close, symbiotic, relationship of production with high value added services (OECD 2016) that is paired with an ability to translate the results of R&D into attractive products and services, and that coincides with a deeper integration into international value chains (W Consult and IW Köln for BusinessEurope

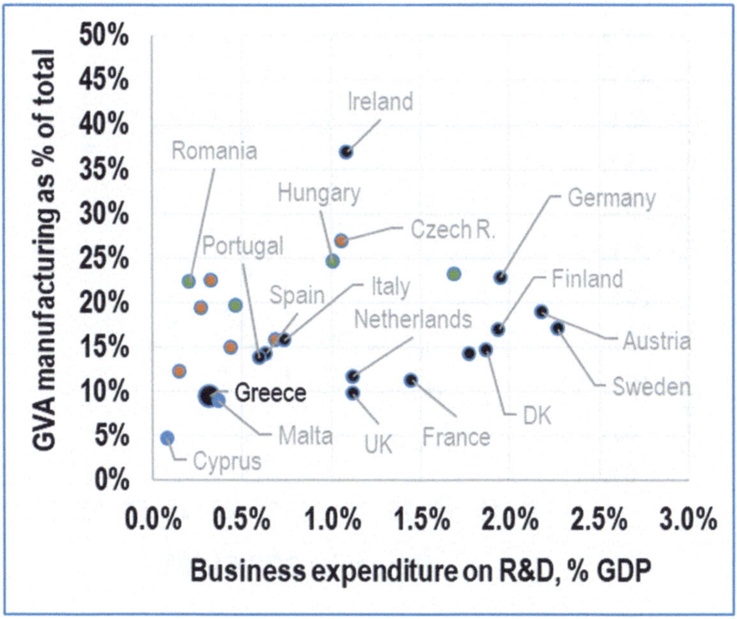

Fig. 4.3 Share of manufacturing to value added and business R&D expenditure (*Eurostat, 2015, SBA Factsheet 2015, Orange color former socialist countries, blue Cyprus and Malta*)

2014). We have to note that in these countries the institutional framework does not raise major tax and regulatory barriers that hinder the growth of companies that combine the manufacturing of products with the integration of services, and allows them to expand their business when, through this combination, they create a competitive advantage. This is, of course, the case when they grow to a larger size and cement their ability to be competitive in the manufacturing of internationally tradable goods. It should be noted here that the company size difference between Greece and the EU averages is quite obvious in the manufacturing sector, Fig. 4.5, and correlated with the presence of the manufacturing sector in the economy. The growth of companies is, in turn, so important because it is the growing companies that create new jobs and introduce innovation in the production lines that increase productivity (Haltiwanger et al. 2013),

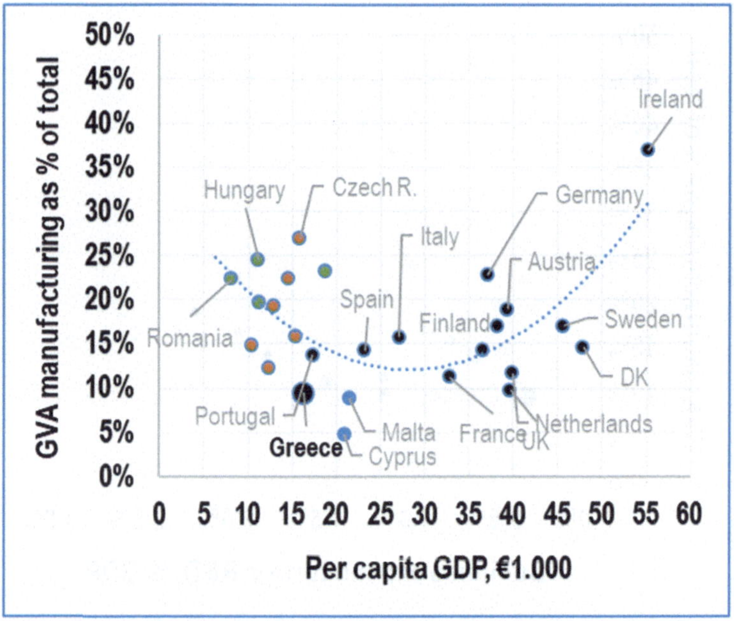

Fig. 4.4 Per capita GDP and value added in manufacturing (*Eurostat, 2015, Orange color former socialist countries, blue Cyprus and Malta*)

creating in the process the preconditions to offer higher annual wages to their employees (Fig. 4.6, Appendix 1).

If we compare all related available dates, it can be shown that the countries for which all these attributes are documented at the same time are usually institutionally strong countries in which the social state is strong and efficient while at the same time important network industries, like that of energy, are regulated and operating efficiently in a way that ultimately offers the productive base of the country access to key services at competitive terms.

The process of growth and welfare creation in our time is built around a constant qualitative transformation that is not always documented easily in the collected statistics, a fact only indicatively reflected in the complicated relationship between manufacturing and per capita GDP, and that poses significant challenges to the vibrant research that attempts to understand the mechanisms that ensure this path towards prosperity.

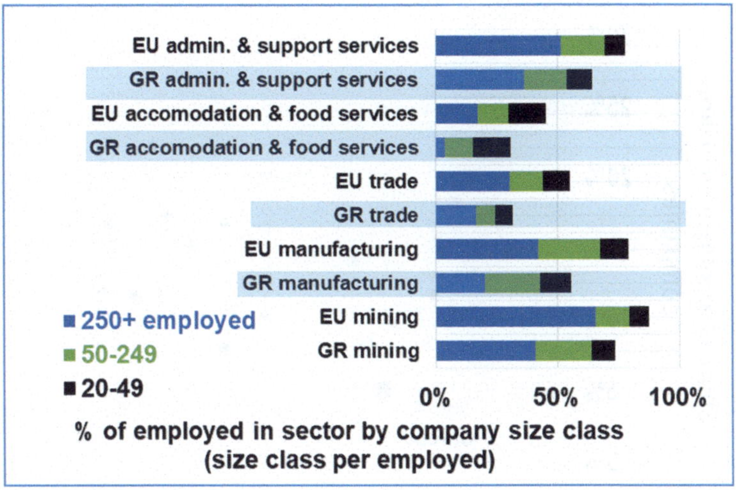

Fig. 4.5 Company size—% of employed in companies by company size (Eurostat, *2015*)

In this context, the classic study of Dertuzos et al. (1989) highlighted already decades ago the problem of the thinning production base in the US, suggesting that even while an economy moves toward becoming a service economy, it should not neglect its production base, a message that apparently has also deeper roots in history (Williamson 2011). More recently, a new research initiative from MIT, titled Production in the Innovation Economy (Berger and the MIT Taskforce on Innovation in the Production Economy 2013), reaffirmed these findings, documenting a relationship that emerges to be very fluid with respect to the attributes that define the relationship between production and services. Recent research stresses in particular the importance of the production base, not only with respect to its size but also regarding the dispersion among many activities, skills, and specializations as well as the ability to interconnect these points of economic (Hausmann et al. 2013).

Thus, even while the manufacturing share of overall economic activity is often documented to decline (Rodrik 2015), the sector is likely to maintain a changing, but key, part of the skills set that enables an economy to produce and offer more complex goods (Hausmann and Hidalgo 2010),

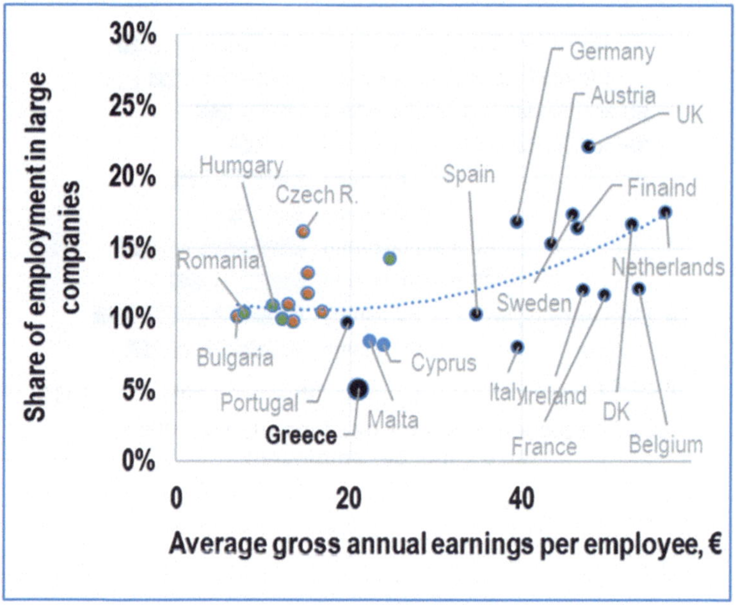

Fig. 4.6 Employment in large businesses and annual gross average employee wage (*Eurostat, 2015, SBA Factsheet 2015, Orange color former socialist countries, blue Cyprus and Malta*)

along a blurred, and less-well-documented, coexistence of services and goods.

In such a setting, and irrespectively of the convergence of productivity among countries in the manufacturing and services sector, the main challenge for each country is to build on the existing economic activities to first establish the basics of a balanced business and knowledge ecosystem, and subsequently to allow it to fulfill its full potential within in a favorable environment of strong institutions (see e.g. Acemoglu and Robinson 2012; but also Olson 1982; North 1990, 1989; Mantzavinos et al. 2003), something that is especially true for countries with less mature institutions like Greece (2014).

Especially in our times, when production and services merge along the value chain, the statistics on the contribution of manufacturing may not always be able to fully document the importance of the sector in an environment in which supportive services may grow also at even higher rates.

Therefore, the relationship that for European countries is still clear between employment and the employment share of manufacturing (Fig. 4.2), becomes already more complicated when one examines value added (Fig. 4.4).

We have already mentioned how in modern times it is critical to allow for those that introduce the new in the economy to grow. Therefore, we now turn to focus on the distribution of companies according to size, which allows to document, overall and beyond the narrow definition of sectors, the contribution, and correlation, of a strong and multidimensional business ecosystem with the various key dimensions of institutional maturity and quality that are, indicatively, selected, and represented in Fig. 4.7.

This change of emphasis to company size is not only supported by the fact that on average manufacturing companies have a larger size (Fig. 4.5, where also the size deficit of Greek companies is once again documented), something that may be challenged in the times of the fourth industrial revolution, at least to some extent, as local to the place of consumption and customized production increases in importance. It is mainly a reflection of the fact that successful value chains that integrate services and production offer, in our times, most growth opportunities, and thus such an environment will allow for enough representation of larger services companies that may grow as key enablers of these value chains, without though excesses that can emerge when competitive pressures are allowed to recede in a market. At the same time, we need to always take into account the findings of the Atlas of Economic Complexity (Hausmann et al. 2013) that stress the importance of skill and activity diversity in the corporate landscape, along with the balanced distribution of companies by size.

Related, according to a recent study (IOVE 2017), manufacturing directly or indirectly contributes about 30% of the Greek GDP and employment, sizeable more than its direct contribution, which is a reflection of the well-established fact that manufacturing activity has important secondary effects on the economy (IW Consult and IW Köln for BusinessEurope 2014) but also a documentation of the important deficit the country posts in this dimension in comparison to key European averages.

The fact that manufacturing emerges to have such large indirect footprints on economic activity, as documented through the input–output tables that trace how each sector is connected with other sector of the

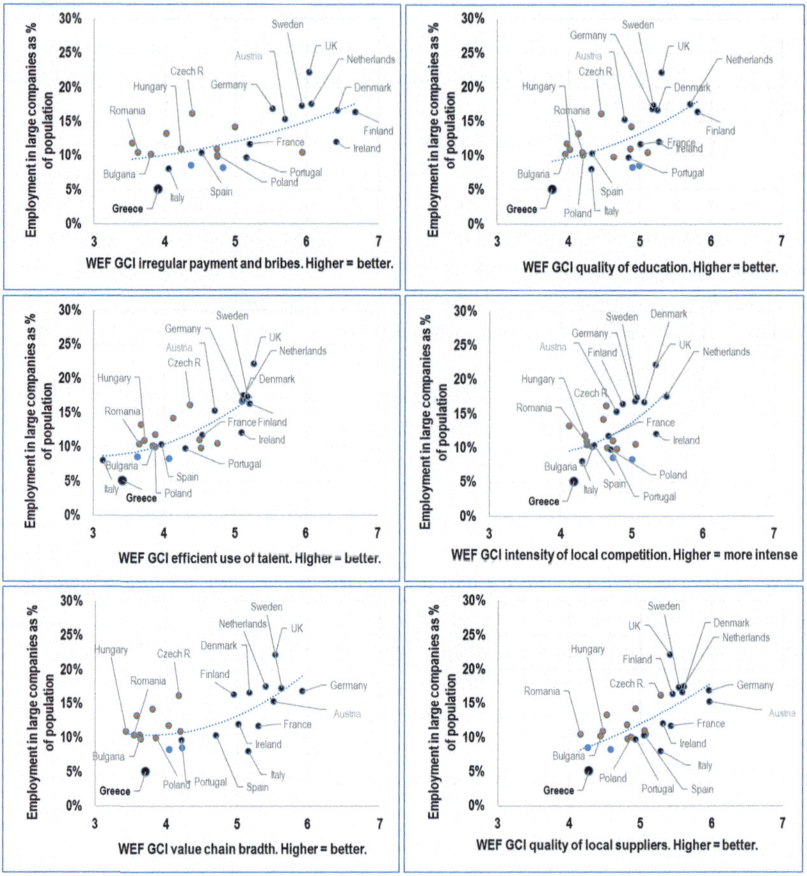

Fig. 4.7 A substantial and balanced contribution of larger companies to the economy is compatible with lower corruption, more competitive markets, better use of talent, better education, the depth of domestic value chains, and the quality of suppliers (*SBA Factsheet, 2015, WEF GCI 2015–2016 components, Orange color former socialist countries, blue Cyprus and Malta*)

economy, stressed the evolving role of the sector along complex value chains in modern economies.

Figure 4.7 relates perceptions indexes collected through the executive opinion survey conducted by the WEF, which documents perceptions of the business community on issues related to the business environment and competitiveness. While the debate regarding the merits of subjective indictors, like the one used, and data collected from hard facts, like, for example, the Doing Business and OECD PMR, is ongoing, it remains a fact that subjective indicators can evaluate the overall reality, even with some measurement error, while fact-based approaches offer the benefit of greater detail, but remain restricted to the specific regulatory or procedural area they focus on. For the aims of our current exposition, the subjective indicators of the WEF thus are appropriate in conveying how the business community overall and taking all facts that shape reality appreciates the examined, key, dimensions of an economy.

All this implies that when policymakers underestimate the crucial contribution of manufacturing toward the ability of a country to build and maintain the forces that support this transformation process, they often conduct a serious mistake. It also means that the mere existence of a strong productive base is not always sufficient to ensure the desired results, nor does it emerge without the establishment of the necessary preconditions. These preconditions are, in the end, directly related to qualities related with the establishment and quality of the democracy, governance, the rule of law, transparency, and the ability to implement efficiently public policies, to formulate appropriate regulations and excel in public policy dimensions like education and health in a way that ensures access to quality services especially for the less privileged. Such an environment "nudges", to paraphrase Thaler and Sunstein (2008), the private sector to create jobs and taxable income, while abiding to reasonable rules that protect the public interest without needless shortcomings and vaguenesses that burden private initiatives with a damaging-for-all ill-conceived dependence on the state. Such an environment supports, in the end, growth through the formulation of appropriate policies (Fig. 4.8).

An ability to reward talent and success that stems either from investment or education during the professional life, at the level of both the corporate entity and the individual is a crucial ingredient of such a framework. The same applies to the establishment of a competitive and, thus inevitably, based on meritocracy environment that gives the incentives to channel effort towards progress and succees in a creative direction. Without these attributes there can exist no incentives to work or to invest, nor to strive for innovations that increase non-wage competitiveness and allow for this to be distributed through the remunerations of those that helped achieve it.

Energy	- Accelerate the phase out of subsidies, levies and taxes driving up energy prices for consumers. - Modernise energy infrastructure to establish an integrated energy market with regional cooperation.
Research and innovation	- Ensure an adequate funding in the next Multiannual Financial Framework as research and innovation remain clearly underfunded. - Secure, the positive approach introduced by Horizon 2020, in particular in balancing EU funding over the whole ecosystem of research and innovation. - Speed up the implementation of the 'innovation principle'.
Circular economy	- Accelerate good practices sharing and raise awareness in member states.
Digitalization	- Secure free flow of data and avoid restrictions on where certain types of data can be physically stored. - Ensure the development of national digitalisation platforms and their coordination, through the creation of a European network of digital innovation hubs. - Avoid pre-empting hypothetical risks of artificial intelligence and focus on opportunities.
Skills	- Take into account sectors with skills shortages for future skills anticipation blueprints. - Increase the speed at which education and training curricula are adapted to changing skills demands on the labour market, including the role of vocational education and training. - Benchmark skills policies as part of the European semester, with a focus on helping member states learn from each other and design skills policies achieving a better use of available resources to improve learning outcomes, thereby contributing to labour productivity growth.

Fig. 4.8 Business Europe report "Building a strong and modern European industry – Views on a renewed industrial strategy", BusinessEurope

The establishment of such an environment is a delicate balancing act, especially during times in which populism encourages societies and politicians to establish prejudices regarding the role of competitive markets and the balanced participation of larger companies in an economy that distributes rewards according to merit (Di Tella and MacCulloch 2009).

This process, it is argued, is directly linked with the deepening of value chains and the qualitative enrichment of the supplier networks in an economy, and such a process includes inescapably a balanced participation by the manufacturing sector (Fig. 4.7).

The evidence presented in Fig. 4.7 demonstrates how the establishment of a balanced corporate landscape with a sufficient participation of larger companies, reflected through their contribution to employment, is linked with key dimensions of institutional maturity, quality of public services that are crucial for social coherence, and mobility and development like access to education meritocracy and competitive conditions in market. Strangely, given the related prejudices, it appears that competitive markets are linked with an increased participation of larger corporates in the business landscape, and this demonstrates how competitive markets in the end allow successful small companies to grow.

In this context, the deficit of manufacturing and larger companies in Greece, also documented in the Figs. 4.1, 4.2, 4.3, 4.4, 4.5, 4.6, 4.7, and 4.8, through a low participation in employment and gross value added of manufacturing, a deficit in employment among larger companies, when compared to other European peer countries, has to be identified as a reflection of the overall weakness of the institutions of the country. At the same time, it becomes evident that changing this undesirable situation cannot come as a result of a piecemeal approach, and thus will entail at the same time both a maturing of institutions in the country and a strengthening of its productive base. This process in turn will imply that the country will be able to offer employment opportunities that are diverse, and thus will match the inevitably diverse preference and talents of any population, rather than offer single dimensional job opportunities that would prevail should one attempt to secure growth through a policy encouragement that focuses on a few sectors of the economy (Hausmann 2012).

3 A Revival of the Productive Base as a Prerequisite for the Survival of Greece

The modern, digital, globalization offers growth opportunities to an unprecedented, in history, degree, but at the same time marginalizes brutally, and to an equally unprecedented degree, those who do not prepare themselves and thus are not adequately equipped to take advantage of these opportunities (Hausmann and Hidalgo 2010). In turn this means that the modern age bears increased risks of marginalization especially for countries, and regions within those countries (The Economist 2017) that are unable to attract the appropriate, from a qualitative aspect, critical mass of investment and talent that allows a society to follow, and benefit from, these fast and decisive for the future of humankind developments.

A solid, and sufficiently diverse, productive base, and of course the preconditions that allow it to grow and prosper, are necessary so that a country can avoid this marginalization. Only that way can a society take full advantage of the various talents and professional career preferences of the population, contributing exponentially to the increase of not only prosperity but also the ability of the economy to follow these developments.

This in turn is strongly correlated with the balanced distribution of small and large companies, production, and services provision that is necessary to form a dynamic economy and coherent society. Such a balanced business ecosystem is, in the end, the foundation for the growth of SMEs in a country, but also the precondition for the growth of successful start-ups that contribute to the growth of companies (Pelagidis and Mitsopoulos 2014).

Also, these are the preconditions to create the tax base that will finance a state that is based on the rule of law to apply these policies, that in turn will support sustainable growth and the economic and social coherence that such growth can secure.

But such a productive base can prosper only under certain preconditions. In particular:

1. Tax policy, and the tax framework in general as well as the policy for social security contributions, has to be sufficiently reciprocal, offering adequate services in return for the burden they impose on the private agents, and it should not discourage the development of complex value chains, the use of salaried employment and the reward of work and talent. In case this happens, the economic activity that is correlated with the development of high value chains and innovation-driven growth is most hit, depriving an economy of the main driver of growth.
2. The quality of laws and regulations and the adequacy of administrative services, and the way it ensures the application of these laws and regulations, should not introduce barriers, or introduce a vagueness and uncertainty that has a similar effect, especially on the creation of complex value chains, the participation in international value chains, and the adoption and investment in innovation both in production and in services. Once again, in such case companies that aim to participate in such value chains are adversely affected to a disproportional way.

3. The design of energy policy in a country has to be realistic and lead to the efficient use of the comparative advantages a country has, ensuring that both household consumers and corporates that produce internationally tradable goods have access to energy with competitive terms.
4. There has to exist a solid and mature financial system that can finance both established activities, of all sizes, but in addition also finance the innovative, new, and risky at all scales (Pelagidis and Mitsopoulos 2014). The importance of linking finance, production, and innovation is often underestimated, in spite of the fact that innovation and progress in the dimension of production has always, historically, been matched by equally important innovations in the tools used to finance the real-economy innovations (Lamoreaux and Sokoloff 2007).

In Greece, these preconditions have gradually been eroded during the past decades. Tax policy, for the past decades but even more during the crisis and adjustment program years (Appendix 2), has been unstable, with vague rules generally compatible with corruption and often openly hostile toward the reward of talent and business success (SEV 2018; Mitsopoulos 2017). It has to be stressed that even though tax policies often influence decisively investment decisions (World Economic Forum 2013a), low tax rates may not have the desired impact on the attraction of investment when other costs and uncertainties cancel out this tax advantage.

The quality of laws, and of their implementation, used to lag. Thus, business initiatives like those that are developing within the context of complex value chains along which "things are being made" had much increased chances to confront at more focal points provisions of regulations or administrative practices that create undue and unrelated to the protection of the public interest obstacles or cost increases. Thus, in the end, the endeavor become noncompetitive or is cancelled outright. The irony here was that these costs were not even a revenue for the state, like taxes, but simply a deadweight loss.

A crucial dimension, especially for the companies "that produce," is energy. Traditionally energy policy in Greece was not planned in a rational way, and as a result unnecessarily risks were created for the national economy depriving the part of Greece "that produces things" from access to energy with competitive terms.

Regarding the access to finance, it has to be stressed that in our country the qualitatively sufficient institutions that ensure the rule of law and the sanctity of contracts were never well established. As a result non-bank financing that depends disproportionally on the delivery of such institutions could never really take off. The same applies to bank finance without material guarantees, like real estate or immovable equipment. This means that the fiscal crisis and its indirect effects on the financial system, that is mainly the banking system, affected disproportionally the intermediate tranches of the Greek business landscape, especially when it found it difficult as a result of the nature of its business line to move to a significant extent into the shadow economy or depended more on complex international financial transactions. This, in turn, was disproportionally the case for Greek intermediate manufacturing that was well integrated in international value chains.

Actually, some of the most unfortunate, for the productive base of the country, policy decisions, and increases in the costs of energy for industrial use coincided with the peak of the crisis and the exclusion of a large share of the productive base of the country from access to finance at competitive terms and the multiplication of tax excesses and the growth of tax uncertainty (Mitsopoulos 2016). This happened at the same time progress at the level of regulations concerning the business environment was, proportionally with the impact of these negative developments, small and reluctant and therefore unable to counterbalance them. Overall, these developments can explain the apparent paradox of the large decline of employment in Greek manufacturing during the adjustment program years, when the aim of the latter was to lead the country to an "export led growth" (Pelagidis and Mitsopoulos 2017).

For Greece, this means, more than ever before and irrespectively of the post-program status of the country that improving the quality of institutions and policy design and delivery has to be a top priority. Only that way can one ensure that nonretributive tax and administrative barriers and obstacles will not slow down the growth and success especially of those that endeavor initiatives that are more complex and integrated in international value chains, and the provisions of services that support such endeavors. Alternatively, Greece will not prosper, and its distance with the countries that will lead in the new digital age of the fourth industrial revolution will simply grow. It should be noted here that following the exit from the adjustment programmes, increased national ownership of the reform agenda has emerged, especially in the areas of taxation with key improvements in the tax system and the applied rates especially for investment and in the area of licencing manufacturing units. Furthermore, there have been taken initiatives to reform the banking sector and to swiftly reduce the stock of non-performing loans accumulated during the years of the adjustment programmes, to introduce a modern framework to handle insolvency promise and to advance numerous other reforms and initiatives to improve infrastructure. Paired together, these initiatives offer the country an opportunity to grow its manufacturing base and to rebalance its corporate landscape, by complementing the existing smaller companies with the parts that are missing through the growth of dynamic smaller companies and the attraction of larger investment.

4 The Importance of a Close Collaboration Between the Private and Public Sector to Support the Productive Base of the Country and Its Growth

In the age of the digital revolution, the developed world will be able to support an increase in prosperity, if it can master the full usage of the appropriate skills, encourage innovation, and ensure the close cooperation of the public and private sector especially as far as the equipment of the population with the necessary skills is concerned (McNelly 2016; World Economic Forum 2016). According to the WEF, this is summarized in the ability to use talent, the present and future use of which will mark the perseverance in a country of the preconditions that will allow it to fully reap the opportunities that the fourth industrial revolution creates. It is stressed that, at the same time, there arise important challenges related to equality, but the response to this challenge through excessively high and progressive taxation does not offer a constructive solution as it will lead to a reduction of the talent pool that remains in the country. On the contrary, the policy tools that will be developed have to ensure social coherence without driving out of the country the most dynamic part of its workforce and business landscape.

The priorities that corporate and political leaders set in a country that advances its productive base, and that is well placed to reap the benefits of these new age, have to be supported by governance structures that can adapt with speed and versatility to the evolving challenges (World Economic Forum 2013). The shape that these structures need to have are already the subject of an ongoing debate (World Economic Forum 2018) but it is certain that the production of regulations that focus on provisions that regulate specific activities on a case-by-case approach, rather than setting general principles, will seriously undermine the ability of a country to grow is such a fast-changing environment. The related, and emerging, debate stresses that a close collaboration between the public and the private sector is a key precondition to achieve the balancing act required to introduce regulations that are expressing general principles, flexible and adaptive to the implementation of these in a changing environment. This is even more the case given the legacy of widespread deficiencies that are documented for the country along the dimensions presented, for example, in Fig. 4.7.

5 Conclusions

Greece "produces" but not as much as it could, or should. This gap in the productive base is translated into a corresponding gap in employment, prosperity, and, overall, all dimensions of economic and fiscal performance. This reality is connected very closely with all the deficits that are documented in the country and in all dimension, from openness, and innovation to qualitative aspects of the job market and the efficiency of social policies. It is also related with the often-documented institutional deficit of the country and the structure of the tax system that used to discourage, and still does so in spite of the improvements legislated during recent years, salaried employment in the private sector and therefore the growth of companies that employ such employees. Challenges were mounted horizontally to all entrepreneurial activity through regulations and taxation, the institutional weaknesses, and the inability to access financing at terms compatible with those accessed by competitors in the otherwise Single Market. This situation hurt constantly, accumulatively, and increasingly especially those companies that strove to develop more complex and elaborate activities that, as a result of their nature, are embedded in the official economy and depend more on the rule of law and therefore cannot bypass the institutional weaknesses of the country with a shift to the shadow economy, with respect to both regulations and taxation.

The establishment in Greece of such a widespread SME population that emphasizes simple business activities and primitive production and services reflects this legacy and reality. The disincentives, from a taxation and regulation perspective, to growth and evolution and the inevitable entanglements that follow when one leaves the trodden path, that is, when one innovates and invests in more complex and advanced processes, are the reason why Greece has the documented deficit in its productive base and why there is such a paucity of larger companies in its business landscape.

This diagnosis incorporates though also a positive message: Removing the obstacles that hold the country back, the improvement of its job market performance toward a situation in which the supply and demand for high-skill employment will be matched in a high-remuneration equilibrium, is not impossible. Upgrading the institutions is based also on a better understanding and dialogue between the private and the public sector during the process of designing and implementing policies. Removing critical obstacles to the use of salaried employment in the private sector, like rationalizing the level and progressivity of the tax wedge, will ultimately increase the tax base and public revenue. Solving specific problems, like the ones faced by the energy market, can pose a challenge, but with good faith and a meticulous approach to meet clear goals, they can be overcome. In the end, realizing the above constitutes more than a simple decision to support the "Greece that produces". It constitutes a decision to revisit, as a country, the way that we design policies, and ensure that a mechanism is put in place that will improve the lives of all Greeks, increase their prosperity and levels of happiness, and transform Greece into a place that is attractive to work, live, and invest. In that sense, during recent years the effort undertaken to advance key reforms that improve the business environment, encourage innovation and rationalize the tax system, among others, offers Greece the best hope to reverse some of the legacies that have hindered its growth towards sustainable prosperity in the past decades.

Appendix 1. Employment and Wages in Manufacturing

Employment in manufacturing is mainly full time, contrary to sectors that have strong seasonality (Fig. 4.9) in their activity, and that are based by the nature of their activities mainly on part-time and flexible employment contracts (e.g. this is the case in retail trade to support flexibility in the operation of stores, and in the hotel and food sectors due to the seasonality of demand in Greece). This results in the fact that part-time employment in the European economy is about 20.5% of the total, but in manufacturing only 7.8% according to Eurostat for 2015. This, along with the fact that employment in manufacturing usually requires higher skills, implies that in the end annual remuneration is higher (Fig. 4.10), but also that

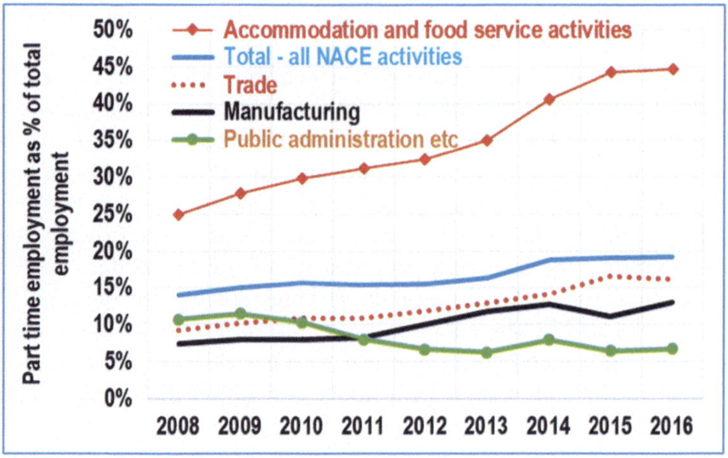

Fig. 4.9 Part-time employment in Greece according to sectors (*Eurostat, 2016. Part-time employment in the public sector follows as a result of seasonal contracts, for example, for education, fire-fighting etc.*)

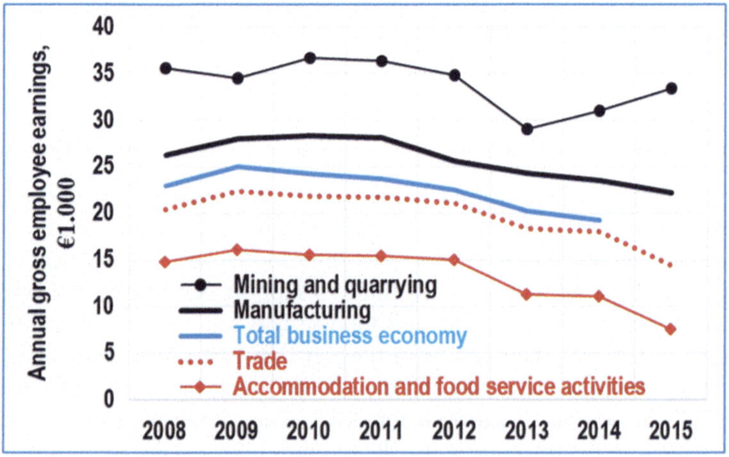

Fig. 4.10 Annual employer cost by sector in Greece (*Eurostat, 2015, data for business economy*)

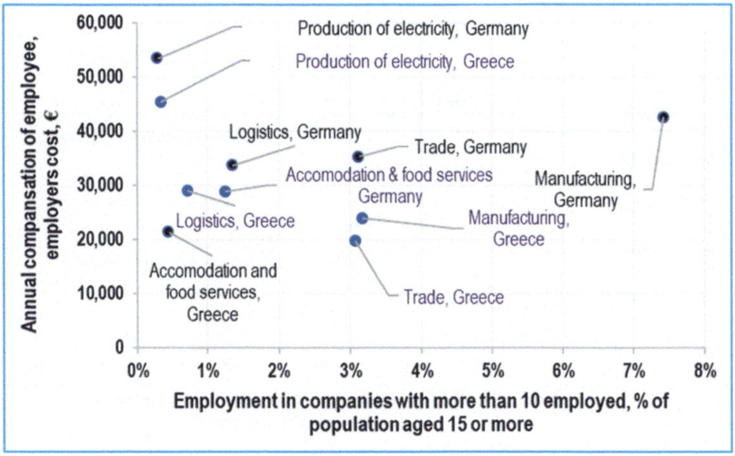

Fig. 4.11 Remuneration and employment in manufacturing, accommodation, food and beverage sector, energy production, transport, and storage (*Eurostat, 2009, businesses with over ten employed persons*)

remuneration is more resilient during crises. Another implication is that these incomes form a more stable and a larger tax base for the public sector to draw on.

The qualitative improvement that comes with the enhancement of the productive base of a country has positive externalities beyond the narrow sector. Even in the services sector the attributes of jobs improve when the sector participates in value chains that include manufacturing. A comparison between Greece and Germany in the precrisis and pre-adjustment program year 2009 that documents data for companies with at least ten employed persons (Figs. 4.11 and 4.12) shows that the employment of manufacturing does not influence, for example, the employment share, to the population, of trade, the food and beverage sectors or accommodation, with the employment share to the population in trade being at notably similar levels and the employment share of food and beverage and accommodation sectors being higher in Greece, as is expected due to its capacity as a prime tourist destination. But on the other hand, in Greece along with employment in manufacturing the employment in logistics

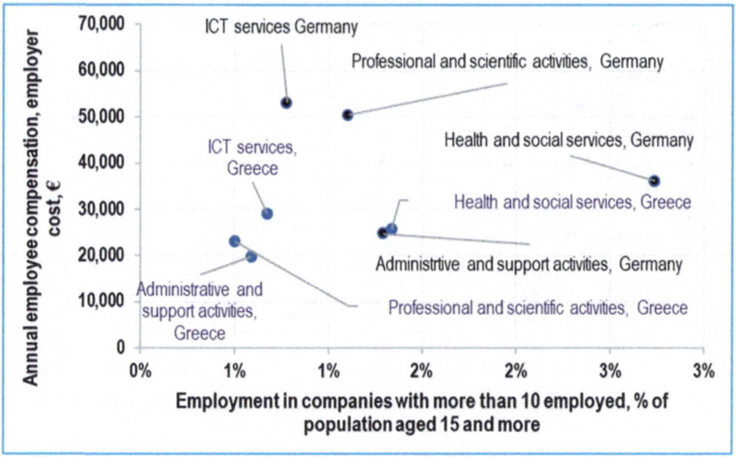

Fig. 4.12 Remuneration and employment in services that support the business sector (*Eurostat, 2009, businesses with over ten employed persons*)

services, administrative business services and scientific activities, ICT professions, and health and social services (that include care for children and elderly dependents of working families) all decline. This important differentiation in the structure of the job market is reflected also beyond wages in qualitative aspects of the job market. Indicatively, the increase of employment in manufacturing is related with a decline in the share of employed that work part-time despite their preferences (Fig. 4.13).

These attributes are documented not only in Greece, but also in other countries, and are a reason why manufacturing jobs are again deemed desirable by policy-makers and researchers (Andes and Muro 2013), especially as progress in health and safety issues guarantees the significant improvement in the work environment these jobs can achieve. The same applies to the fact that high skill services and manufacturing merge to an ever-closer relationship that is a prerequisite to build the balanced skill and business population landscape that guarantees the ability to take advantage of the modern age (Muro et al. 2016).

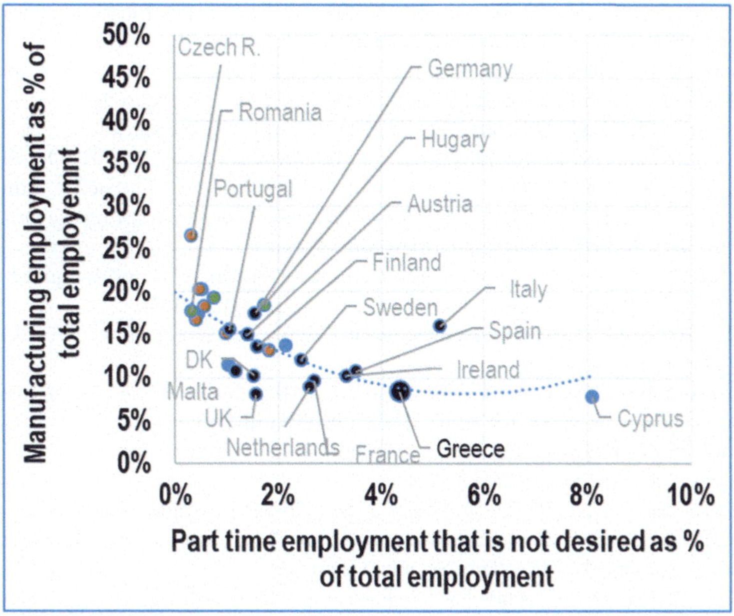

Fig. 4.13 Employment in manufacturing and share of employment that is part-time despite the preferences of the employed person (*Eurostat, 2015, Orange color former socialist countries. Part-time employment according to Eurostat is employment for less than 35 h/week*)

References

Acemoglu, D. and Robinson J. (2012). *Why Nations Fail: The Origins of Power, Prosperity, and Poverty*. New York: Crown Publishers.

Andes, S. and Muro, M. (2013). Jobs Alone Do Not Explain the Importance of Manufacturing, Brookings Institution Report, April 3.

Berger, S with the MIT Task Force on Production in the Innovation Economy (2013). Making in America. From Innovation to Market. In Locke, R.M. and Wellhausen, R. (eds), *Production in the Innovation Economy*. Cambridge, MA: MIT Press.

Dertouzos, M.L., Solow, R.M. and Lester, R.K. (1989). *Made in America: Regaining the Productive Edge*. Cambridge, MA: MIT Press.

Di Tella R. and MacCulloch R. (2009). Why Doesn't Capitalism Flow to Poor Countries? Brookings Paper on Economic Activity No 1.

Haltiwanger J., Jarmin R. and Miranda J (2013). Who Creates Jobss? Small versus Large versus Young. *Review of Economics and Statistics*, 95(2), 347–361.

Hausmann, R. (2012). Ireland Can Show Greece a Way out of the Crisis. Exports Hold the Key to Economic Survival. *Financial Times.* February 8.

Hausmann, R. and Hidalgo, C. (2010). Country Diversification, Product Ubiquity, and Economic Divergence. CID Working Paper No. 201, October.

Hausmann, R., Hidalgo C., Bustos S., Coscia M., Chung S., Jimenez J., Simoes A. and M. Yildirim (2013). *The Atlas of Economic Complexity: Mapping Paths to Prosperity* 2nd ed.. Cambridge, MA: MIT Press.

IMF (2018). Manufacturing Jobs: Implications for Productivity and Inequality. In IMF (ed) *World Economic Outlook* (Ch. 3). Washington: IMF.

IOVE (2017). *Ο Τομέας Μεταποίησης στην Ελλάδα: Τάσεις και Προοπτικές*, IOBE (In Greek).

IW Consult and IW Köln for BusinessEurope (2014). *Industry as a Growth Engine in the Global Economy.* IW Köln/ IW Consult GmbH, Cologne.

Lamoreaux N. and Sokoloff K. ed. (2007). Financing Innovation in the United States, 1870 to Present. MIT Press.

Mantzavinos, C., North, D. and Shariq, S. (2003). Learning, Institutions and Economic Performance. *Preprints* of the Max Planck Institute for Research on Collective Goods, Max Plank Society, Germany.

McNelly, J. (2016). 3 Trends for the Future of Manufacturing. *World Economic Forum,* Article.

Mitsopoulos M. (2016). Greek Export and Labor Market Performance: Facts and Myths that Can Help Devise a Useful Growth Strategy. In Luigi Paganetto (Ed), *Stagnation Versus Growth in Europe: Capitalism in the 21st Century.* Switzerland: Springer.

Mitsopoulos, M. (2017). Overtaxation of Private Sector Salaried Employment as a Key Impediment to the Recovery of Greece and The Reaction of the Greek Private Sector Job Market to Changes in Tax Rates and Uncertainty (pp. 289–357). In Thomakos, D., and Nikolopoulos, K. (Eds.), *Taxation in Crisis: Tax Policy and the Quest for Economic Growth.* UK: Palgrave Macmillan.

Muro M., Kulkarni S. D. Hart (2016). America's Advanced Industries: New Trends. *Brookings Institution Report*, August 4.

North, D. (1990). *Institutions, Institutional Change and Economic Performance.* Cambridge: Cambridge University Press.

North, D. (1989). Institutions and Economic Growth: A Historical Introduction, *World Development* 17(9), 1319–1332.

OECD (2016). Enabling the Next Production Revolution: The Future of Manufacturing and Services. *Interim Report*, Meeting of the OECD Council at Ministerial Level Paris, 1–2 June 2016.

OECD and IMF (2017). Tax Certainty. *Report* for the G20 Ministers, IMF and OECD.

Olson, M. (1982). *The Rise and Decline of Nations.* New Haven: Yale University Press.

Pelagidis T. and Mitsopoulos M. (2014). *Greece: From Exit to Recovery?* Brookings Institution Press.

Pelagidis T. and Mitsopoulos M. (2017). *Who's to Blame for Greece? How Austerity and Populism are Destroying a Country with High Potential.* Second Edition. Palgrave Macmillan.

Rodrik, D. (2015). Premature Deindustrialization. *Journal of Economic Growth*, 21, 1–33.

SEV Tax Committee (2018). *All Encompassing Supertaxation in Greece. Can we Still Hope for Growth?* SEV Hellenic Federation of Enterprises.

Thaler R. and Sunstein C (2008). *Nudge Improving Decisions about Health, Wealth, and Happiness.* New Haven: Yale University Press.

The Economist (2017). Left in the Lurch. Globalisation has Marginalised many Regions in the Rich World. What can be done to help them? Print edition, Oct 21st, 2017.

Williamson, J. (2011). *Trade and Poverty: When the Third World Fell Behind.* Cambridge, MA: MIT Press.

World Economic Forum (2013). *Manufacturing for Growth Strategies for Driving Growth and Employment.* A World Economic Forum Report in Collaboration with Deloitte Touche Tohmatsu Limited. World Economic Forum Geneva.

World Economic Forum (2013a). Going Deep on Critical Policy Issues. Competitive Tax Policy: A Strategic Lever. In *Manufacturing for Growth Strategies for Driving Growth and Employment.* A World Economic Forum Report in Collaboration with Deloitte Touche Tohmatsu Limited. World Economic Forum Geneva.

World Economic Forum (2016). *Manufacturing Our Future: Cases on the Future of Manufacturing*, Report released by the World Economic Forum Global Agenda Council on Manufacturing. World Economic Forum White Paper.

World Economic Forum (2018). *Agile Governance Reimagining Policy-making in the Fourth Industrial Revolution.* World Economic Forum White Paper.

CHAPTER 5

Greek Shipping Receipts Revisited: A Freight Market and Country Risk Perspective

Zacharias G. Bragoudakis, Stelios Th. Panagiotou, and Helen A. Thanopoulou

1 Introduction

The years since 2009 have been marked for Greek shipping—still leading the world fleet for more than four decades—by two major trends: high volatility in the main freight markets and a turbulent country environment. Both these could potentially severely impact shipping receipts. Despite the international character of almost the totality of Greek-owned tonnage, Greek shipping is mainly managed from Piraeus, with the share of

---

A previous version of the chapter was presented at the European Conference on Shipping and Intermodalism—ECONSHIP 2015 at Chios, Greece, during 24–27 June 2015. The views expressed in this chapter are those of the authors and do not necessarily reflect those of the Bank of Greece.

Z. G. Bragoudakis (✉)
Economic Analysis and Research Department, Bank of Greece, Athens, Greece

Department of Economics, National and Kapodistrian University of Athens, Athens, Greece
e-mail: zbragoudakis@bankofgreece.gr

I. T. Kokores et al. (eds.), *Money, Trade and Finance*,
https://doi.org/10.1007/978-3-030-73219-6_5

foreign-based headquarters diminishing in past decades (Harlaftis et al. 2010). As almost the entirety of the fleet is being managed now from Greek headquarters, country risk emerged, since early 2010, as potentially critical especially in a period of long-term decline of freight rates—which reached historic record lows in early 2016—to be followed by a fickle and questionably sustainable recovery. Investigating the way shipping inflows evolved—in this period of high market volatility—during the Greek sovereign crisis period, allows making a number of inferences about both the role of the maritime cluster itself in securing a minimum of inflows destined to finance its operations and the impact of country risk on shipping inflows.

Adding to the existing literature, the approach of the authors is novel as it compares advanced cointegration methods like Fully Modified OLS (FMOLS) and Dynamic OLS (DOLS) considered statistically more robust compared to simple OLS. The ECM framework allows estimating adjustment process to the long-run equilibrium level. The analysis also includes an attempt to measure the impact of country risk on the gross shipping inflows. The spread of the ten-year Greek bond over the German Bund was used as a proxy to the country risk. As the sovereign crisis was peaking, there were increasing concerns—based on anecdotal evidence—on the ability of the shipping sector to maintain a stable level of inflows similar to the one seen in the past due to: (a) the freight market volatility and (b) the Greek-sovereign risk. The current chapter attempts to answer these two questions and to reveal, also, the role of the sovereign risk in the course of shipping inflows in the recent turbulent years.

The chapter is organized as follows: Following the introduction, Sect. 2 proceeds to a literature review on shipping receipts. Section 3 discusses freight market developments and Greek country risk since the end of the last

S. T. Panagiotou
Economic Analysis and Research Department, Bank of Greece, Athens, Greece

Department of Shipping, Trade and Transport, University of the Aegean, Chios, Greece

H. A. Thanopoulou
Department of Shipping, Trade and Transport, University of the Aegean, Chios, Greece

Bayes Business School, City, University of London, London, UK decade. Data, methodology and results of the statistical analysis of shipping receipts in long-run market disequilibria and the impact of the country risk are discussed in Sect. 4. Conclusions are presented in Sect. 5.

2 Literature Review on Greek Shipping Inflows

The case of Greece in terms of Greek shipping inflows is idiosyncratic compared with both traditional cross-trading shipowning countries, such as Norway and the UK, or cargo-owning countries with large trades such as Japan or, today, China. For all the aforementioned countries, the maritime cluster of activities is significantly larger than mainly shipowning and ship-managing, and this despite the decline of the use of nationals for crewing and independently of the size (Harlaftis et al. 2010) of the national trade; this is due to the survival of a long tradition in maritime-related services—including international shipping finance—for the UK and Norway with the addition of shipbuilding and related activities (as, for instance, classification societies) being very significant in the past decades for Japan and later China.

The importance of the inflows from shipping services to the Greek economy is well documented. In the period 2002–2014, the inflows from shipping services amounted to more than 6.0% of the GDP annually and covered more than 40% of the goods' trade deficit (Table 5.1). However, the collapse in the freight rate market in the second half of 2008 had a significant negative effect on the receipts from shipping services which recorded a decline of 30% in 2009. This development came at a critical juncture for the Greek economy just entering then into recession territory; a year later, the first economic adjustment programme was concluded. The Greek economy experienced a great recession in 2009–2013, which amounted to more than a 25% decrease in real GDP terms.

In this economic environment, the identification of growth sectors and the contributions from the Greek shipping activity became an important policy requirement. Against this backdrop, there were a number of studies identifying shipping as a potential growth industry and quantifying its potential value added (Boston Consulting Group 2013; IOBE 2013; Bank of Greece 2014). In terms of shipping inflows, Bragoudakis and Panagiotou (2010) and Panagiotou and Bragoudakis (2010) investigated the determinants of receipts from Greek shipping services by the use of an error correction model (ECM). The authors have identified the existence of a stable long-run relationship between freight rates and the stock of

Table 5.1 Evolution of shipping inflows 2002–2014

	2002	2003	2004	2005	2006	2007	2008	2009	2010	2011	2012	2013	2014
Receipts from shipping													
-in USD million	7547	10,161	15,425	16,136	16,676	21,562	26,037	17,073	18,542	17,692	15,118	14,178	15,193
-in EUR million	7997	8961	12,404	12,953	13,280	15,679	17,624	12,262	14,013	12,711	11,761	10,672	11,449
-as % of GDP	4.9	5.0	6.4	6.5	6.1	6.7	7.3	5.2	6.2	6.1	6.2	5.9	6.4
-as % of total exports (goods & services)	24.7	27.0	30.7	30.5	28.8	30.1	31.4	27.4	28.3	24.2	21.5	19.4	19.8
- as % of services exports	37.8	41.7	46.3	47.4	46.7	49.9	51.6	45.2	49.1	44.4	42.7	38.1	36.9
- as % of goods trade balance	35.5	35.6	44.0	44.1	37.7	36.6	39.7	37.0	46.1	48.3	55.9	51.4	51.4

Source: Bank of Greece and EL.STAT

loans to the Greek shipping sector—as a proxy of the Greek shipping cluster—and the inflows of shipping receipts in the Greek economy. In addition, it was revealed that the selected specification of the proposed model is more accurate compared to other benchmark time series models as autoregressive or random walk.

Bragoudakis, Panagiotou and Thanopoulou (2015) further analysed the determinants of Greek net shipping inflows on the basis of recent data in relation to freight rates and to Greek investment strategy incorporating monthly data until mid-2012. They have also taken into account the composition of the Greek-owned tonnage to accurately reflect the impact of market developments. Kasimati and Veranos (2011), following a similar methodology as Bragoudakis and Panagiotou (2010), estimated an ECM that related the inflows from shipping services with the freight rates and the size of the Greek-flagged fleet on a quarterly basis with results in line with the aforementioned literature. Prandeka and Zarkos (2014) investigated the relationship between the net receipts from shipping services and related these with the level of freight rates and the size of Greek flagged fleet on a quarterly basis with similar methodology and results in line with the aforementioned research.

3 Freight Market Developments and Greece-Related Country Risk

The period following the Lehman Brothers collapse was one of abrupt freight rate declines followed by short market recoveries, albeit within an overall recessionary trend (Fig. 5.1). However, until 2014 shipping markets seemed unwilling to "capitulate" most evidently due to the increased speed of mean reversion (Alizadeh, Strandenes and Thanopoulou, 2014) and a combination of still-healthy cash flows holding strong since the previous super-cycle (Stopford 2009). Refinancing facilities by banks unwilling to write down more bad loans and the entry into the market of funds—eager to provide fresh capital in exchange of equity—contributed to sustaining the continued growth of world tonnage not affected by the limited scrapping taking place. Yet, following the "false dawn" of the summer of 2013, the long-term freight decline continued especially in dry bulk carriers. A succession of absolute lows of the BDI index—since its creation in 1985—followed since 2015, with the index landing at a historic low below 300 points of the index in early February 2016.

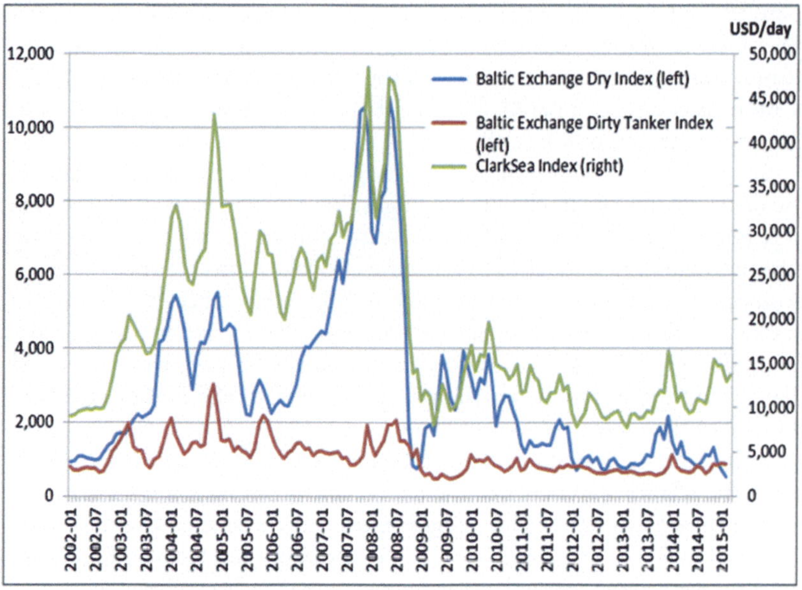

Fig. 5.1 Freight rates—monthly data. (Source: Clarkson Research Services)

Following the creation of the EMU, the introduction of the euro and the elimination of the exchange rate risk, it can be argued—with hindsight—that the assessment of the sovereign risk of individual euro area member countries by the market participants was underestimated. The collapse of the Lehman Brothers in September 2008 and the emergence of the financial crisis led to the reassessment of the risk associated with sovereigns as well as with private sector corporations—financial or non-financial. This reassessment of the sovereign risk is evident in the case of the Greece, as depicted by the spread of the ten-year Greek bond over the German Bund. The average spread from 2002 until the collapse of the Lehman Brothers was around 30 basis points (i.e. 0.3%). During the first episodes of the financial crises and before the emergence of the euro area sovereign crisis (September 2008–April 2010), this spread increased almost sevenfold to more than 200 bps. The upward movement continued during the first two economic adjustment programmes period (May 2010–December 2014) and amounted—on average—to 1251 bps. The middle of 2012, however, was precisely the time of a number

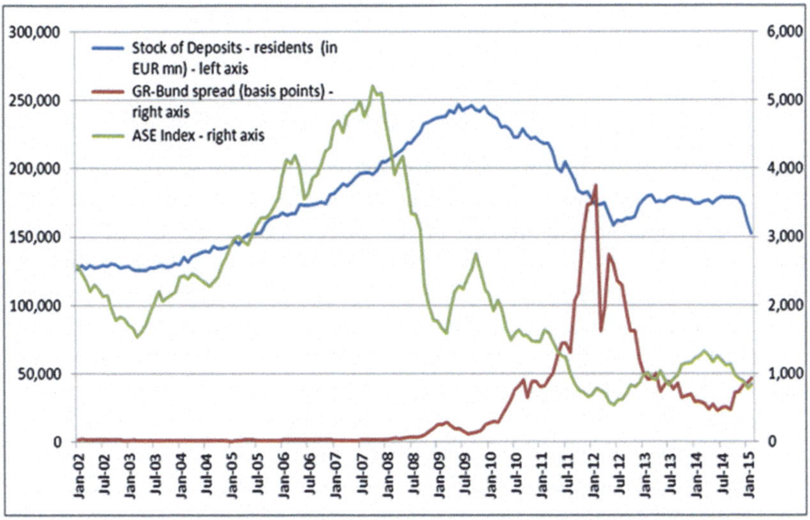

Fig. 5.2 Stock of deposits, ASE Index and spread of the Greek ten-year bond over the German Bund—monthly data. (Sources: Bloomberg and Bank of Greece)

of major political developments in Greece with two elections and an almost-catastrophic loss of trust in the banking sector within the context of political uncertainty. The spreads reached levels close to 2700 bps around the period of the first of the two successive national elections which took place in May and June 2012. A full liquidity crisis was averted only through resort to central bank financing and ELA liquidity to unprecedented levels. In the first half of 2015, just before the agreement on the third economic adjustment programme, the spread was at elevated levels of around 1150 bps. It peaked around the time of the referendum on 5 July 2015, before returning to its previous level just after the Euro Summit of 13 July 2015. The development in the spread seems to be closely—and negatively—related to both the index of the Athens Stock Exchange and the stock of deposits and repos of residents with Greek financial institutions (Fig. 5.2).

4 Econometric Methodology and Empirical Results

4.1 Data

The Greek shipping inflows (TSI) are the receipts from sea transportation (international) services,[1] which reflect the operation of ocean-going shipping. These data were compiled by the Bank of Greece external statistics department and transcribed in USD on the basis of ECB published monthly average exchange rates. The ClarkSea Index (IND) was sourced from the Clarkson Research database. End-of-month outstanding loan data (LS) are published by the Bank of Greece; the data represent outstanding loans from what the Greek banking system[2] has provided to Greek shipping companies. These data were also expressed in USD as in the case of the balance of payments data. Finally, the USD Libor (three months) rates (Libor) were obtained by www.global-rates.com, while the spread of the Greek ten-year bond over the respective German bund (spread) was calculated on the basis of Bloomberg data. The period of our study spans from January 2002 to December 2014.[3]

4.2 Econometric Methodology and Theoretical Considerations

The baseline specification of the long-run equation is an extension of the previous work by Bragoudakis and Panagiotou (2010) and Bragoudakis et al. (2015), which investigated the determinants of the shipping foreign exchange inflows. The first extension is the inclusion of the USD Libor, as

[1] The data, which are compiled by the Bank of Greece Statistics Department, are the aggregation of the Greek shipping companies' individual transactions which are facilitated by the domestic banking system (both Greek and foreign banks).

[2] Financial institutions based in Greece which record their shipping loans in the Greek offices/branches.

[3] The sample period ended in December 2014 in order to avoid distortions resulting by the events that occurred in the first half of 2015 and the introduction of capital controls. It is reminded that political uncertainty was raised significantly in the first half of 2015 on the back of a number of events such as the call of snap parliamentary elections for January, the initially scheduled expiry of the second adjustment programme at the end of February, the calling of a referendum and the introduction of capital controls in late June 2015 coupled with a period of banks being not open to the public. Since the introduction of capital controls in June 2015, the receipts from shipping services recorded an overwhelming decrease, although there continued to be a strong inflow amidst the dearth of others at the time.

it reflects the financing cost of the bank loans that the shipping companies have received.

Firstly, the time series properties of all the variables are initially evaluated employing the Augmented Dickey-Fuller (1981) and DF-GLS (Elliot et al.1996) unit root tests. More specifically, we examined the rank of integration I(d) for the series of the TSI, IND, LS, the exchange rate (EXR) and Libor. Secondly, an error correction model (ECM) in two steps, proposed by Engle-Granger (1987), was employed in order to investigate the structure of the shipping inflows. As the first step, the existence of a long-run relationship was tested. In particular, the relationship between TSI and IND, LS, EXR, Libor is investigated. All series have been logarithmicaly transformed except for Libor; hence, the estimated coefficients denote elasticities.

The baseline specification of the long-run relationship for shipping inflows (TSI) can be written as follows:

$$\text{TSI}_t = \mu + \alpha_1\text{IND}_t + \alpha_2\text{LS}_t + \alpha_3\text{EXR}_t + \alpha_4\text{Libor}_t + d_t, \tag{5.1}$$

This implies that in the long run it is assumed that the endogenous variable of shipping inflows (TSI) is determined by the exogenous variables of the freight index (IND), the outstanding loans (LS), the exchange rate (EXR) and the London interbank overnight interest rate of three months (Libor). A deterministic dummy shift variable (DVSHIFT0807) has also been added in the long-run relationship to account for the change of the regime before and after July of 2008 due to the global financial crisis which substantially affected the freight rates and thus the Greek shipping inflows. If IND, LS, EXR and TSI are I(1) and d_t ~I(0), the series would be cointegrated. The term of μ is the constant parameter, while the parameters of α_1, α_2, α_3, α_4 denote the long-run elasticities. The term of d_t is the long-run vector of residuals of Eq. (5.1), and in case of the existence of cointegration denotes the error correction term.

Estimating (5.1) by static OLS method achieves a consistent estimate of the long-run steady-state relationships between the variables, and all dynamics and endogeneity issues can be ignored asymptotically. This arises because of what is termed the "super-consistency property" of the OLS estimator when the series are cointegrated. In this chapter, we propose a more sophisticated approach by taking into consideration both FMOLS and DOLS methods for the estimation of the long–run relationship. FMOLS and DOLS are considered statistically more robust methods compared to simple OLS static method. In particular, according to Phillips and Hansen (1990), the resulting FMOLS estimator is asymptotically unbiased, and has fully efficient mixture normal asymptotics allowing for standard Wald tests using asymptotic χ^2 statistical inference. Saikkonen (1992) and Stock and Watson (1993) propose the DOLS method, which specifies the cointegrating regression with lags and leads resulting in orthogonal cointegrating error term to the entire history of the stochastic regressor innovation. The numbers of lags and leads are chosen using the Bayesian information criterion (BIC). Using DOLS increases the efficiency and reduces the small sample bias relative to the OLS estimator.

The criterion of residual sum of squares (RSS) was employed to assess the estimated results of the above three alternative methods. The method which provides the lower value of RSS is selected as the best. Consequently, the residuals provided from the best method are employed to test for the existence of cointegration. To test the null hypothesis of no cointegration, the well-known Engle-Granger (1987) and Phillips-Ouliaris (1990) cointegration tests were employed. The best-selected cointegration method for the long-run relationship (5.1) provides results of the following disequilibrium vector:

$$d_{t-1} = \text{TSI}_{t-1} - \mu - \alpha_1 \text{IND}_{t-1} - \alpha_2 \text{LS}_{t-1} - \alpha_3 \text{EXR}_{t-1} - \alpha_4 \text{Libor}_{t-1}.$$

In the second step, we estimate the correspondence error correction model (ECM) by using the disequilibrium vector $d_{t-1.}$ The ECM framework allows for capturing any short-run dynamics and also measuring the speed of adjustment to equilibrium of the endogenous variable TSI. Engle and Granger's ECM in its original form (5.2) is based on the following assumptions: (a) residuals have a zero mean; (b) residual values (either higher or lower than their mean) revert to their mean, that is, at the same speed ρ; and (c) the dependent variable responds to any deviation from equilibrium. It should be noted that the Hendry–type "general to specific" process is employed to reduce the ECM to its parsimonious form. The specification of the symmetric ECM for the TSI can be written in a general form as follows:

$$\Delta(TSI)_t = \delta_0 + \delta_{1,i} \sum_{i=1}^{k_1} \Delta(TSI)_{t-i} + \delta_{2,i} \sum_{i=0}^{k_2} \Delta(IND)_{t-i} + \delta_{3,i} \sum_{i=0}^{k_3} \Delta(LS)_{t-i} + \gamma d_{t-1} + \varepsilon_{1t}, \tag{5.2}$$

where Δ denotes first differences in logarithms and $\varepsilon_{1t} \sim N(0, \sigma^2)$. The k_1, k_2 ... k_5, denote the maximum lag lengths of each explanatory variable. An impulse dummy (DV0807) have been also added in the model (5.2) to capture any impulse disturbance of the endogenous series due to the collapse of financial markets after the Lehman Brothers bankruptcy. The coefficient γ denotes the speed of adjustment to the long-run equilibrium and takes negatives values: high γ value in absolute terms means fast adjustment to the long-run equilibrium. This implies that when the variable TSI_t deviates from the long-run equilibrium relationship (5.1) in period *t*-1, there is a tendency of TSI_t to return to the long-run equilibrium in the following period *t*. Essentially, when the errors d_t exceed their mean value in period *t*-1, TSI_t will tend to move downwards to reach the long-run equilibrium value in period *t*, whereas when errors are below their mean, TSI_t will tend to move upwards, to reach the long-run equilibrium value in period *t*.

4.3 Empirical Results

The hypothesis of a unit root in the logarithmic levels of the series cannot be rejected. By contrast, the hypothesis of a unit root in the first differences is rejected in all cases in favour of the alternative of stationarity. This finding suggests that all employed series are I(1). Table 5.2 presents the results of the unit root tests.

4.3.1 Long-Run Estimation Results

The baseline long-run estimation[4] refers to the period from January 2002 to December 2014, and the results of three competitive long-run estimation methods are presented in Table 5.3. The empirical findings suggest that the method of DOLS performs better than those of OLS and FMOLS. The value of RSS in (5.1) is much lower using DOLS

[4] All series have been logarithmically transformed except for Libor which is interest rate. Hence, the estimated coefficients denote elasticities.

Table 5.2 ADF and DF-GLS unit-root tests

ADF Statistics	(TSI)	Δ(TSI)	(IND)	Δ(IND)	(LS)	Δ(LS)	(EXR)	Δ(EXR)	Libor	Δ(Libor)
Intercept	-2.772	-5.965**	-2.269	-6.556**	-2.01	-11.510**	-3.062	-9.106**	-2.016	-11.510**
Lags	3	2	1	0	0	0	1	0	0	0
Trend and Intercept	-2.218	-6.234**	-2.922	-9.985**	-0.456	-11.751**	-2.503	-9.327**	-0.456	-11.751**
Lags	3	2	1	0	0	0	1	0	0	0
None	0.688	-5.915**	-0.127	-10.008**	2.506	-11.091**	-0.616	-9.084**	-2.506	-11.091**
Lags	3	2	1	0	0	0	1	0	0	0
DF-GLS Statistics	(TSI)	Δ(TSI)	(IND)	Δ(IND)	(LS)	Δ(LS)	(EXR)	Δ(EXR)	Libor	Δ(Libor)
Intercept	-0.583	-0.743	-1.556	-6.556**	0.91	-7.180**	-1.313	-6.966**	0.910	-7.810**
Lags	3	11	1	0	0	0	1	0	0	0
Trend and Intercept	-1.201	-1.165	-1.819	-8.466**	-0.514	-9.248**	-1.678	-8.090**	-0.514	-9.248**
Lags	3	0	1	0	0	0	1	0	0	0

Notes: ** Denotes rejection of the null hypothesis for 5% significance. Critical values being provided by MacKinnon (1996) and Elliot, Rothenberg and Stock (1996). All series have been logarithmic transformed exept for Libor, because it is an interest rate. The selected lag length for no serial correlation of the ADF residuals is based on the Swartz Information Criterion

Table 5.3 Long-run estimations comparison

		Cointegrating methods			
		Baseline models			
Long-run regression methods (HAC standard errors & covariance)		*OLS*	*FMOLS*	*DOLS*	*DOLS including spread*
Explanatory variables	*Coefficients*				
Constant	μ	1.612**	1.480**	1.431**	1.559**
		(2.371)	(2.250)	(2.300)	(2.044)
$(IND)_t$	α_1	0.351**	0.386**	0.364**	0.351**
		(7.763)	(8.819)	(8.855)	(7.854)
$(LS)_t$	α_2	0.174**	0.151**	0.183**	0.181**
		(3.710)	(2.984)	(3.954)	(3.058)
$(EXR)_t$	α_3	1.114**	1.098**	1.091**	1.101**
		(5.092)	(5.641)	(5.058)	(4.729)
$(Libor)_t$	α_4	0.048**	0.045**	0.041**	0.048**
		(4.301)	(4.918)	(3.936)	(4.104)
DVSHIFT087	α_5	0.288**	0.252**	0.201**	0.225**
		(2.982)	(3.968)	(2.565)	(2.937)
$(Spread)_t$	α_6				-0.0003
					(-0.197)
Adjusted R^2		0.929	0.928	0.940	0.930
RSS		1.126	1.158	0.932	1.126
S.E. of regression		0.086	0.088	0.080	0.087

Notes: The numbers in parenthesis are the t-statistics

**indicate significance at the 5% level. Critical values being provided by MacKinnon (1996)

OLS: HAC standard errors & covariance (Prewhitening with lags = 0 from SIC maxlags = 5, Bartlett kernel, Newey-West automatic bandwidth = 8.4682, NW automatic lag length = 4)

FMOLS: Long-run covariance estimate (Prewhitening with lags = 0 from SIC maxlags = 5, Bartlett kernel, Newey-West fixed bandwidth = 5.0000)

DOLS: HAC standard errors & covariance (Prewhitening with lags = 0 from SIC maxlags = 5, Bartlett kernel, Newey-West automatic bandwidth = 8.3396, NW automatic lag length = 4)

(RSS_{TSI}=0.932) compared to OLS (RSS_{TSI}=1.126) and FMOLS (RSS_{TSI}=1.158). Hence, the comparison results presented in Table 5.3 provide evidence in favour of DOLS method. In addition, when the spread is included, the residuals of sum squares using DOLS (RSS_{TSI}=1.126) are worsening.

Table 5.4 Cointegration tests based on DOLS

Long-run regression method DOLS			*Residuals (dt)*
ADF Statistics			
	Intercept		-5.233**
		Lags	3
	Trend and Intercept		-5.207**
		Lags	3
DF-GLS Statistics			
	Intercept		-3.520**
		Lags	3
	Trend and Intercept		-4.566**
		Lags	3
Engle-Granger t-statistic			-5.134**
Engle-Granger z-statistic			-76.845**
Phillips-Ouliaris t-statistic			-9.032**
Phillips-Ouliaris z-statistic			-129.463**

Notes: Critical values being provided by MacKinnon (1996) and Elliot, Rothenberg and Stock (1996). The selected lag length for no serial correlation of the ADF residuals based on Swartz Information Criterion

**indicate significance at the 5% level

Consequently, the residuals provided from the DOLS method according to the baseline specification (without spread variable) are employed to test for the existence of cointegration. It is worth noting that the estimated parameters among three methods are very close, implying the well specification of the models.

The results of unit root tests for the existence of cointegration for the long run relationship which has been identified from the DOLS method are presented in Table 5.4. So, the cointegration tests are based on the results of DOLS method of estimation.

The standard ADF (1981) and DF-GLS (1996) unit root tests provide evidence in favour of stationarity of the long-run residuals of TSI. This means that d_t~I(0), indicating that the corresponding series are cointegrated. These findings are also strongly supported by the results of the complementary residual-based Engle-Granger (1987) and Phillips-Ouliaris (1990) cointegration tests.

The coefficients estimated by DOLS (Table 5.3) represent the long-run cointegrating relation among variables. It is clear that all explanatory variables (freight index, outstanding loans, exchange rate and Libor) are statistically significant, and they have the expected signs. More specifically, the results indicate a partial pass-through rate of α_1=0.364 for the freight rate ClarkSea index (IND), which means that a 10% increase in index leads to 3.6% increase in the inflows. In the case of the outstanding loans (LS), the pass-through rate is estimated at α_2=0.183, meaning that a 10% rise in outstanding loans tends to increase the shipping inflows by 1.8%. The significance of outstanding loans can be explained by the fact that when shipowners receive a loan from a bank, they are also required to open an operating account for the financed vessel in the same bank and to perform all the vessel's trading transactions (including freight receipts) through this account. The amount of the outstanding loans can be deemed as a proxy for the increase of the Greek shipping cluster and its impact on the shipping inflows. Although the amount of outstanding loans relates to advancements and decisions taken place in previous periods, it also indicates the amount of loans that have been provided by the domestic banking system through the Greek-based branches. Moreover, the pass-through rate of Libor to the shipping inflows amounts to 0.041%, meaning that a 10% change in the interest rate corresponds to 0.4% respective increase in the inflows. Taking into account that Libor acts as the reference interest rate for the shipping loans, an increase (decrease) in Libor increases (decreases) the interest cost of a shipping company's loans, and hence increases (decreases) the need for shipping inflows needed for servicing the interest payment. It shall be mentioned that contrary to the level of loans that refers to decisions taken in previous periods, Libor indicates the current cost of servicing a loan. Finally, the positive sign of the coefficient of exchange rate USD/Euro (EXR) α_3=1.091 indicates that when the USD depreciates against the euro, then the inflows in USD terms increase as well (see also Haralambides 1986). The coefficient should be expected to be close to unity. A Wald F statistic (p-value = 0.67) of the restriction that α_3=1 is accepted. These results are in line with those reported in Bragoudakis and Panagiotou (2010) and Bragoudakis et al. (2015).

4.3.2 Results for the Short-Run Dynamics of Shipping Inflows

The parsimonious ECM estimations for the short-run dynamics of shipping inflows (TSI) are presented in Table 5.5. The estimated short-run shipping inflows dynamic equations are characterized by relatively good fitness, and pass all diagnostics χ^2 tests for the hypotheses that there is no serial correlation (LM test) and autoregressive conditional heteroscedasticity (ARCH test), the equations are well specified (Ramsey test), and the

Table 5.5 ECM estimations of shipping inflows

Sample		*Jan. 2002–Dec. 2014*
Regression method (HAC standard errors & covariance)		*OLS*
Explanatory variables	*Coefficients*	
Constant	δ_0	0.001 (0.239)
$\Delta(TSI)_{t-1}$	$\delta_{1,1}$	-0.159** (-3.716)
$\Delta(IND)_t$	$\delta_{2,1}$	0.210** (4.305)
$\Delta(LS)_t$	$\delta_{3,1}$	0.364** (5.098)
$\Delta(Spread)_t$		-0.002** (-2.593)
d_{t-1}	ν	-0.554** (-6.662)
Adjusted R^2		0.336
DW		2.193
F-statistic		15.785
RSS		0.820
S.E. of regression		0.076
AIC		-2.269
SIC		-2.146
Diagnostic tests [p-value]		
Ramsey – Reset (1)		0.959
LM(1)		0.376
LM(3)		0.147
ARCH(1)		0.640
Jarque-Bera Normality test		0.991

Notes: The number in parenthesis are the t-statistics

**indicate significance at the 5% level. Critical values being provided by MacKinnon (1996)

errors follow the normal distribution (Jarque-Berra test). One remaining issue concerns the stability of the estimated parameters. For this reason, the CUSUM and CUSUM Square tests were applied over the period January 2002 to December 2014. As Fig. 5.3 shows, the null hypothesis of the parameter stability cannot be rejected at the 5% significance level.

The error correction term coefficient is γ_1= -0.554, indicating that the speed of adjustment to the equilibrium steady state is relatively quick in

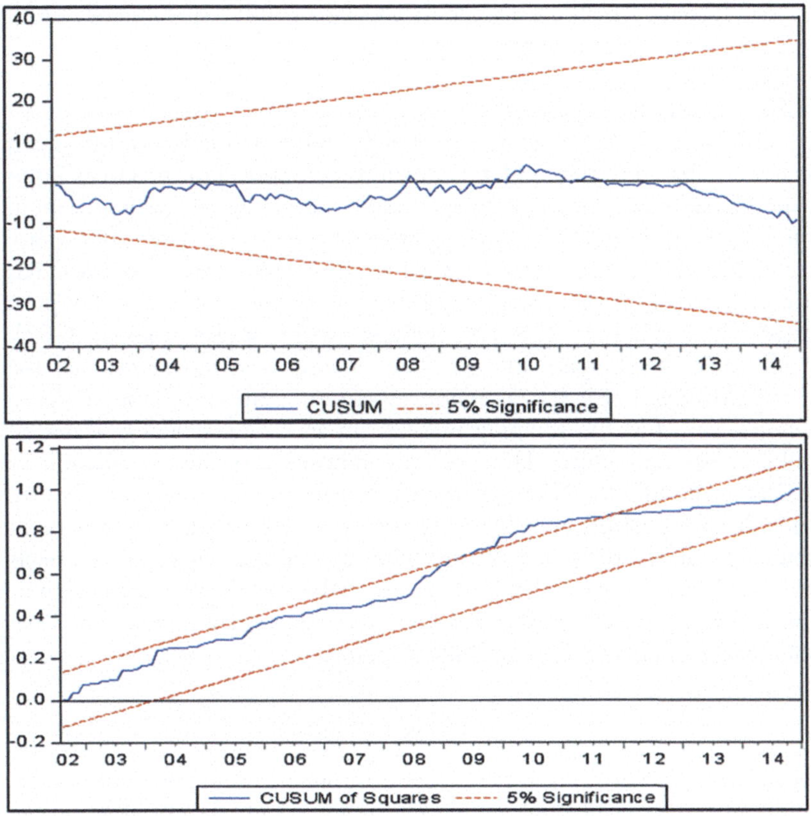

Fig. 5.3 Stability tests

the sense that the system needs around two months to reach the equilibrium level. The contemporaneous shipping freight index affects the shipping inflows by 0.21% in terms of positive growth rate. In the case of outstanding loans to shipping, the short-run elasticity is estimated at $\delta_{3,1}$=0.364, implying that a 10% increase in growth rate of outstanding loans leads to 3.6% higher shipping inflows considered (see also Bragoudakis et al. 2015) to reflect the increase of Greek-owned tonnage, especially managed from inside the wider Piraeus as well as the strengthening of the maritime cluster. Also, the spread is statistically significant but has a very low coefficient, which means that in the short run the spread plays a limited role in shipping receipts.

4.3.3 *Assessing the Impact of Sovereign Risk*

In the long term, the baseline model with DOLS method performs much better compared to the model that includes the spread of the Greek bond over the German bund. The spread variable was statistically insignificant in the long run, though a negative coefficient was found. Then, the short-term effect of the spread was investigated. It was found that the spread has a short-term negative impact on the shipping inflows; this effect though is extremely small, that is, a 10% increase in the spread leads to 0.02% decrease in the shipping inflows. This finding is an indication that the Greek sovereign risk has a minor short-term impact on the shipping inflows, and thus the shipping inflows can act as a stabilizing source of inflows into the country. However, the imposition of the capital controls and corresponding restrictions in cross-border capital movements in late June 2015—a period outside our sample—led to a significant decrease in shipping inflows; they have not yet fully recovered as the capital controls are largely still in place (Bank of Greece 2016), while an awaited significantly strong market recovery has still to emerge in major large traditional shipping segments such as dry bulk shipping.

5 Conclusions

Against the background of the Greek economic crisis since 2009, understanding the determinants of shipping inflows and the existence of any asymmetries in a highly volatile market environment compounded by country risk has research and policy interest. The empirical analysis by employing FMOLS and DOLS cointegration methods for the estimation of the long-run relationships for inflows, which are more robust compared to simple OLS method, moved technically a step forward the literature compared to previous econometric attempts. The results suggest that the shipping inflows—in the long run—are determined mainly by developments in the freight market and the amount of outstanding loans to the shipping sector by Greek-based financial institutions.

The chapter then investigated the effect of the sovereign risk to the shipping inflows. It is revealed that in the long term the sovereign risk does not have a significant impact on the shipping inflows. In contrast, the short-term effect of the sovereign risk has a statistically significant negative effect on the shipping inflows, but the impact still remains minimal. The latter indicates the stabilizing role that shipping inflows played even in periods of alleviated sovereign risk levels, such as those of increased concerns about the future of Greece in euro area.

References

Alizadeh, A, Strandenes, S. P. and Thanopoulou, H. (2014). Decision to Lay-up Vessels under the Assumption of Stochastic Freight Rate: Time-Varying Mean Reversion and Volatility. Proceedings of the IAME 2014 Conference, Norfolk, VA.

Bank of Greece (2014). Annual Report on the Monetary Policy. *Special Issue III.2. Bank of Greece*, June.

Bank of Greece (2016). Annual Report on the Monetary Policy. *Special Issue IV.2. Bank of Greece*, June.

Boston Consulting Group (2013). Impact Assessment of the Shipping Cluster on the Greek Economy & Society.

Bragoudakis, Z. and Panagiotou, S. (2010). Determinants of the Receipts from Shipping Services: The Case of Greece. *Bank of Greece, Economic Analysis and Research Department, Economic Bulletin* 34: 43–58.

Bragoudakis, Z., Panagiotou, S. and Thanopoulou, H. (2015). Greek Shipping Earnings and Investment Expenditure: Exploring the Pre & Post "Ordering-Frenzy" Period. *SPOUDAI- Journal of Economics and Business* 65(3–4): 3–28.

Clarkson Research Services – Shipping Intelligence Network at www.Clarksons.net.

Dickey, D.A, Fuller, W.A. (1981). Likelihood Ratio Statistics for Autoregressive Time Series with a Unit Root. *Econometrica* 49: 1057–1072.

Elliott, G., Rothenberg, T. and Stock, J. (1996). Efficient Tests for an Autoregressive Unit Root. *Econometrica* 64: 813–36.

Engle, R. and Granger, C. (1987). Cointegration and Error-Correction: Representation, Estimation and Testing. *Econometrica* 55: 251–76.

Haralambides, H. (1986). Shipping and Economic Development. Center for Planning & Economic Research, Report No 30.

Harlaftis, G., Thanopoulou, H. and Theotokas, I. (2010). *The Present and the Future of Greek Merchant Shipping*. Academy of Athens Study No. 10, Academy of Athens, Athens.

IOBE (2013). *The Contribution of Ocean-going Shipping to the Greek Economy: Performance and Outlook*. Athens: IOBE.

Kasimati, E. and Veranos, N. (2011). Contributing of the Greek Merchant Fleet in the Greek Economy: Evaluation and Policy Suggestions. *Centre of Planning and Economic Research, Greek Economic Outlook*, Issue 16.

MacKinnon, J.G. (1996). Numerical Distribution Functions for Unit Root and Cointegration Tests. *Journal of Applied Econometrics* 11: 601–618.

Panagiotou, St. and Bragoudakis, Z. (2010). Maritime Transportation & Ocean-going Shipping. Ch.2.5, pp. 221–234, in Bank of Greece Special Edition, *The Greek Current Account: Causes for imbalances and policy suggestions*, July 2010.

Phillips, P.C.B. and Hansen, B. (1990). Statistical Inference in Instrumental Variables Regression with I(1) Processes. *The Review of Economic Studies* 57(1): 99–125.

Phillips, P. and Ouliaris, S. (1990). Asymptotic Properties of Residual Based Tests for Cointegration. *Econometrica* 58: 165–193.

Prandeka, M. and Zarkos, V. (2014). The Greek Maritime Transport Industry and its Influence on the Greek economy. *Eurobank Economy and Markets* IX (5), May.

Saikkonen, P. (1992). Estimation and Testing of Cointegrated Systems by an Autoregressive Approximation. *Econometric Theory* 8(1): 1–27.

Stock, J. and Watson, M. (1993). A Simple Estimator of Cointegrating Vectors in Higher Order Integrated Systems. *Econometrica* 61(4): 783–820.

Stopford, M. (2009). Globalisation and the Long Shipping Cycle'. Guest Lecture, Royal Institute of Naval Architects, November 11, 2009 viewed on: 16 February 2015, http://www.clarksons.net/archive/research/freestuff/RINA%20President%27s%20Invitation%20Lecture%2011%20Nov%202009.pdf

PART III

Trends in Policy Analysis

CHAPTER 6

Fiscal Policy and Growth in the Euro Area Periphery: Does the Business Cycle Matter?

Sotiris K. Papaioannou

1 Introduction

The influence of fiscal policy on growth is one of the most heavily researched topics in modern macroeconomics. However, the evidence provided so far has been quite controversial with the most recent studies advocating that such effects depend on time and country-specific factors related to monetary policy, exchange rate regime, trade openness and public debt (Ilzetzaki et al. 2013).

We argue that fiscal policy transmissions to the real economy are much different during recessions, and therefore the effects of public spending on growth depend on the state of the economy. In normal periods, the economy is mainly financed by the private sector, and therefore the importance of public spending in raising aggregate demand remains low. However, in periods of recession, fiscal policy might be an effective tool to increase output. The main channels through which fiscal policy becomes relevant are monetary policy accommodation as well as credit and/or liquidity constraints. In the first case, the interest rate remains low, and therefore

S. K. Papaioannou (✉)
Centre of Planning and Economic Research (KEPE), Athens, Greece
e-mail: sopa@kepe.gr

I. T. Kokores et al. (eds.), *Money, Trade and Finance*,
https://doi.org/10.1007/978-3-030-73219-6_6

private consumption and investment are not adversely affected. In the second case, the marginal propensity to consume increases as a higher number of households and firms become financially constrained.

Despite relevance of such theoretical underpinnings, few studies have so far assessed the influence of fiscal policy in periods of slack or have distinguished on the differentiation of such effects in periods of recession and in periods of expansion (Auerbach and Gorodnichenko 2012; Blanchard and Leigh 2013). Scarceness of evidence partly reflects assumptions of linearity in most of the employed vector autoregression and dynamic stochastic general equilibrium models. This study aims to contribute in this direction and studies whether the effects of fiscal policy on growth can be asymmetric under different business cycle regimes. We do this by using Markov Switching regression in models where the output gap is used to determine the state of the regime.

Unlike other studies, we focus on countries of the euro area periphery as they constitute recent cases of a combination of tight fiscal policies and deep or prolonged recession.[1] Fiscal consolidation in these countries has received much criticism, and its effectiveness has been questioned recently due to their disappointing growth performance.

Econometric results are reported on quarterly data for five countries (Spain, Italy, Portugal, Ireland and Cyprus), and show us that the effects of public spending on growth are asymmetric over the business cycle. The highest influence on output is observed when the output gap is low. On the contrary, in periods of high and positive output gaps, the impact of public spending remains is weak.

The chapter proceeds as follows: Section 2 presents the theoretical framework and discusses the results of the empirical literature. Section 3 presents the data, introduces the econometric methodology and examines the link between public spending and growth from the perspective of a Markov Switching regression model. Section 4 concludes.

[1] Crisis mainly concerns public debt sustainability, banking and financial stability and chronic imbalances in the current account. As a means to respond to such difficulties, most of these countries have received international aid in the form of funding and under the provision that a strict program of fiscal adjustment, accompanied with structural reforms, should be followed in order to restore structural weaknesses. Greece was the first country to receive international aid in 2010, and is still under an adjustment program. Ireland, Portugal and Cyprus received aid in 2010, 2011 and 2013, respectively. Spain also received assistance for its financial sector in 2012. The only country that remains within an economic adjustment program is now Greece.

2 Theoretical Framework and Related Literature

2.1 *Theoretical Framework*

Predictions of the existing theoretical literature are ambiguous as regards the impact of fiscal policy on output. General equilibrium new Keynesian models show that the government spending multiplier can be close or above one (Gali et al. 2007; Monacelli and Perotti 2008), while standard real business cycle models are in sharp contrast and predict that consumption declines (Baxter and King 1993; Burnside et al. 2004; Ramey 2011). The main reason for such a significant difference is the implicit assumption of infinitely lived Ricardian households, whose consumption depends on an intertemporal budget constraint. Any increase in government spending lowers the present value of income after taxes, which in turn generates negative wealth effects and decreases consumption.[2]

However, in periods of economic slack, an increasing number of households becomes credit constrained, as the uncertainly about income and wealth developments makes borrowing less easy.[3] Models featuring non-Ricardian households show that the presence of credit constraints raises the marginal propensity to consume, and hence makes fiscal policy a more powerful tool for short-run stabilization. Credit-constrained households differ from Ricardian households in that they face collateral constraints on their borrowing, and therefore they raise their consumption after an increase in public spending.

[2] Several studies have tried to reconcile predictions of neoclassical models with observed evidence which were in favor of a raise in consumption after an increase in government spending. Gali et al. (2007) extended a standard new Keynesian model to allow for the coexistence of infinite horizon Ricardian consumers and 'rule of thumb' consumers, which do not save and do not borrow. They showed that an interaction of rule-of-thumb consumers with sticky prices and deficit financing of government spending can account for higher consumption when spending increases. In a similar way, Hall (2009) developed a dynamic general equilibrium model which has as main features the decline in markups of prices over costs when output raises and the elastic response of employment when demand increases. With these features, the model delivers quite high multipliers and increase in consumption. Recently, Cogan et al. (2010) showed that government spending multipliers are much smaller in new Keynesian models than old Keynesian ones, with the estimated stimulus in GDP being one-sixth of what is predicted in old Keynesian ones.

[3] Ratto et al. (2009), in their model for the euro area, estimated that half of the nonliquidity-constrained households to be credit constrained.

During recession, the influence of fiscal policy can be affected by monetary policy conditions and particularly by the interest rate. Theoretically, the influence of government spending on growth can become positive when monetary policy does not respond to changes in fiscal policy, mostly in cases when the interest rate is close to zero. In such a case, an increase in government spending leads to an initial rise in output. With nominal interest rates held constant at zero, the expected rise in inflation drives down the real interest rate. Thus, private spending increases, and this in turn leads to a further increase of output. On the contrary, when monetary policy responds by increasing the nominal interest rate, the impact of public spending on growth lowers.

2.2 *Related Literature*

The evidence of the empirical literature on the effects of fiscal policy is not uniform. Blanchard and Perotti (2002) show that shocks in government spending were associated with higher output of the US economy during the postwar period, with the size of the multiplier being close to one. The results of Monacelli et al. (2010) are also in favor of a multiplier which is larger than one in the US economy. However, influences of fiscal policy on output seem to have weakened, with the impact being particularly stronger in the period before the 1980s (Perotti 2005, 2007). Alesina and Ardagna (2010) have shown that fiscal stimulus based on tax cuts is more likely to increase growth as compared to fiscal expansion based on spending increases. They also show that adjustments based on spending cuts rather than tax increases are less likely to create recessions.

Another strand of the literature shows that the response of output depends on country-specific characteristics related to the exchange rate regime, trade openness, level of development and public sector debt (Chung and Leeper 2007; Favero and Giavazzi 2007; Ilzetzaki et al. 2013). Also a number of recent studies demonstrate that the stance of monetary policy matters in determining the growth influence of public spending. Christiano et al. (2011) show that the government spending multiplier can be very large when monetary policy does not respond to changes in prices, mostly in cases when the nominal interest is very close to zero. In contrast, when the central bank follows a Taylor rule, then the value of the government spending multiplier is less than one. Similarly, Christiano et al. (2011), Woodford (2011), Davig and Leeper (2011), Eggertsson (2011) and Conenen et al. (2012) conclude that fiscal policy can be effective in raising output when monetary policy remains accommodative and interest rates are kept low.

The latest literature shows us that the state of the economy indeed matters in determining the impact of fiscal policy on growth. Blanchard and Leigh (2013) showed that stronger fiscal consolidation of the EU countries has been associated with lower than expected growth especially in the early period of the crisis. In the same spirit, Auerbach and Gorodnichenko (2012) showed that the output effects of fiscal policy are more severe in recessions than in expansions.

3 Empirical Results

3.1 Major Stylized Facts

For each country (Spain, Italy, Portugal, Ireland and Cyprus), a quarterly dataset has been compiled from the National Accounts' database of Eurostat (2016), which covers the variables of output and public spending (defined as the sum of public consumption and public investment).[4] The annual time series of the output gap is obtained from the AMECO (2016) database. The two different techniques which are used to convert its frequency from annual to quarterly are the linear and the cubic frequency conversion method. The variables of output and public spending enter in real terms and are seasonally adjusted. The length of the time span for which all three variables are available differs across countries.[5]

Average quarterly changes of output growth and public spending are shown in Figs. 6.1 and 6.2. It is very clear that output growth rates present a highly asymmetric behavior among the two periods of 2001–2007 and 2008–2015. Average GDP growth rates of Cyprus, Italy, Portugal and Spain have remained negative for the whole period of 2008–2015, while in Ireland they have shrunk substantially. Figure 6.2 briefly illustrates the evolution of public spending growth rates during 2001–2007 and 2008–2015. In a similar fashion, public spending patterns are quite

[4] Greece has not been included in countries under examination as the statistical properties of its GDP variable indicate that it is not first difference stationary.

[5] For Spain, the sample covers the period from the fourth quarter of 1995 to the first quarter of 2016. For Cyprus, the data starts from the third quarter of 1998 and ends in the first quarter of 2016. For Italy and Portugal, the data starts in the second quarter of 1999 and ends in the first quarter of 2016. For Ireland, the data starts in the second quarter of 2002 and ends in the first quarter of 2016.

different between the two periods. While all governments increased their public expenditure during 2001–2007, in the subsequent period public spending growth rates became negative as a response to high public sector deficits and subsequent fiscal tightening measures. Similarly, the output gap variable has switched from positive to negative in all five countries (Fig. 6.3).

3.2 Econometric Results

We now examine the relationship between public spending and growth. Given that both variables display an asymmetric behavior over time (Figs. 6.1 and 6.2), a Markov Switching model is appropriate to explore whether the impact of public spending on growth is uneven in the EU countries. For each individual country, we consider the following Markov Switching model with two regimes:

$$growth_t = a + \sum_{i=-m}^{0} \beta_i(s_t)\Delta PUB_{t+i} + u_t \tag{1}$$

where *growth* is the quarterly growth rate of output and ΔPUB is the quarterly public spending growth rate. Public spending is defined as the sum of government consumption and government investment, while both variables of output and public spending enter real terms and are seasonally adjusted. As this process requires stationarity, both variables of output growth and public spending growth have been checked and found to be stationary (Table 6.1).

The variable of *growth* is assumed to have been generated by a Markov Switch model with two regimes and m lags in the regressor of public spending growth. The value of the intercept α does not differ between the two regimes, while the β coefficients depend on the current regime represented by s_t. We allow for regime-dependent heteroskedasticity, and, therefore, the error term u_t is represented by $u_t|s_t \sim N(0, \sigma^2(s_t))$. This class of models was initially developed by Goldfeld and Quandt (1973) as a response to the asymmetric evolution of key economic variables during the business cycle. The state of the regime, represented by the variable s_t, is determined by the quarterly output gap. We assume two different regimes, the first representing high and positive output gaps and the second low or negative output gaps. We specify s_t as a first-order Markov chain, where the transition probability between the two regimes depends on the past value of the most recent regime: $P(s_t = j | s_{t-1} = i) = p_{ij}$.

The selection criteria that were followed for the choice of the value of m in each country regression were that convergence in the estimation should be achieved and no serial correlation should be present in the estimated residuals. As the number of observations for each country is not very high, the number of lags m of the public spending growth variable was also chosen to be the least high, provided that the two basic criteria (convergence and no serial correlation in the residuals) were first met. Therefore, the number of the chosen lags differs in each country.

Regression results are shown for each country in Tables 6.2, 6.3, 6.4, 6.5 and 6.6. The number of lags of the variable of public spending varies across tables, while a common constant term is assumed in both regimes. Also, econometric estimates have included the impact of the lagged dependent variable. In order to test the robustness of the obtained results, a number of different assumptions is made, with tables displaying results after (a) having included a variable for tax revenues, (b) having followed the cubic frequency conversion method to obtain the quarterly output gap series and (c) having distinguished on the effects of public investment and public consumption.

Relying primarily on results encompassing the highest number of lags, we note that in Spain (Table 6.2) the coefficient estimates of public spending are higher in the low-output gap regime. We verify this result when the variable of taxes enters in the regression or when the output gap variable is obtained by the cubic frequency conversion method. When considering on the effects of public investments and public consumption, we obtain results that are in favor of a statistically significant and positive effect of public investment only in the high-output gap regime. By contrast, government consumption seems to affect output equally and positively in both regimes.

In Italy (Table 6.3), the effect of fiscal policy seems to be stronger when the output gap is low. Also, Column 7 shows us that public investments are more effective as a growth driver during downturns. Similarly, the estimates for Portugal (Table 6.4) confirm that public spending is more effective when the economy is in the low-output gap regime, while the influence of public investment seems to stronger during expansions. When considering the case of Ireland (Table 6.5), we observe that public expenditure in general exerts a negative impact on GDP in boom periods. By contrast, when being in periods with low- or negative-output gaps, its influence on output is mainly positive. Similar results are obtained when considering Cyprus (Table 6.6) where the impact of public spending is negative when the economy grows. However, during recessions, public expenditure and its individual components, that is, public consumption and public investment, exert a positive and statistically significant influence on output. Figure 6.4 illustrates graphically each of the two regimes' probabilities over time.

In light of the obtained results, we assess the effects of fiscal policy under these two regimes. We conduct a series of simulations to trace the impact of a hypothetical fiscal shock in contraction and expansion which lasts for five quarters (current quarter and four lagged quarters). The shocks are set equal to a one standard deviation of the variable of public spending, and their impact is illustrated numerically In Table 6.7. Two main conclusions can be derived from this table. First, the response of output after an increase government spending differs substantially between expansions and contractions with the highest influence observed in recessions. By contrast, in expansion periods, we also observe negative changes of output in Spain, Cyprus and Ireland. Second, the accumulated effects of public spending on growth vary substantially across countries in both contractions and booms.

3.3 Discussion

The obtained results confirm that the effects of public spending on growth are cyclically dependent with higher effects observed during downturns. It is obvious that for all five countries of the euro area periphery, the growth influence of public spending is positive when the output gap variable is low. It is also much stronger when compared to its influence during expansions. We agree with Hernandez de Cos and Moral Benito (2016) having demonstrated for Spain that the government spending multiplier is higher during recessions and in periods of banking stress. We attribute this evidence on the high percentage of credit- and liquidity-constrained consumers as well as on the consistently low interest rates having prevailed in the last years. Reinhart and Rogoff (2008) have stressed that the recent crisis has been characterized by sharp falls in house prices, which in turn have led to higher default levels and tightening of credit conditions. Ratto et al. (2009), in their model for the euro area, estimated that half of the nonliquidity-constrained households is credit constrained.

By contrast, in normal times, low or even negative responses of output after a shock in government spending indicate that households and firms do not respond with higher consumption and higher investment. Afonso and Alegre (2011) have identified crowding-out effects of certain components of public spending (e.g. consumption and transfers) and crowding-in effects associated with public investments in a panel of EU countries.

It seems that the arguments in favor of a more expansive fiscal policy mix are sensible when the economy is in recession. On the contrary, the effectiveness of a tight fiscal policy during recession is well under question as disappointing growth performance of most peripheral EU countries might partly be owed to the adverse impact of recent fiscal consolidation. Countercyclical fiscal policy can be effective in the spirit of Keynes, in that increases in government spending may have significant positive effects on output and consumption if and only if there are significant slack resources in the economy (Parker 2011). In this view, the markets are failing during recessions, and the impact of such failures can be partly offset by fiscal policy.

By contrast, in normal times this relationship weakens as households and businesses have more opportunities to finance their consumption and investment through borrowing by the private financial sector. In this case, there are no benefits to expansionary fiscal policy as it would primarily raise interest rates and crowd out private consumption and investment, as analytically described in neoclassical models.

4 Conclusion

The purpose of this study was to econometrically quantify the impact of public spending on growth of countries on the euro area periphery (Spain, Italy, Portugal, Ireland and Cyprus) and across different business cycle regimes. We focused on a period starting from the late 1990s and reaching 2016, and therefore we have included in our analysis periods of high growth succeeded by recession as well as periods of fiscal expansion followed by fiscal consolidation.

Markov Switching regression results show us that the effects of public spending on growth are asymmetric over the business cycle. The highest influence on output is observed when the output gap is low. On the contrary, in periods of high and positive output gaps, the impact of public spending remains weak or even becomes negative. Future research could focus on whether certain characteristics like corruption or market regulation exacerbate the influence of the business cycle on growth.

Appendix

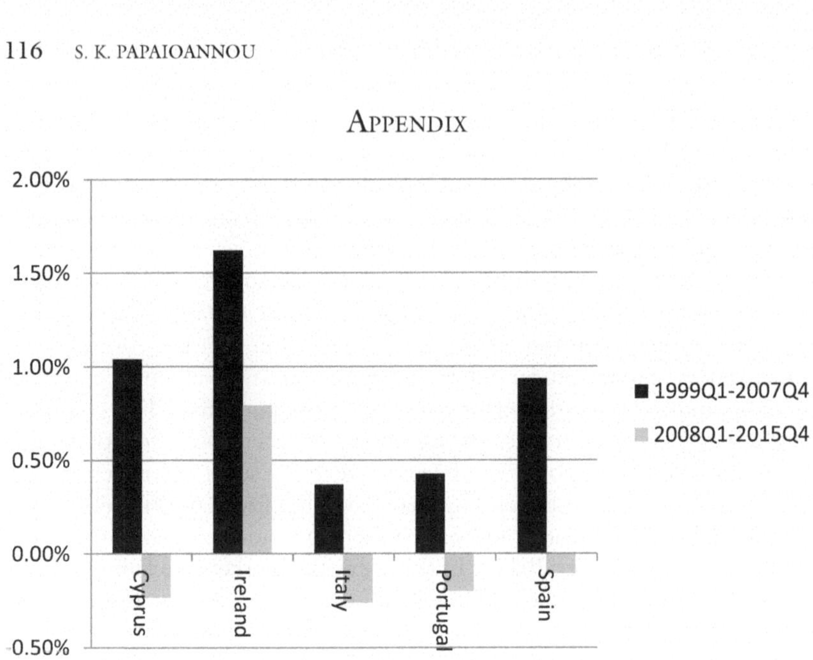

Fig. 6.1 Quarterly GDP growth across (average 1999–2007 and average 2008–2015). (Source: Eurostat, National Accounts)

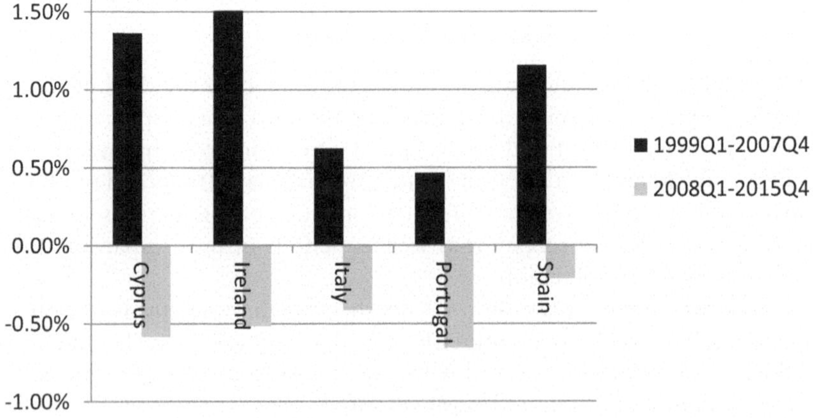

Fig. 6.2 Quarterly public spending growth (average 1999–2007 and average 2008–2015, Sum of public consumption and public investment). (Source: Eurostat, National Accounts. 1. Data for Ireland start in the first quarter of 2002)

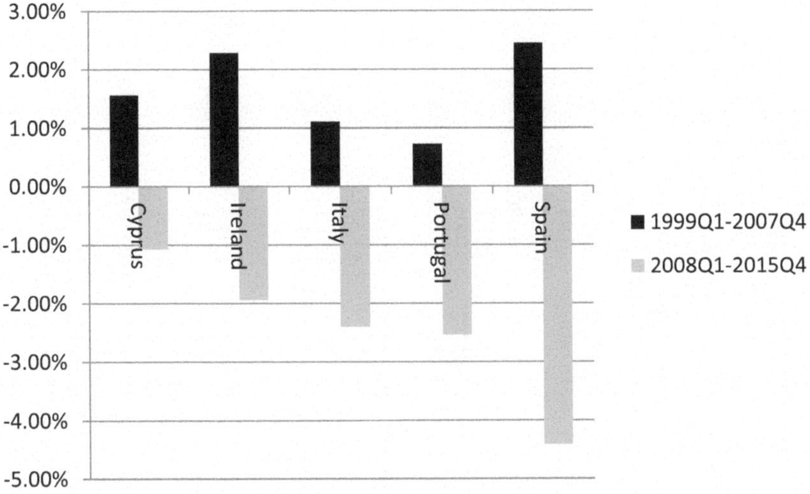

Fig. 6.3 Quarterly output gap (%, average 1999–2007 and average 2008–2015). (Source: AMECO, Annual Macroeconomics Database)

Table 6.1 Unit root test (Augmented Dickey Fuller test)

	GDP (in logs)[b]	*Public spending (in logs)*[b]	*GDP (in first differences)*[b]	*Public spending (in first differences)*[b]
Spain	-0.22 (0.93)[a]	-1.80 (0.37)	-9.27 (0.00)	-2.76 (0.06)
Italy	-2.20 (0.20)	-2.12 (0.23)	-4.66 (0.00)	-13.05 (0.0)
Portugal	-3.45 (0.01)	-1.13 (0.69)	-5.78 (0.00)	-17.06 (0.00)
Ireland	-1.42 (0.56)	-1.86 (0.34)	-9.96 (0.00)	-9.31 (0.00)
Cyprus	-1.98 (0.29)	-2.51 (0.11)	-2.83 (0.05)	-12.17 (0.00)

[a] *P*-values in parentheses

[b] Initial hypothesis: Nonstationary variable

Table 6.2 Regression results of Markov Switch model (Spain)

Dependent variable: Output growth

	1	*2*	*3*	*4*	*5*	*6*	*7*	*8*	*9*
	No lag	*1 lag*	*2 lags*	*3 lags*	*4 lags*	*Taxes*	*Output gap (cubic spline)*	*Public investment*	*Public consumption*
Constant tem	0.004 (1.54)	0.005*** (2.55)	0.005*** (2.52)	0.003*** (8.22)	0.004*** (19.05)	-0.015*** (-2.92)	0.007*** (16.60)	0.006*** (3.98)	0.005*** (9.75)
Regime: Low or negative output gap									
Public spending	0.015* (1.66)	-0.037 (-1.18)	0.049*** (5.88)	0.030*** (7.23)	0.061*** (15.97)	0.058** (2.11)	0.055*** (24.37)	-0.0005 (-0.09)	0.084*** (24.61)
Public spending (t - 1)		-0.015 (-0.85)	0.028*** (2.93)	0.114*** (12.92)	0.051*** (8.08)	0.029 (0.72)	0.026*** (7.19)	0.004 (0.62)	0.071*** (14.14)
Public spending (t - 2)			0.023*** (2.91)	0.155*** (14.80)	0.055*** (8.44)	0.019 (0.49)	0.046*** (8.02)	0.011 (1.57)	0.061*** (12.14)
Public spending (t - 3)				0.016*** (3.76)	-0.011* (-1.92)	-0.050 (-1.43)	0.007 (1.39)	-0.001 (-0.10)	0.035*** (6.91)
Public spending (t - 4)					-0.055*** (-14.36)	-0.060** (-2.02)	0.017*** (4.68)	0.002 (0.41)	0.017*** (3.71)
Regime: High–positive output gap									
Public spending	-0.027 (-1.07)	0.013 (1.20)	0.006 (0.41)	0.068*** (5.29)	0.003 (0.43)	0.004 (0.33)	0.035*** (6.94)	0.008*** (2.06)	0.002 (0.56)
Public spending (t - 1)		0.002 (0.15)	0.086*** (4.03)	0.072*** (6.43)	0.014 (1.38)	-0.005 (-0.28)	0.040*** (5.15)	-0.005 (-0.80)	0.119*** (21.51)

Public spending (t - 2)	0.043** (2.40)	0.045*** (7.61)	0.015** (2.01)	-0.007 (-0.42)	0.020*** (4.07)	0.018*** (3.26)	0.133*** (21.97)
Public spending (t - 3)		0.042*** (11.07)	-0.045*** (-7.66)	-0.020 (-0.99)	0.015*** (3.63)	0.005 (1.01)	0.016** (2.42)
Public spending (t - 4)			-0.024*** (-5.45)	0.003 (0.22)	0.018*** (3.86)	0.009 (1.45)	-0.063*** (-14.85)
Test-equal variances (*p*-value)			-13.777 (0.00)				
Test-equal coefficients (*p*-value)			12.644 (0.00)				

Table 6.3 Regression results of Markov Switch model (Italy)

Dependent variable: Output growth

	1	*2*	*3*	*4*	*5*	*6*	*7*	*8*
	No lag	*1 lag*	*2 lags*	*3 lags*	*Taxes*	*Output gap (cubic spline)*	*Public investment*	*Public consumption*
Constant tem	0.0002 (0.24)	-0.0009 (-1.06)	0.0009** (2.42)	0.001*** (3.13)	-0.042*** (-4.83)	0.002*** (15.16)	0.0008 (0.89)	0.0006** (2.06)
Regime: Low–negative output gap								
Public spending	0.002 (0.30)	0.0008 (0.11)	0.001 (0.23)	-0.001 (-0.38)	0.010 (1.40)	0.021*** (6.42)	0.0003 (0.48)	0.079*** (12.31)
Public spending (t - 1)		0.009 (0.89)	0.050*** (5.11)	0.038*** (5.73)	0.077*** (5.87)	0.043*** (7.43)	0.003** (2.32)	0.092*** (5.14)
Public spending (t - 2)			0.095*** (8.39)	0.082*** (10.23)	0.029*** (3.52)	0.095*** (12.53)	0.007*** (4.24)	0.097*** (4.45)
Public spending (t - 3)				0.058*** (7.16)		0.077*** (10.20)	0.006*** (3.37)	0.043*** (2.53)
Public spending (t - 4)						0.012*** (4.81)	0.002* (1.90)	-0.012 (-1.35)
Regime: High–positive output gap								
Public spending	0.022** (2.21)	-0.069*** (-4.13)	0.016 (1.60)	-0.038*** (-2.67)	-0.009* (-1.67)	-0.030*** (-4.58)	-0.003 (-0.86)	-0.058*** (-3.99)
Public spending (t - 1)		-0.054*** (-6.88)	0.057*** (3.12)	0.068*** (4.01)	0.002 (0.29)	0.042*** (3.56)	-0.009** (-2.07)	0.253*** (9.81)

Public spending (t - 2)	-0.012 (-1.53)	0.089*** (5.51)	0.016*** (3.44)	0.067*** (3.86)		-0.005 (-1.13)	0.311*** (11.67)
Public spending (t - 3)		-0.015** (-2.10)		-0.022 (-1.55)		-0.002 (-0.47)	0.094*** (5.74)
Public spending (t - 4)				-0.056*** (-4.68)		0.003** (2.47)	-0.016*** (-2.76)
Equal variances		-12.119 (0.00)					
Equal coefficients		2.512 (0.01)					

Table 6.4 Regression results of Markov Switch model (Portugal)

Dependent variable: Output growth							
	1	*2*	*3*	*4*	*5*	*6*	*7*
	No lag	*1 lag*	*2 lags*	*Taxes*	*Output gap (cubic spline)*	*Public investment*	*Public consumption*
Constant tem	0.0004 (0.23)	0.001 (0.80)	0.001 (1.50)	0.002 (0.36)	0.001* (1.70)	-0.0004 (-0.19)	0.0006** (2.03)
Regime: Low–negative output gap							
Public spending	0.006 (0.69)	0.031 (1.19)	0.049*** (2.59)	-0.031*** (-3.96)	0.062*** (2.89)	0.002 (0.35)	0.125*** (25.02)
Public spending (t - 1)		0.032 (1.32)	0.045** (2.08)	-0.049** (-2.15)	0.090*** (3.20)	0.005 (0.46)	0.142*** (27.74)
Public spending (t - 2)			0.042*** (2.89)	0.113*** (3.83)	0.094*** (3.86)	0.014 (1.58)	0.144*** (22.23)
Public spending (t - 3)				0.187*** (8.74)	0.060** (2.28)	0.009* (1.80)	0.099*** (13.24)
Public spending (t - 4)				0.030* (1.77)	-0.019 (-1.05)		-0.010** (-2.02)
Regime: High–positive output gap							
Public spending	0.034 (1.27)	-0.007 (-0.26)	0.005 (0.11)	-0.005 (-0.49)	-0.038 (-0.92)	-0.005 (-0.33)	0.071*** (2.74)
Public spending (t - 1)		-0.036** (-2.31)	0.054 (0.94)	0.018 (1.26)	-0.025 (-0.63)	-0.006 (-0.52)	0.113*** (3.48)
Public spending (t - 2)			0.016 (0.24)	0.091*** (5.79)	0.016 (0.35)	-0.020* (-1.82)	0.074*** (4.72)
Public spending (t - 3)				0.059*** (4.24)	-0.008 (-0.19)	-0.020** (-2.26)	0.128*** (5.26)
Public spending (t - 4)				0.016*** (2.60)	-0.005 (-0.19)		0.055** (2.37)
Equal variances			-3.040 (0.00)				
Equal coefficients			19.475 (0.00)				

*, ** and *** indicate significance at the 10%, 5% and 1% levels, respectively. z-statistics are reported in parentheses

Table 6.5 Regression results of Markov Switch model (Ireland)

Dependent variable: Output growth								
	1	*2*	*3*	*4*	*5*	*6*	*7*	*8*
	No lag	*1 lag*	*2 lags*	*3 lags*	*Taxes*	*Output gap (cubic spline)*	*Public investment*	*Public consumption*
Constant tem	0.008*	0.009*	0.010**	0.009**	0.003***	0.010**	0.011**	-0.0004
	(1.68)	(1.76)	(2.36)	(2.20)	(2.64)	(2.38)	(2.19)	(-0.55)
Regime: Low–negative output gap								
Public spending	-0.005	-0.005	0.042	0.040	-0.056***	0.059	0.011	0.070***
	(-0.09)	(-0.08)	(0.75)	(0.64)	(-4.65)	(0.91)	(1.47)	(4.53)
Public spending (t - 1)		0.011	0.070	0.054	0.034***	0.068	0.005	0.323***
		(0.17)	(1.11)	(0.80)	(4.11)	(0.97)	(0.63)	(21.12)
Public spending (t - 2)			0.150***	0.148**	0.198***	0.173**	0.020**	0.060***
			(2.38)	(1.98)	(18.26)	(2.15)	(2.09)	(3.22)
Public spending (t - 3)				-0.034	-0.113***	-0.018	-0.004	0.187***
				(-0.54)	(-12.19)	(-0.27)	(-0.53)	(14.38)
Public spending (t - 4)					0.077***	0.040	0.0008	0.104***
					(5.32)	(0.59)	(0.10)	(5.70)
Regime: High–positive output gap								
Public spending	-0.147	-0.159	-0.005	-0.289	-0.843***	-0.326	-0.007	-0.229**
	(-0.39)	(-0.38)	(-0.03)	(-0.73)	(-11.54)	(-0.75)	(-0.07)	(-2.40)

(*continued*)

Table 6.5 (continued)

Dependent variable: Output growth								
	1	*2*	*3*	*4*	*5*	*6*	*7*	*8*
	No lag	*1 lag*	*2 lags*	*3 lags*	*Taxes*	*Output gap (cubic spline)*	*Public investment*	*Public consumption*
Public spending (t - 1)		-0.136 (-0.25)	-0.544 (-1.17)	-0.138 (-0.36)	-0.924*** (-18.41)	-0.228 (-0.52)	-0.125 (-0.69)	0.046 (0.63)
Public spending (t - 2)			-0.844** (-2.43)	-0.389 (-1.13)	-1.538*** (-21.01)	-0.480 (-1.15)	0.0007 (0.02)	-0.614*** (-10.14)
Public spending (t - 3)				0.403 (1.12)	-1.145*** (-14.98)	0.345 (0.87)	0.092 (1.20)	0.482*** (5.45)
Public spending (t - 4)					0.004 (0.91)	0.332 (0.68)	0.047 (0.28)	0.688*** (11.42)
Equal variances				4.319 (0.00)				
Equal coefficients				-0.809 (0.42)				

*, ** and *** indicate significance at the 10%, 5% and 1% levels, respectively. z-statistics are reported in parentheses

Table 6.6 Regression results of Markov Switch model (Cyprus)

Dependent variable: Output growth								
	1	*2*	*3*	*4*	*5*	*6*	*7*	*8*
	No lag	*1 lag*	*2 lags*	*3 lags*	*Taxes*	*Output gap (cubic spline)*	*Public investment*	*Public consumption*
Constant tem	0.006***	0.004	0.004**	0.006***	0.040***	0.006***	0.005**	0.003**
	(2.47)	(0.96)	(2.18)	(3.11)	(2.76)	(3.70)	(2.10)	(2.09)
Regime: Low–negative output gap								
Public spending	0.050***	0.025	-0.006	0.023	0.068***	0.030	0.044***	0.070***
	(5.02)	(1.20)	(-0.42)	(1.54)	(3.54)	(1.37)	(9.89)	(3.05)
Public spending (t - 1)		0.013	0.061*	0.077***	0.088***	0.074***	-0.008	0.098***
		(0.53)	(1.87)	(3.06)	(4.37)	(3.94)	(-1.29)	(4.74)
Public spending (t - 2)			0.146***	0.158***	0.253***	0.157***	0.034***	0.105***
			(5.55)	(8.37)	(11.94)	(11.01)	(6.85)	(3.58)
Public spending (t - 3)				0.018	0.026	-0.020	0.042***	0.118***
				(1.08)	(1.41)	(-1.35)	(6.39)	(5.67)
Public spending (t - 4)					0.089***	0.022	0.007	0.090***
					(5.07)	(1.53)	(1.12)	(5.86)
Regime: High–positive output gap								
Public spending	-0.020	-0.046	0.040***	0.061***	-0.016	0.058***	-0.002	-0.013
	(-1.13)	(-1.09)	(3.33)	(6.43)	(-1.22)	(4.08)	(-0.58)	(-0.87)

(*continued*)

Table 6.6 (continued)

Dependent variable: Output growth								
	1	*2*	*3*	*4*	*5*	*6*	*7*	*8*
	No lag	*1 lag*	*2 lags*	*3 lags*	*Taxes*	*Output gap (cubic spline)*	*Public investment*	*Public consumption*
Public spending (t - 1)		-0.004 (-0.129)	0.022** (2.36)	0.028*** (3.69)	-0.019 (-1.12)	0.044*** (2.74)	-0.005 (-0.91)	-0.022 (-0.99)
Public spending (t - 2)			-0.046*** (-5.72)	-0.028*** (-4.00)	-0.060*** (-4.33)	-0.026** (-2.22)	-0.012*** (-2.48)	-0.005 (-0.26)
Public spending (t - 3)				0.027*** (2.63)	-0.023 (-1.37)	0.036* (1.91)	-0.006 (-1.08)	-0.059*** (-2.64)
Public spending (t - 4)					-0.045*** (-3.27)	-0.012 (-1.16)	-0.002 (-0.49)	-0.047** (-2.22)
Equal variances				6.026 (0.00)				
Equal coefficients				4.365 (0.00)				

*, ** and *** indicate significance at the 10%, 5% and 1% levels, respectively. z-statistics are reported in parentheses

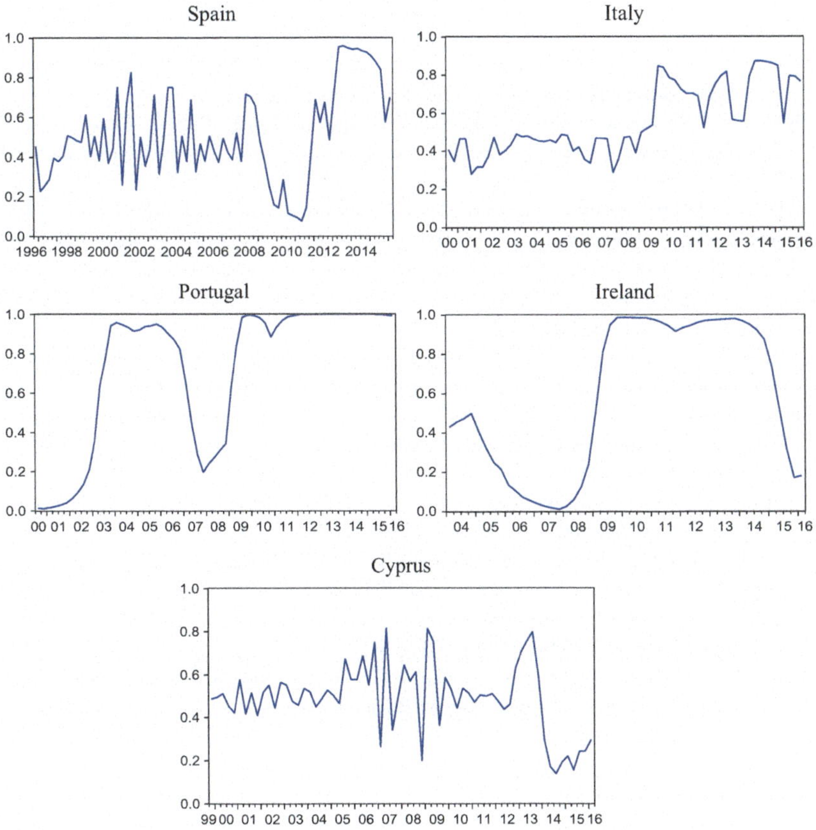

Fig. 6.4 Regime probabilities (Low–negative output gap)

Table 6.7 Predicted accumulated change in GDP growth

	High–positive output gap	*Low–negative output gap*
Spain	-0.070%	0.191%
Italy	0.002%	0.607%
Portugal	1.222%	1.707%
Ireland	-1.552%	1.400%
Cyprus	-0.878%	2.823%

References

Afonso A., Alegre JG (2011). Economic Growth and Budgetary Components: a Panel Assessment for the EU. *Empirical Economics*, 41:703–723.

Alesina A., Ardagna S (2010). Large Changes in Fiscal Policy: Taxes versus Spending. In Brown J (ed) *Tax Policy and the Economy*, University of Chicago Press, 35–68.

AMECO (2016). *Annual Macroeconomic Database*, European Commission.

Auerbach A., Gorodnichenko Y. (2012). Measuring the Output Responses to Fiscal Policy. *American Economic Journal-Economic Policy*, 4: 1–27.

Baxter M., King R. (1993). Fiscal Policy in General Equilibrium. *American Economic Review*, 83: 315–334.

Blanchard O., Leigh D. (2013). Growth Forecast Errors and Fiscal Multipliers. *American Economic Review Papers and Proceedings*, 103: 117–120.

Blanchard O., Perotti R. (2002). An Empirical Characterization of the Dynamic Effects of Changes in Government Spending and Taxes on Output. *Quarterly Journal of Economics*, 117: 1329–1368.

Burnside C., Eichenbaum M., Fisher J. (2004). Fiscal Shocks and Their Consequences. *Journal of Economic Theory*, 115: 89–117.

Christiano L., Eichenbaum M., Rebelo S (2011). When is the Government Spending Multiplier Large?. *Journal of Political Economy*, 119: 78–121.

Chung H., Leeper M (2007). What Has Financed Government Debt?. NBER Working Paper No. 13425, Cambridge MA.

Cogan J.F., Cwik T, Taylor J.B., Wieland V. (2010). New Keynesian versus Old Keynesian Government Spending Multipliers. *Journal of Economic Dynamics and Control*, 34: 281–295.

Conenen G., Erceg C., Fredman C., Furceri D., Kumhof M., Lalonde R., Laxton D., Linde J., Mourougane A., Muir D., Mursula S., De Resende C., Roberts J., Roeger W., Snudden S., Trabanst M., Veld J. (2012). Effects of Fiscal Stimulus in Structural Models. *American Economic Journal- Macroeconomics*, 4: 22–68.

Davig T, Leeper E.M. (2011). Monetary-Fiscal Policy Interactions and Fiscal Stimulus. *European Economic Review*, 55: 211–227.

Eggertsson G. (2011). What Fiscal Policy is Effective at Zero Interest Rates?. *NBER Macroeconomics Annual*, 25: 59 – 112.

Eurostat (2016) *National Accounts Database*.

Favero C., Giavazzi F. (2007). Debt and The Effects of Fiscal Policy. NBER Working Paper No. 12822, Cambridge MA.

Gali J., Lopez-Salido J.D., Valles J. (2007). Understanding the Effects of Government Spending on Consumption. *Journal of the European Economic Association* 5: 227–270.

Goldfeld S.M., Quandt R.E. (1973). A Markov Model for Switching Regressions. *Journal of Econometrics* 1: 3–15.

Hall R.E. (2009). By How Much Does GDP Rise if the Government Buys More Output?. *Brookings Papers of Economic Activity*, 40: 183–249.

Hernandez de Cos P., Moral Benito E. (2016) 'Fiscal Multipliers in Turbulent Times: the Case of Spain', *Empirical Economics*, 50: 1589–1625.

Ilzetzaki E., Mendoza G., Vegh C. (2013). How Big (Small) are Fiscal Multipliers? *Journal of Monetary Economics*, 60: 239–254.

Monacelli T., Perotti R. (2008). Fiscal Policy, Wealth Effects and Markups', NBER Working Paper No. 14584, Cambridge MA.

Monacelli T., Perotti R., Trigari A. (2010). Unemployment Fiscal Multipliers. *Journal of Monetary Economics*, 57: 531–553.

Parker J. (2011). On Measuring the Effects of Fiscal Policy in Recessions. *Journal of Economic Literature*, 49: 703–18.

Perotti R. (2005). Estimating the Effects of Fiscal Policy in OECD Countries. Proceedings, Federal Reserve Bank of San Francisco.

Perotti R. (2007). In Search of the Transmission Mechanism of Fiscal Policy. *NBER Macroeconomics Annual*, 22: 169–226.

Ramey V. (2011). Identifying Government Expenditure Shocks: It is All in the Timing. *Quarterly Journal of Economics*, 126: 1–50.

Ratto M., Roeger W., Veld J. (2009). QUEST III: an Estimated Open Economy DSGE Model of the Euro Area with Fiscal and Monetary Policy. *Economic Modelling*, 26: 222–233.

Reinhart C, Rogoff K. (2008). Is the 2007 US Sub-Prime Financial Crisis so Different? An International Historical Comparison. *American Economic Review Papers and Proceedings*, 98: 339–344.

Woodford M (2011). Simple Analytics of the Government Expenditure Multiplier. *American Economic Journal- Macroeconomics*, 3: 1–35.

CHAPTER 7

Monetary Policy and Systemic Risk: U.S. Evidence

Ioanna T. Kokores and Angelos Kanas

1 Introduction

Systemic risk arises when there is a breakdown in aggregate financial intermediation that accompanies a financial institution's failure to meet its obligations, and is related to financial markets' questioning the ability of the financial system to absorb losses. An example of systemic risk is the 2008 episode of the market equity value of several firms being close to zero (Fannie Mae, Freddie Mac, Lehman Brothers, AIG, Merrill Lynch, Washington Mutual, Wachovia, and Citigroup), thereby rendering them insolvent and no longer able to provide financial intermediation (see e.g. Engle and Richardson 2015). The effect of systemic risk on monetary

I. T. Kokores
Department of Economics, University of Piraeus, Piraeus, Greece

A. Kanas (✉)
Department of Economics, University of Piraeus, Piraeus, Greece

Scientific Committee, Parliamentary Budget Office,
Hellenic Parliament, Athens, Greece
e-mail: akanas@unipi.gr

I. T. Kokores et al. (eds.), *Money, Trade and Finance*,
https://doi.org/10.1007/978-3-030-73219-6_7

policy has been the focus of recent contributions, mainly examining the notion that policy rates affect the risk-taking behavior of banks (Faia and Karau 2017). Addressing causality toward the opposite direction, recent research also investigates the effect of financial fragility to the monetary policy decision-making process (see e.g. Barrett et al. 2016).

In the present chapter, we assess if monetary policymakers follow systemic risk in adjusting monetary policy for the US over the period 1960–2011. Specifically, we focus on the causal link *from* systemic risk *to* monetary policy, and evaluate the reactions of monetary policy variables during periods of high and low systemic risk.

Within this framework, we address the issue of whether monetary policy reacts differently when systemic risk exceeds a particular threshold level. This approach is motivated by and is consistent with the Federal Reserve's (FED) statutory mandate (FED 1917), which points out that among the FED's macro areas of intervention is the aim of 'maintaining the stability of the financial system and containing systemic risk that may arise in financial markets', and, in particular, 'shall maintain long run growth of the monetary and credit aggregates commensurate with the economy's long run potential to increase production, so as to promote effectively the goals of maximum employment, stable prices, and moderate long-term interest rates' (FED's mandate effective amendment as of 2000). Additionally, in the recent Federal Reserve Act's amendment effective as of 2016, the FED passed over technical amendments to its rule identifying global systemically important bank holding companies and requiring those firms to hold additional amounts of risk-based capital to avoid restrictions on capital distributions and discretionary bonus payments.

Thus, in consistency with the above FED's mandate, when systemic risk increases above a threshold level and 'severe' systemic instability arises, the reaction of the monetary policy should be assessed as to whether monetary policy is eased and is compliant with these statements.

Measurement of systemic risk is based on the CATFIN factor proposed by Allen et al. (2012), and employed in recent contributions (Giglio et al. 2016). Our findings are twofold. First, monetary policy does respond to CATFIN. Second, its response is asymmetric between regimes of high CATFIN and low CATFIN values. The threshold CATFIN value is estimated in the area of 0.047–0.056. The implications of these findings are that FED does follow systemic risk, as approximated by CATFIN, in monetary policy decision-making, and, thus, this factor may be included into an inflation targeting policy regime in assessing the sensitivity of the target interest rate.

The chapter is structured as follows: Section 2 outlines CATFIN as a measure of systemic risk. The next section presents the data and the method. Section 4 discusses the empirical results and draws policy implications. The last section concludes.

2 Systemic Risk: CATFIN

Factor CATFIN, proposed by Allen et al. (2012), measures the catastrophic risk in the financial sector, and is a Value-at-Risk (VaR) measure derived by looking at the cross-section of financial firms at any point in time. It is defined as the average of three different Value-at-Risk (measures: two using parametric distributions and one using the nonparametric method.[1] It is a macro-measure of systemic risk, adopting the view that systemic risk can emerge through general economic factors that cause markets to freeze up. This measure captures the system-wide level of risk-taking and is calculated using the historical distribution of equity returns. In other words, CATFIN determines the macroeconomic implications of aggregate risk-taking in the financial system. CATFIN was developed to forecast potential detrimental effects of financial risk-taking by the overall financial sector on the macroeconomy. The intuition is that banks do not internalize the costs on the society when making risk-taking decisions, and CATFIN is supposed to capture these externalities. CATFIN has attracted considerable attention in the literature as a systemic risk factor. Allen and Tang (2014) and Cai et al. (2017) considered CATFIN as a market aggregate measure of systemic risk in the financial and the banking sector.

3 Data and Methodology

The data set comprises of monthly observations for CATFIN, the log difference of M1, the log difference of M3, and the difference in the effective federal funds rate. In line with the extant literature, the latter rate is considered as the monetary policy rate. We, additionally, proxy the process of the FED's monetary policymaking by individually addressing the 'narrow' and the 'broad' monetary aggregates (M1 and M3 respectively, as defined

[1] In the present analysis, we consider the nonparametric method, in line with Giglio et al. (2016).

by the FED). The latter is considered relevant, initially, from a methodological aspect, in that our data set spans over several decades prior to the official use of inflation targeting by central banks, when, in fact, monetary aggregates had been closely monitored. Furthermore, it also employs a theoretical connotation. Since the workings of the risk-taking channel of the monetary transmission mechanism have been under special scrutiny after the global financial turmoil of 2007–2008, the effectiveness of interest rate monetary policy has been put into question (see e.g. Maddaloni and Peydro 2011). The above measures of the money supply, reflecting the provision of liquidity that may stimulate the economy, may help the monetary authorities determine the type and extent of intervention (conventional and unconventional) that they could introduce to influence the economy.

CATFIN is obtained from Giglio et al. (2016), and the other data from the FRED database.[2] The sample period starts from January 1960 and ends at December 2011 due to the availability of CATFIN, and comprises of 621 monthly observations. Over the sample period, the average value of CATFIN is 0.044, with a minimum value of 0.016 and a maximum of 0.28. A pictorial representation of the data is given in Fig. 7.1.

Our empirical methodology is based on Balke (2000). Consider the following 'structural' threshold VAR model:

$$Y_t = A^1 Y_t + B^1(L)Y_{t-1} + \left[A^2 Y_t + B^2(L)Y_{t-1}\right]\mathrm{I}(\mathrm{c}_{t-d} > \gamma) + U_t,$$

where Y_t is an 2×1 vector of variables comprising of a monetary policy variable and CATFIN; $B^1(L)$ and $B^2(L)$ are lag polynomial matrices; U_t are structural disturbances; c_{t-d} is the threshold variable that determines which regime the system is in and $I(c_{t-d} > \gamma)$ is an indicator function that equals 1 when $c_{t-d} > \gamma$, and 0 otherwise. A^1 and A^2 reflect the structural contemporaneous relationships in the two regimes, respectively, and are assumed to have a recursive structure. In order to test the threshold value, the threshold model is estimated by least squares for all possible threshold values. Three separate test statistics were calculated, namely sup-Wald, avg-Wald, exp-Wald, as shown in Table 7.1.

The simulation method of Hansen (1996) was used to conduct inference. The estimated threshold value is one that maximized the log

[2]The Fred codes are: FEDFUNDS for the federal funds rate, M1SL for M1, and MABMM301USM189S for M3.

determinants of the structural residuals. Asymmetries in terms of magnitude, persistence and significance of the responses can be seen by comparing the regime-dependent functions. The regime-dependent impulse response function describes the effect of CATFIN on monetary policy variables within each regime. Our functions are conditional on a given regime prevailing at the time of the disturbance and throughout the duration of the response. The validity of regime conditioning depends on the time horizon of the impulse response and the expected duration of the regime. As long as the horizon is not excessive and the transition matrix predicts regimes, which are highly persistent, the conditioning is valid, and regime-dependent impulse response functions can be a useful analytical tool. The empirical estimation follows Balke (2000).

4 Empirical Findings and Policy Implications

U.S. monetary policy aims to promote maximum employment, stable prices and moderate long-term interest rates by setting a *symmetric* inflation target (FED statutory mandate effective amendment 2016). In its assessment of the balance of risks (encompassing risks to the financial system) that could impede the attainment of the aforementioned monetary policy goals, the FED responds to projections of systemic risk incidents, as measured by CATFIN. However, the response of the FED's interest rate monetary policy is asymmetric (Fig. 7.2).

When the CATFIN value exceeds 0.048, there is a short-lived (three-month) impulse response of the policy rate to increases in systemic risk. When CATFIN is at a relatively low level (below the 0.048 level), the policy rate does not response to systemic risk. Thus, there is an asymmetric policy rate impulse response with the asymmetry being triggered by the magnitude of systemic risk. The FED appears to be reading the CATFIN value, and decides to respond only after CATFIN exceeds that value. So, for the FED, relatively high systemic risk arises when CATFIN is higher than 0.048. A policy implication is that the U.S. interest rate monetary policy should include CATFIN only for relatively high values of this factor. The periods during which CATFIN exceeded that threshold and thus monetary policy responded to systemic risk are shown in Fig. 7.3.

Conventional monetary policy strategy changes to the money supply are initially reflected to changes in M1. Since M1 does not include financial assets, it actually covers the types of money most commonly used as a medium of exchange, and, thus, may incorporate (to a certain extent) a considerable impact of previous monetary policy strategy. The change in log M1 appears to respond to systemic risk differently across the high CATFIN and the low CATFIN regime. When the CATFIN exceeds 0.054, M1 increases when systemic risk increases, while when CATFIN is below 0.054, M1 decreases after systemic risk increases. Thus, similarly to the policy rate, even for M1 there is an asymmetric response between periods of high and low systemic risk. An important feature of the response of M1 is the long-term tendency for this response to die out, with the response lasting about 10 to 12 months. Thus, the effect of systemic risk on M1 does not appear to be persistent in both regimes.

However, the asymmetry in the response of U.S. monetary policy to CATFIN is *not* maintained when the former is viewed in terms of the initial part of the interest rate monetary policy transmission process, as reflected in changes to the M3 monetary aggregate. The change in log M3 does not appear to be asymmetric between periods of high and low CATFIN values. In addition, the response of M3 appears to be persistent, with systemic risk effects remaining present even after 12 months. This is consistent with a priori expectations given that M3 includes large liquid financial assets (like short-term repurchase agreements and institutional money market funds) and CATFIN measures the risk of the broader financial sector which includes the assets similar to the ones comprising M3. Even though M3 is a monetary aggregate that has not been explicitly tracked by the FED since 2006 (when the FED stopped publishing reports on M3), our results, especially in view of the recent global financial turmoil, point toward the opposite. Since M3 appears to have a persistent symmetric response to CATFIN, then M3 monitoring by the FED (irrespective of the shortcomings in its precise measurement due, for example, to acute global financial interdependence) seems to be equivalent to the incorporation of risks to financial stability (upside and downside) in the monetary policy strategy (see e.g. Yellen 2014, p. 2).

5 Conclusion

In the present chapter, we assess if monetary policymakers follow systemic risk in adjusting monetary policy for the US over the period 1960–2011. We focus on the causal link *from* systemic risk *to* monetary policy, and evaluate the reactions of monetary policy variables during periods of high and low systemic risk. Measurement of systemic risk is based on the CATFIN factor proposed by Allen et al. (2012), and employed in recent contributions (Giglio et al. 2016). The Federal Reserve's monetary policy strategy is presented in terms of the evolution of both the federal funds rate, as well as of the pertinent 'narrow' and 'broad' definition of monetary aggregates (namely M1 and M3).

Our findings are twofold. First, U.S. monetary policy as measured by the three proxies proposed, does respond to CATFIN. Second, its response is asymmetric between regimes of high CATFIN and low CATFIN values. The threshold CATFIN value is estimated in the area of 0.047–0.056. The implications of these findings is that FED does actually follow systemic risk, as approximated by CATFIN, in monetary policy decision-making, and, thus, this factor may be included into an inflation targeting policy regime in assessing the sensitivity of the target interest rate.

Appendix

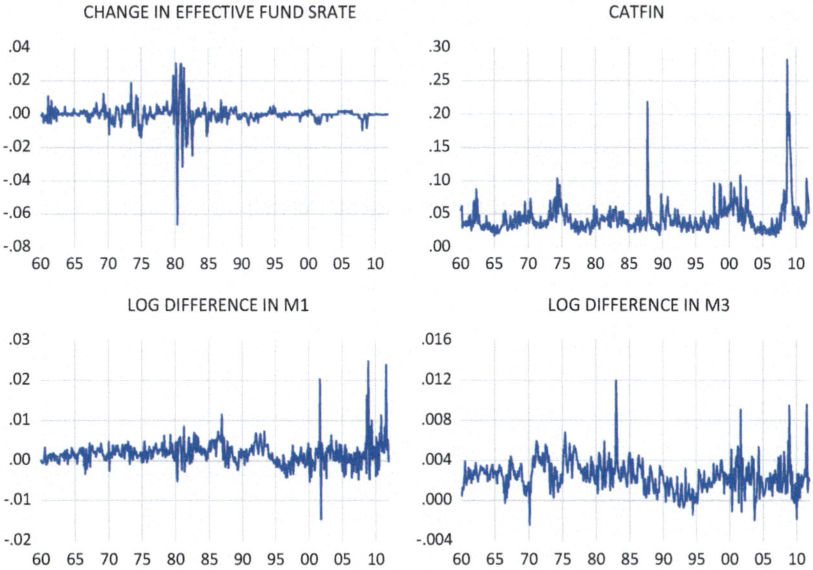

Fig. 7.1 Data

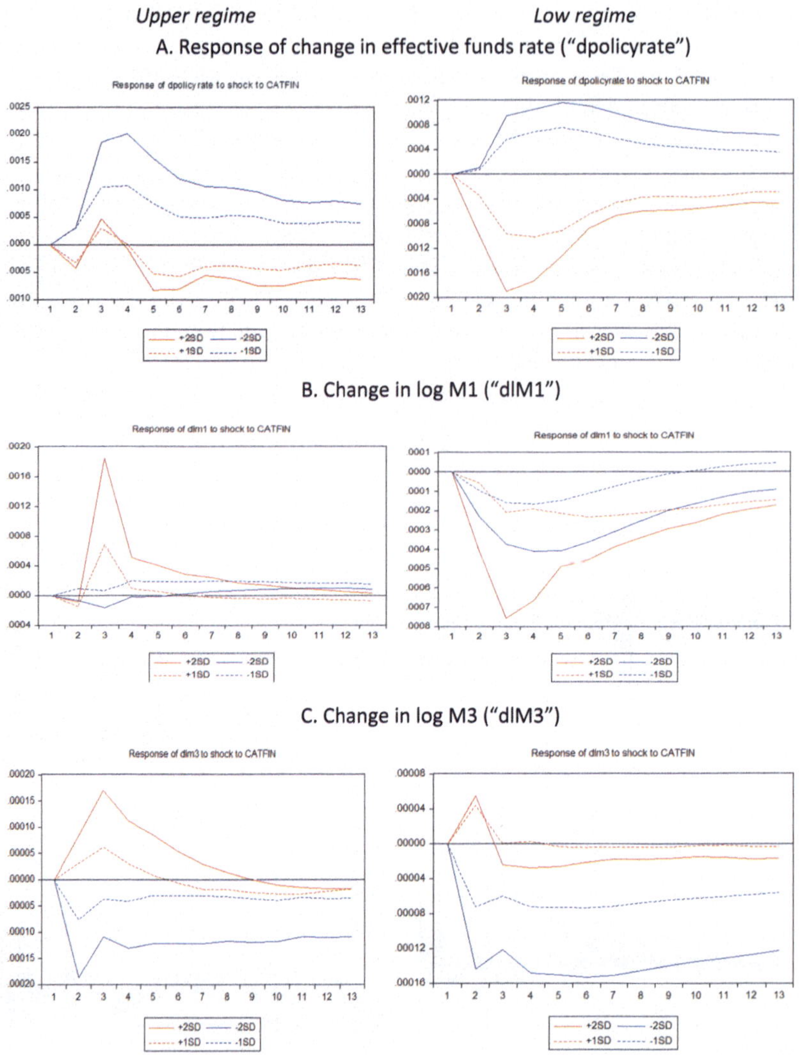

Fig. 7.2 Response of monetary policy variables to CATFIN. (**a**) Response of change in effective funds rate ("dpolicyrate"). (**b**) Change in log M1 ("dlM1"). (**c**) Change in log M3 ("dlM3")

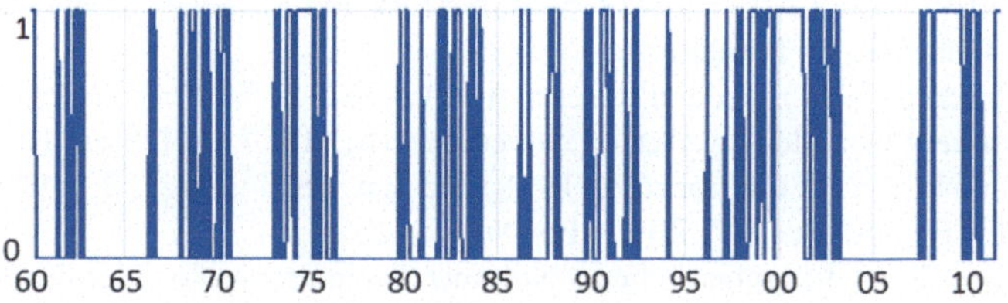

Fig. 7.3 Periods when CATFIN exceeded 0.048

Table 7.1 Tests for threshold SVAR

Monetary policy variables	*Test statistics*	*for threshold*	*in SVAR*	*CATFIN threshold value*
	sup-Wald	*avg-Wald*	*exp-Wald*	
Change in effective funds rate	57.11 (0.00)	23.79 (0.00)	24.21 (0.00)	0.048
Change in log of M1	101.33 (0.00)	46.71 (0.00)	46.99 (0.00)	0.054
Change in log of M3	60.51 (0.00)	23.43 (0.00)	25.61 (0.00)	0.052

Note: In parentheses next to test statistics are the *p*-values for rejecting the null of no threshold

References

Allen, L., T. G. Bali, and Y. Tang (2012). Does Systemic Risk in the Financial Sector Predict Future Economic Downturns?. *Review of Financial Studies* 25(10): 3000–3036.

Allen, L. and Y. Tang (2014). What's Contingency? A Proposal for Bank Contingent Capital Triggered by Systemic Risk. *Federal Reserve Bank of Atlanta*, Working Paper.

Balke, N.S. (2000). Credit and Economic Activity: Credit regimes and Nonlinear Propagation of Shocks. *The Review of Economics and Statistics,* 82: 344–349.

Barrett, C.R., I. Kokores and S. Sen (2016). Monetary Policy Games, Financial Instability and Incomplete Information. *Annals of Finance,* 12(2): 161–178.

Cai, J., Eidam F., Saunders A. and Steffen S. (2017). Syndication, Interconnectedness and Systemic Risk. Available online at SSRN: https://ssrn.com/abstract=1508642

Engle, R. and M. Richardson (2015). Systemic Risk and the Prospect of Global Financial Stability. *Banking Perspective*, Quarter 2: 26–22.

Faia, E and S. Karau (2017). Banks' Systemic Risk and Monetary Policy. Working Paper University of Frankfurt.
Federal Reserve (1917). Federal Reserve Act. 12 USC 225a. *Federal Reserve Act's Amendment* as added by Act of November 16, (1977) (91 Stat. 1387) and amended by Acts of October 27, (1978) (92 Stat. 1897); Aug. 23, (1988) (102 Stat. 1375); and Dec. 27, 2000 (114 Stat. 3028).
Hansen, B. (1996). Inference When a Nuisance Parameter is Not Identified Under the Null Hypothesis. *Econometrica*, 64: 413–430.
Giglio S., B. Kelly and S. Pruitt (2016). Systemic Risk and the Macroeconomy: An Empirical Evaluation. *Journal of Financial Economics*, 119: 457–471.
Maddaloni, A., and J.-L. Peydro (2011). Bank Risk-Taking, Securitization, Supervision, and Low Interest Rates: Evidence from Euro-Area and US Lending Standards', *Review of Financial Studies*, 24: 2121–2165.
Yellen, J. L. (2014). Monetary Policy and Financial Stability. *Remarks by the Chair of the Board of Governors of the Federal Reserve System*, at The 2014 Michel Camdessus Central Banking Lecture International Monetary Fund, Washington, DC, July 2. Available online: https://www.federalreserve.gov/newsevents/speech/files/yellen20140702a.pdf.

PART IV

Financial Markets and the Macroeconomy

CHAPTER 8

What Drives the Default Risk of Restructured Loans

Yannis Dendramis, Elias Tzavalis, Petros Varthalitis, and Eleni Athanasiou

1 Introduction

Loan restructuring is a well-known procedure in which banks are involved to avoid massive losses and accommodate borrowers' financial difficulties. This is more acute under financially distressed and severe recession conditions of the economy. This procedure often involves the extension of the maturity of a loan, reduction of its instalment rates and/or allowance of

We thank Dimitris Georgarakos, Peter McAdam and Rachel Slaymaker for their insightful comments and suggestions. We have also benefited from comments by seminar participants at the Athens University of Economics & Business, Czech National Bank and the 5th Paris Financial Management Conference. The views presented in the paper are those of the authors alone and do not present official views of their institutions.

Y. Dendramis • E. Tzavalis (✉) • P. Varthalitis
Department of Economics, Athens University of Economics and Business, Athens, Greece
e-mail: e.tsavalis@aueb.gr

I. T. Kokores et al. (eds.), *Money, Trade and Finance*,
https://doi.org/10.1007/978-3-030-73219-6_8

grace period (usually six months) during which no loan payments are made. The extension of the maturity of a loan plays a key role in loan restructuring. If borrowers' ability-to-pay conditions improve during the extended maturity interval, the defaulted loans may be cured, and lenders may avoid losses.

Because of the importance of loan restructuring for the whole economy and society, many governments have introduced legal and institutional frameworks supporting it in order to deal with the effects of the 2008 financial crisis on household debt and non-performing loans (NPLs). Some governments have also introduced laws banning foreclosures (see Laeven and Laryea (2009) for a survey). These procedures favor loan restructuring based on criteria like borrowers' income, employment status, family size and potential disabilities inter alia.

Although loan restructuring and the legal framework supporting it can be proved mutually beneficial for lenders and borrowers, they may also raise moral hazard incentives. That is, borrowers with ability-to-pay and without liquidity problems may not pay back their loans by repeatedly exploiting allowance of debt payment moratorium. Existence of such incentives make debt servicing and credit risk modeling a difficult task for banks especially during systemic financial crises.[1] Almost certainly, these incentives will lead to an increase in the rate of loan defaults in the long run and tend to make the financially distressed conditions of the economy permanent.[2] Thus, they have macroprudential and financial stability interest.[3]

E. Athanasiou
Retail Banking Credit Risk Division, Alpha Bank Greece, Athens, Greece

[1] See Chan et al. (2016) and Dendramis et al. (2018) for the mortgage loan market.

[2] See Andritzky (2014), for a recent comprehensive survey of the negative effects of loan restructuring and debt moratorium procedures on the economy and banking sector.

[3] For a detailed discussion on how high default rates and NPLs shape macroprudential and financial stability policies, see the ESRB (European Systemic Risk Board) Recommendations 2013 and 2017 considering moral hazard at the core of policies to the resolution of NPLs.

The aim of this paper is to address the following questions using data on consumer loans from the Greek economy over the recent years of the economic and financial crisis. First, if there exist substantial differences in the hazard (default) rates and covariates determining the PD between restructured and non-restructured loans. If yes, we examine whether these differences can be attributed to moral hazard effects. Second, we investigate if there exist covariates which can predict reduction of the PD for restructured loans. Answering these questions can improve credit risk management policies leading to successful debt restructuring and thus help borrowers without moral hazard incentives in servicing their debt.

In this paper, we rely on a panel data binary choice model and use loan-specific covariates, such as personal income, the instalment or/and actual payments of a loan, the balance and delinquent amount of a loan, as well as delinquency buckets of a loan measuring the number of times that a borrower is past due for up to 1, 2 and 3 months over the history of a loan. These covariates can capture attitudes of borrowers that strategically default, thus are referred to as behavioral variables (see e.g., Crook and Bellotti 2010). In addition, we also employ macroeconomic covariates such as the unemployment rate, the real GDP growth rate and the inflation rate which are often used in stress testing (see Crook and Bellotti 2012). These covariates capture the macroeconomic and business cycles effects on the PD. They will also reflect the severe economic conditions held in the Greek economy from 2009 to 2015 which are expected to have influenced the ability of borrowers to pay back their loans. In our econometric analysis, we use two alternative distributions as binary link functions, namely the logit and the cloglog. The latter allows for asymmetric responses of the PD to the covariates of the model. Finally, the panel data nature of the model enables us to include in it a function of the duration of a loan, known as baseline hazard rate function in the literature (see Shumway 2001).

We provide a number of interesting results. First, we show that asymmetric binary link functions such as the cloglog distribution can better fit PD models into the data. Second, we provide clear cut evidence that the group of loan-specific covariates, capturing behavioral attitudes of borrowers, have much bigger marginal effects on the PD than the macroeconomic covariates. This result holds across both types of loans, restructured and non-restructured, as well as across the two binary link functions. Third, we find that the ratio the delinquent amount of a loan over its total balance and the ratio of the actual payments of a loan over the personal income of the borrower have the larger effects on the PD of consumer loans. These effects are consistently higher for the restructured than the non-restructured loans. The former effect provides evidence of moral hazard behavior in the market of consumer loans which arises from the ability of borrowers to restructure their loans repeatedly. On the other hand, the negative sign and large effects of the latter ratio found for the restructured loans indicate evidence of borrowers' commitment without moral hazard motives to service their debt. The above results are consistent across the two different binary functions considered. Finally, we find that the macroeconomic covariates with the larger marginal effects on the PD are the unemployment rate changes followed by the GDP growth rate. The marginal effects of these variables are also bigger for the group of restructured loans.

The paper is organized as follows. Section 2 presents the panel data model employed in our analysis and discusses some of its key properties. Section 3 presents our data set and gives the definition of the covariates employed to estimate the model. Section 4 presents the estimation results of the model and calculates descriptive statistics of the marginal effects of the key covariates of the model. Section 5 concludes the paper.

2 Model Setup

2.1 *The Discrete-Time Proportional Hazard Model*

Assume discrete-time $t = 0, 1, \ldots, T$ and that, at time t, a loan default event can happen for an individual loan account $i = 1, 2, \ldots, N$. This event can be captured by a binary random variable $Y_{i,t}$ which takes the value 1 (i.e., $Y_{i,t} = 1$) if the default event occurs, and zero otherwise (i.e., $Y_{i,t} = 0$, for the no-default event). The panel data proportional survival analysis model assumes that the probability of default (PD) of a loan i, at time t, denoted as $P_{i,t}$ is given by the following reduced form equation[4]:

$$
\begin{aligned}
P_{i,t} &= \Pr\left(Y_{i,t} = 1 \mid Y_{i,l} = 0; \varphi_{d_i}; \xi_i; x_{i,t-m}; z_{t-p}\right), \\
&\forall l < t, i = 1,2,\ldots N \text{ and } t = 1,2,\ldots T_i \qquad (8.1) \\
&= \Phi\left(\omega_i\left(t,s\right)\right),
\end{aligned}
$$

[4] See, for example, Hwang (2012), Bellotti and Crook (2013) and Hwang and Chu (2014).

where $\Phi(\omega)$ is a distribution function, referred to as binary link function, and

$$\omega_i(t,s) \equiv b'W_{i,t-s} = c + b_1'\varphi_{d_i} + b_2'\xi_i + b_3'x_{i,t-s} + b_4'z_{t-s},$$

is a linear in $W_{i,t-s}$ index function, where $W_{i,t-s}$ and b are vectors collecting the covariates of the model and their corresponding slope coefficients (i.e., $b' = (c, b_1', b_2', b_3')$ and $W_{i,t-s}' = \left(1, \varphi_{d_i}', \xi_i', x_{i,t-s}', z_{t-s}'\right)$, respectively, and $s = \{m, p\}$denotes lag structure. Note that s can differ across the covariates of the model $x_{i,t-s}$ and z_{t-s}. Also, T_i denotes the last observation of a loan account i in the sample. For notational convenience, the subscript $i$is dropped from T_i, that is, we assume $T \equiv T_i$.

In model (8.1), the binary function $\Phi(.)$ links the probability of default $P_{i,t}$ of a loan account i, at time t, to different groups (vectors) of covariates defined by linear index function $\omega_i(t, s)$. As a binary function, in our analysis we consider the following two parametric distributions: The standard logit, defined as $\Phi(\omega) = \frac{1}{1+e^{-\omega}}, \omega \in (-\infty, +\infty)$, often used in practice (see Green 2012), and the cloglog, defined as $\Phi(\omega) = 1 - e^{-e^{\omega}}$. The latter allows for an asymmetric pattern of the responses of $P_{i,t}$ to the covariates of the model and the index function $\omega_i(t, s)$ (see Koenker and Yoon 2009).

The vectors of covariates of the link function $\omega_i(t, s)$ are defined as follows: First, $\varphi_{d_i} = \left(d_i, d_i^2, \log(d_i), \log(d_i)^2\right)$ is a vector of linear and nonlinear functions of the duration time (age) of a loan account i, denoted as d_i, which reflects the number of periods (months in our sample) that loan account i is opened and served until period t, where the default event can occur. The inner product of the vectors of slope coefficients b_1 and duration functions collected in vector φ_{d_i} (i.e., $b_1'\varphi_{d_i}$), is known as the baseline hazard rate function of the model. This will be henceforth defined as $h(d_i) \equiv b_1'\varphi_{d_i}$. This is a smooth function of duration time d_i, which enables us to obtain values of $P_{i,t}$ conditional on the values of d_i, for all i. In the empirical literature for mortgages (see, e.g., Deng et al. 2000; Glennon and Nigro 2005), function $h\left(\varphi_{d_i}\right)$ is often found to have an inverse-U scheme, reflecting the fact that loan defaults do not often occur at the very early and/or very late stage of their maturity horizon. The elements of vector φ_{d_i}, assumed above, render $h\left(\varphi_{d_i}\right)$ a quite flexible one, allowing for nonlinear patterns of it with respect to d_i (see, for instance, Bellotti and Crook 2013). By conditioning $P_{i,t}$ on d_i (or $h\left(\varphi_{d_i}\right)$), model (8.1) can show if a consumer loan is more likely to default in early, or late, stages of its maturity horizon and how this compares to other categories of loans which are collateralized (e.g., mortgages).

Second, vector ξ_i consists of application covariates which are defined over the cross-section (N) dimension of the data and their values are known at the time where a loan account i was opened, that is, d_i periods back. Third, vector $x_{i,\,t-s}$ consists of loan-specific covariates which are defined both over the cross- and time-dimension of the data. Their values are given at any time-point t of the life of a loan account i. Finally, z_{t-s} denotes a vector of macroeconomic covariates. The values of this vector is common across all individual loan accounts, i, at any point t of the sample. The lag structure of vectors $x_{i,\,t-s}$ and z_{t-s} enables us to obtain dynamic forecasts of $P_{i,\,t}$ based on current, or past, values of $x_{i,\,t-s}$ and z_{t-s}. This is done for given values of duration d_i and vector ξ_i. A detailed description of the above all covariates included in vectors ξ_i, $x_{i,\,t-s}$ and z_{t-s} are given in the next section.

3 Data and Covariates

In this section, we present our data set and the covariates employed to estimate model (8.1) in more detail. We define the default rates and the restructured loans, and we discuss the predictions of theory about the effects of the covariates of the model on the PD.

3.1 *Data on Consumer Loan Defaults*

Our data set consists of a large set of $N = 55,805$ restructured and non-restructured consumer loan accounts of the Greek economy. These are short-term loans with maturity of about 8 years. Their frequency is monthly and they cover the period from 2009:04 to 2015:12. Following the Basel II definition of default, we assume that a consumer loan is defaulted (i.e., non-performing) when its principal and payments of interest are past due by 90 days or more. The percentage of the defaulted loans in our sample is high which improves considerably the efficiency of the estimation and the inference procedures for model (8.1). Note that a big number of the restructured loans in our sample is protected by the Greek laws 3869/2010, 3986/2011 and 4224/2013 which bans foreclosures and favors debt payment moratorium. A restructured loan is treated as a new entry in our sample with a new account opened at the time that the old loan is defaulted and exit the sample. The new loan account has a new duration time, d_i, new instalments, application and other characteristics.

Figures 8.1a and 8.1b graphically present default rates, over time, for the two categories of loans defined above, namely the non-restructured and restructured loans. In addition to these series, they also present the default loan rates conditional on the duration time d_i (defined in months), given the whole sample period 2009:04–2015:12. The conditional default of a loan rate corresponding to a value of d_i (say δ, for all i) gives the percentage rate of defaulted loans in our sample with elapsed time equal to δ, since the origination of the loan. The inspection of the figures indicates that the default rates exhibit very high volatility, over time, for both cate-

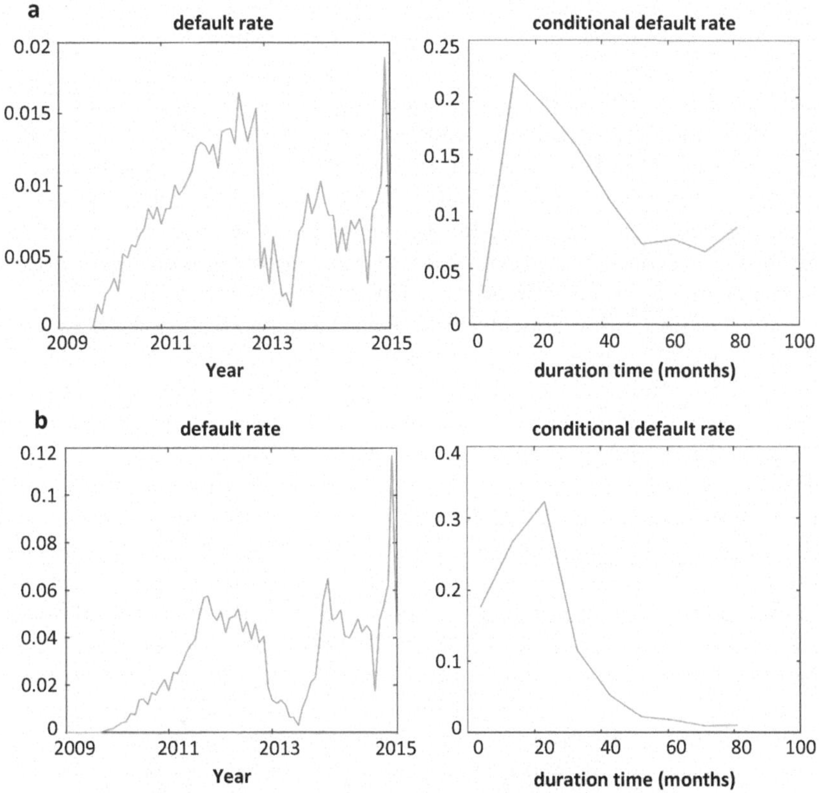

Fig. 8.1a Default and conditional default rates (non-restructured loans)

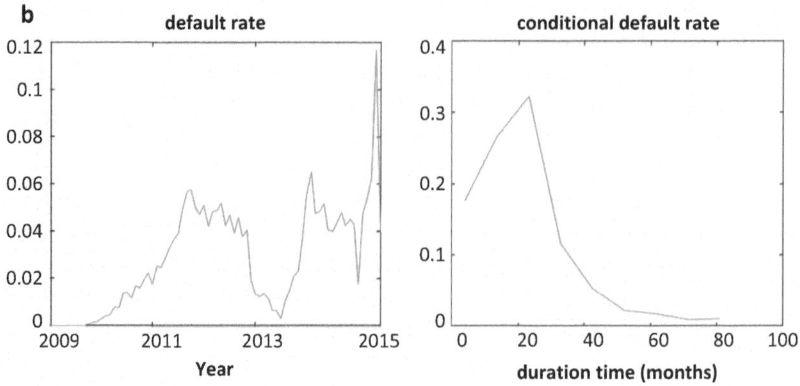

Fig. 8.1b Default and conditional default rates (restructured loans)

gories of loans. They steadily increase in most periods of the sample, but also decrease, substantially, in some years, like 2014, and they reach the peak in year 2015. This pattern of the default rates can be associated with changes in the consumer loan market due to the recession and distressed financial conditions occurring during our sample. The drops of the default rates in year 2014 can be associated with the improving conditions of the Greek economy in this year (see also Charalambakis et al. 2017).

Another interesting conclusion that can be drawn from Figs. 8.1a and 8.1b is that the series of the restructured loans default rates is always higher than the non-restructured ones by an almost constant amount, over all periods of the sample. This may be obviously attributed to differences in the attitudes of the obligors between the two categories of loans. The obligors of the restructured loans may be more tempted toward strategic default. A similar argument can be supported by the inspection of the graphs of the conditional on duration default rates, reported also in the figures. These graphs clearly show that these default rates are always higher for the restructured loans, compared to the non-restructured ones, for all duration intervals d_i, given at the horizontal axis. However, the graphs of them have the same pattern for both categories of loans considered. They are concave with respect to d_i and have an inverse-U shape, which is similar to that observed in other loan markets, for example, mortgages (see Deng et al. 2000; Dendramis et al. 2018). That is, the default rate increases with d_i, initially, and it reaches its peak at a value of d_i about 20 months. After this peak, it starts declining toward zero, as d_i increases, implying that consumer loans are less likely to default as they approach maturity. The shorter duration interval d_i where the consumer default rate reaches its peak, compared to the mortgage loans, can be obviously attributed to the short-term nature of the consumer loans.

3.2 The Covariates of the Model

3.2.1 Application Covariates

The group of application covariates of the model, collected in vector ξ_i, includes the following qualitative dummy variables, defined over the cross-section dimension of the data: (i) ***urban effects***, (ii) ***age effects***, associated with the age of a borrower at the application date, and (iii) ***consumer*** and/or ***car*** categories of loans. In particular, the dummy variable capturing urban effects takes one for the loans around Athens (Attica), and zero otherwise. The age effects are categorized by the following years of age intervals: age < 30 and 30 < age < 45. The car loans differ from the remaining categories of consumer loans of our sample, since they are secured through the dealer. The dealer will not transfer the car title to the borrower until she/he pays off the loan. That is, the car is being used as collateral in a secured loan. Finally, note that, since some of the restructured loans have a grace period of six months, we have also considered a 0/1 dummy variable for this category of loans denoted as grace period. This dummy takes one if a restructured loan is in grace period, and zero otherwise. As the loan-specific covariates, discussed next, this dummy may capture differences in behavioral attitudes of borrowers on the PD between the two categories of loans considered.

3.2.2 Loan-Specific Covariates

The group of loan-level covariates collected in vector $x_{i,\,t-s}$, defined over both the cross-section (N) and time (T) dimensions of the data, includes the following ratios of covariates: the ratio of the delinquent amount of a loan over its total balance (denoted as $\frac{\text{delinquent amount}}{\text{balance}}$), the ratios of the instalment and actual payments of a loan over the personal income of its obligor (denoted as $\frac{\text{instalment}}{\text{income}}$ and $\frac{\text{payment}}{\text{income}}$, respectively), the ratio of the actual payments of the loan over its total balance and that of the total balance of a loan over its instalment (denoted as $\frac{\text{payment}}{\text{balance}}$ and $\frac{\text{balance}}{\text{instalment}}$, respectively). In the above definitions, note that the total balance of a loan includes arrears (i.e., penalties, unpaid instalments, extra interest rates, etc.). The payments of loans reflect payoffs of borrowers, over time, which are less than instalments. The banks allow for such payments on servicing loan debt in order to help borrowers to service their loans, especially under distressed financial and recession conditions where systemic bank risks may appear.

As noted in the introduction, loan-specific covariates like the above ratios are known as behavioral covariates, as they can capture behavioral characteristics of obligors, like moral hazard effects, apart from risk premium attitudes. The sign of the effects of these covariates on PD can be justified as follows. Consumer loans with higher values of $\frac{\text{instalment}}{\text{income}}$ are more likely to default in the future, compared to loans with lower values of this ratio, due to individual income shocks or liquidity constraints that borrowers can face. The same can be argued for the inverse of ratio $\frac{\text{balance}}{\text{instalment}}$. On the other hand, a loan with higher values of ratios $\frac{\text{payment}}{\text{balance}}$ and/or $\frac{\text{payment}}{\text{income}}$ may be less likely to default in the future, compared to one with lower values, reflecting borrower's incentives to meet his/her obligations and avoid defaulting. By doing so, she/he can manage to have access to new credit.

The ratio $\frac{\text{delinquent amount}}{\text{balance}}$ constitutes a measure of consistency of the borrower to pay his/her loan. Another measure of this consistency often used, in practice, is the number of times that a delinquent obligor has a positive amount in buckets 1, 2 and 3, cumulatively. That is, the loan is past due for up to one, two and three months, over its history. This variable is defined as ***delinquency buckets.*** It may be thought of as reflecting a different aspect of borrowers' delinquency risk than $\frac{\text{delinquent amount}}{\text{balance}}$. One may argue that the ratio $\frac{\text{delinquent amount}}{\text{balance}}$ captures borrowers' delinquency risk on default probability Pi, t, while the delinquency buckets variable captures the magnitude of this risk. To see this, consider consumer loans with a small value of $\frac{\text{delinquent amount}}{\text{balance}}$, due, for instance, to low instalments or balloon payments. These loans may exhibit high delinquency buckets risk, due to borrowers' attitude to delay their payments.

3.2.3 *Macroeconomic Covariates*

The group of macroeconomic covariates, collected in vector z_{t-s}, includes the following variables: the inflation rate, the unemployment rate change and the real GDP (gross domestic product) growth rate. All these variables are seasonally adjusted and are measured on monthly basis. Note that the real GDP growth rate is interpolated monthly, since GDP is given quarterly. The above set of macroeconomic variables can capture the effects of changes in the business cycle conditions, occurred during the sample, on $P_{i,t}$. These conditions are measured at aggregate (macroeconomic) level and are expected to influence the ability of borrowers to pay back their loans. As noted in the introduction, they are considered as the main determinants of PD in the empirical credit risk literature and stress testing for consumer loans.

4 Empirical Analysis

In this section, we present and discuss the estimation results of model (8.1). The section is organized as follows. First, we present the econometric method suggested to estimate the model. Second, we present and discuss the estimation results. Third, based on the parameter estimates of the model, we calculate the marginal effects for the most significant covariates of the model on $P_{i,t}$.

4.1 *Estimation Method*

To estimate the vector of the slope parameters of model (8.1), we rely on the maximum likelihood (ML) estimation procedure (see Alllison 1982). The log-likelihood function is given as

$$\log L(\theta) = \sum_{N}^{i=1} \log L_i(\theta), \tag{8.2}$$

where θ denotes the vector of the parameters of the model and $\log L_i(\theta)$ is the log-likelihood function which corresponds to each individual loan account i. This function is given as

$$\log L_i(\theta) = \sum_{T}^{t=1} Y_{i,t} \log P_{i,t} + (1 - Y_{i,t}) \log(1 - P_{i,t}), \ \forall i, i \in \{1, 2, \ldots, N\}. \quad (8.3)$$

The maximization of the log-likelihood function $\log L(\theta)$ yields to asymptotically unbiased and efficient estimates of θ (see, e.g., Harvey 1990).

4.2 *Estimation Results*

The estimation results are presented in Table 8.1; Panel A of the table presents the estimates for the non-restructured loans, while Panel B for the restructured ones. In each of panel, we present estimates based on the logit and cloglog binary functions (see columns (i) and (ii)). For all the above-mentioned different results, we have set the lag order of both the loan-specific and macroeconomic covariates of the model to $s = 3$ months. This lag structure is chosen based on BIC (Bayesian Information Criterion). It can be also justified by the fact that loan default occurs when principal and payments of interest are past due by 90 days (i.e., three-periods back), or more.

To appraise the ability of the model to fit the data and predict the probability of default events, satisfactorily, in the table we present a number of useful statistics and prediction performance metrics. In particular, we report values of the Type I and II errors of the default and non-default events. These errors and metrics, described in more detail in the Appendix, can evaluate the ability of the model to predict default, or non-default, events (namely, $Y_{i,t} = 1$, or $Y_{i,t} = 0$, known as point forecasts (see, e.g., Lahiri and Yang 2013). This can be done based on a threshold value of probability, denoted as p^*, which is estimated by the data (see the table). Finally, the table reports values of the following set of metrics: the minus log-likelihood function value (denoted as *loglik*) obtained by the ML optimization procedure, Schwarz's Bayesian information criterion (denoted as *BIC*), and McFaddens' coefficients of determination R^2 and R^2-adjusted.[5] These metrics can be also used to evaluate how well the model fits into the data.

[5] These coefficients are defined as follows: $R^2 = 1 - \frac{\log L(\theta)}{\log L(\theta_R)}$ and $R^2 - \text{adjusted} = 1 - \frac{\log L(\theta) - K}{\log L(\theta_R)}$, where θ is the vector of the K-slope coefficients of the model and θ_R is that of a restricted version of the model which assumes zero values of the slope coefficients, apart from the intercept.

Table 8.1 Estimates of model (1)

	Panel A: non-restructured loans				*Panel B: restructured loans*			
Binary functions:	*(i) logit*		*(ii) cloglog*		*(i) logit*		*(ii) cloglog*	
Intercept	-91.33	(3.80)	-22.08	(1.06)	-98.08	(4.90)	-32.48	(1.86)
d_i	1.73	(0.11)	0.39	(0.03)	2.25	(0.16)	0.77	(0.06)
d_i^2	-0.006	(0.0004)	-0.001	(0.0001)	-0.008	(0.0006)	-0.002	(0.0002)
$\log(d_i)$	65.02	(3.09)	15.30	(0.87)	73.05	(4.05)	24.46	(1.54)
$\log\left(d_i^2\right)$	-15.72	(0.84)	-3.68	(0.23)	-18.39	(0.84)	-6.21	(0.42)
Age effects: (18,30)	0.03	(0.06)	0.01	(0.02)	-0.16	(0.14)	-0.10	(0.06)
(30,45)	0.002	(0.02)	-0.007	(0.005)	-0.06	(0.02)	-0.02	(0.008)
Consumer loans	0.13	(0.04)	0.023	(0.007)	-0.17	(0.03)	-0.05	(0.01)
Car loans	-0.12	(0.03)	-0.06	(0.009)	-0.25	(0.04)	-0.08	(0.01)
Urban effects	-0.08	(0.02)	-0.01	(0.005)	-0.02	(0.02)	-0.01	(0.008)
Grace period	0.76	(0.003)	0.19	(0.007)	0.20	(0.03)	0.06	(0.01)
$\frac{\text{delinquent amount}}{\text{balance}}$	11.91	(0.07)	7.61	(0.08)	17.14	(0.13)	12.79	(0.20)
Delinquency buckets	0.05	(0.0007)	0.01	(0.0003)	0.03	(0.001)	0.007	(0.0006)
$\frac{\text{instalment}}{\text{income}}$	21.53	(0.58)	6.71	(0.25)	12.95	(0.65)	5.28	(0.34)
$\frac{\text{payment}}{\text{income}}$	-7.04	(0.22)	-9.65	(0.28)	-51.48	(2.28)	-8.66	(0.43)
$\frac{\text{payment}}{\text{balance}}$	-3.97	(0.07)	-3.19	(0.09)	-23.55	(0.07)	-8.37	(0.17)
$\frac{\text{balance}}{\text{instalment}}$	-0.003	(0.0003)	0.0002	(0.0001)	-0.003	(0.0004)	0.0006	(0.0001)
Inflation rate	0.07	(0.009)	0.02	(0.003)	0.08	(0.01)	0.02	(0.003)
Unemployment rate change	0.45	(0.02)	0.10	(0.005)	0.02	(0.02)	-0.0003	(0.009)
GDP	-0.03	(0.01)	-0.007	(0.003)	-0.03	(0.015)	-0.008	(0.005)

(*continued*)

Table 8.1 (continued)

	Panel A: non-restructured loans		*Panel B: restructured loans*	
Binary functions:	*(i) logit*	*(ii) cloglog*	*(i) logit*	*(ii) cloglog*
−loglik	55903.65	52756.50	28758.70	27968.05
BIC	112107.21	105812.91	57804.78	56223.46
R^2	0.26	0.30	0.22	0.24
R^2-adjusted	0.25	0.30	0.22	0.24
p^*	0.01	0.01	0.04	0.05
Type I	0.13	0.06	0.14	0.12
Type II	0.15	0.15	0.23	0.14

Notes: Panels A and B of the table present ML estimates of model (8.1) for non-restructured and restructured loans, respectively. Columns (i) and (ii) present results for the logit and cloglog link functions, respectively. Standard errors are in parentheses. Values of the following fit measures for the model are given: the minus log- likelihood function value (denoted -***loglik***), McFaddens' coefficients of determination R2 and R2-adjusted, defined as $R^2 = 1 - \frac{\log L(\theta)}{\log L(\theta_R)}$ and $R^2 - \textbf{adjusted} = 1 - \frac{\log L(\theta) - K}{\log L(\theta_R)}$, where θ is the vector of the slope coefficients of the model, while θR consists only of the intercept and BIC (the Bayesian information criterion). Type I and Type II are the errors that a loan is predicted as non-defaulted and defaulted, respectively. $p^* \in [0, 1]$ is the threshold value that minimizes the sum of Type I and Type II errors under the constraint that the Type I error is less than $\boldsymbol{u} \in [0, 1]$

A number of interesting conclusions can be drawn from the results of the table. These are summarized as follows.

First, all the measures of fit and prediction performance metrics reported in the table clearly indicate that the specification of the model with the cloglog binary function performs better than that with the logit. This conclusion holds for both the restructured and non-restructured loans. The cloglog function improves the fit of the model, substantially. It reduces considerably the Type I and II errors of the model and improves its fit into the data, as can be seen by the values of the R^2 (R^2-adjusted) reported in the table.

Second, as shown by the table and Figs. 8.2a and 8.2b, the estimates of the baseline hazard rate function $h(d_i)$, capturing the total effects of the duration of a loan d_i on $P_{i,t}$, and its slope parameters indicate that this function has an inverse-U shape. Its maximum with respect to d_i is reached at an interval of about 20 months. These features of $h(d_i)$ are consistent across the two binary link functions and the two categories of loans considered. As was expected, the graphs of $h(d_i)$ are related to the descriptive conditional duration default rates, presented in Figs. 8.1a and 8.1b. However, they do not correspond one-to-one to them, given that model (1) is also proportional to the covariates of the model. Another interesting con-

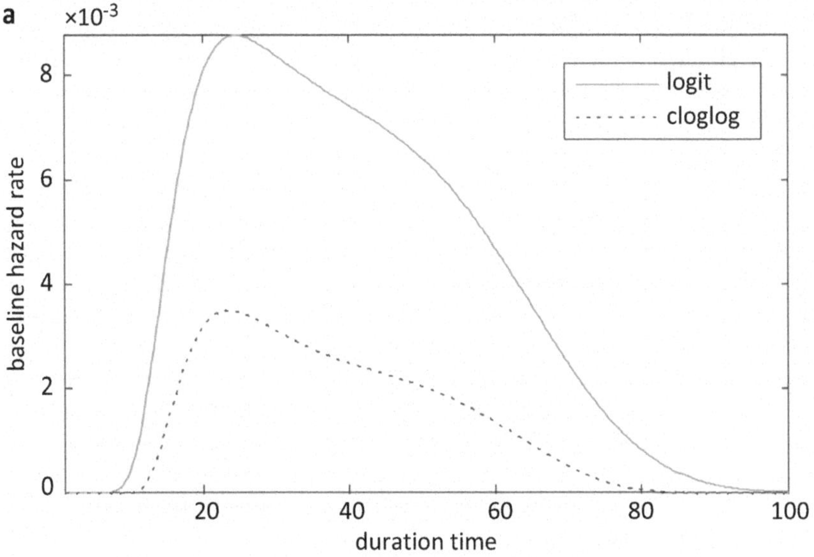

Fig. 8.2a Estimates of the baseline hazard rate function—non-restructured loans

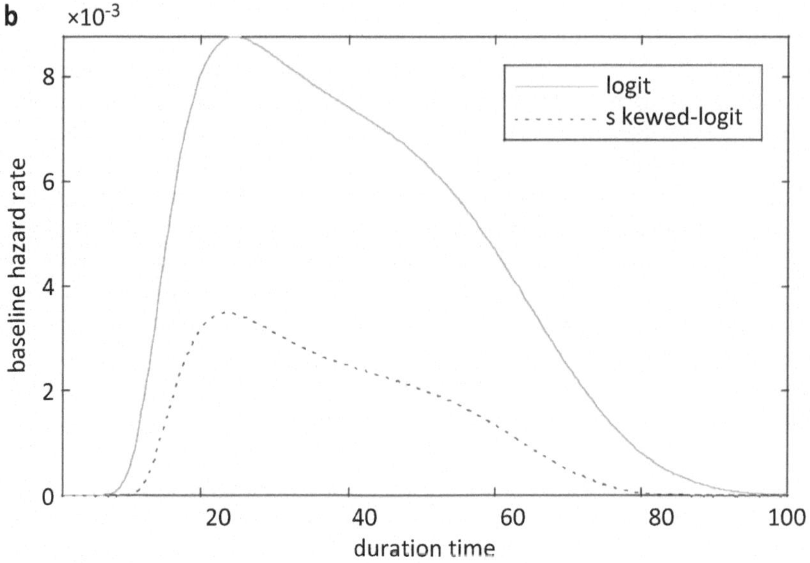

Fig. 8.2b Estimates of the baseline hazard rate function—restructured loans

clusion that can be drawn from Figs. 8.2a and 8.2b is that the logit distribution implies much higher estimates of $P_{i,t}$ conditional on d_i, compared to the cloglog, which is found to fit better the data. This result can be attributed to the fact that the logit distribution does not account for the asymmetries in the binary link function $\Phi(\omega)$, as mentioned before.

Third, for the group of application covariates, the results of the table indicate that the *urban* and *age* (especially, those in interval (30,45)) *effects* on $P_{i,t}$ are negative and significant, for both panels of the table. The same is true for the *car loans* effects, which are found to be clearly bigger than the *consumer loans* ones. As noted before, this can be attributed to the fact that car loans are secured by the dealer. These results are also consistent across the two binary functions considered. Another interesting conclusion that can be drawn from the table for the group of application variables concerns the effects of the *grace period* qualitative dummy on $P_{i,t}$. This variable is also significant for both categories of loans considered.

Fourth, regarding the loan-specific covariates, the results of the table indicate that this constitutes a very important group of information of the consumer loan market about $P_{i,t}$. All of these covariates are found to be significant, at the 5% level, for both the non-restructured and restructured loans examined. The sign of their slope coefficient estimates is also in accordance to the theory. The positive sign effects of $\frac{\text{delinquent amount}}{\text{balance}}$ and *delinquency buckets* on $P_{i,t}$ highlight the importance of borrower's delinquency risk and attitude on loan defaulting. On the other hand, the positive sign of the effects of $\frac{\text{instalment}}{\text{income}}$ and $\frac{\text{balance}}{\text{instalment}}$ on $P_{i,t}$ can be attributed to the inability of borrowers to pay back their loans, due to the recession conditions of the economy. The significant negative effects of $\frac{\text{payment}}{\text{income}}$ and $\frac{\text{payment}}{\text{balance}}$ on $P_{i,\,t}$ can be interpreted as reflecting borrowers' commitment to service their debt. As argued before, by paying off their loans, borrowers in the consumer loan market may keep servicing their debt and manage to have access to credit and liquidity.

Although the effects of the loan-specific covariates on $P_{i,t}$ seem to be qualitatively the same across the restructured and non-restructured loans, there are important differences in the size of some of these effects between the two categories of loans, as is shown by their slope coefficient estimates. In particular, for ratios $\frac{\text{delinquent amount}}{\text{balance}}$ and $\frac{\text{payment}}{\text{balance}}$ the effects on $P_{i,t}$ are much bigger for the restructured loans than the non-restructured, while the opposite happens for $\frac{\text{instalment}}{\text{income}}$. These results are consistent across the two different binary functions considered. To see how important these differences are between restructured and non-restructured loans, in the next section we calculate their marginal effects.

Finally, regarding the effects of the macroeconomic variables on $P_{i,t}$, the results of the table are qualitatively consistent with the ability-to-pay hypothesis (see Elul et al. 2010), implying that a rise in unemployment rate changes (which is associated with a fall of the real GDP level) will affect the ability of borrower to pay their loans and will increase $P_{i,t}$. The insignificant effects of the unemployment rate changes on $P_{i,t}$ for the restructured loans can be attributed to the fact that these changes (or shocks) on $P_{i,t}$ may have been absorbed for this category of loans. The positive effect of a rise in inflation on $P_{i,t}$ can be attributed to a fall in real per capita income which is implied by it. As was expected this effect is common for both categories of loans, as that of the real GDP level.

4.3 *Marginal Effects*

The estimates of slope coefficients of the model, discussed in the previous section, cannot fully indicate the size effects of the model covariates on $P_{i,t}$, as these effects also depend on the density function of the binary link function $\Phi(.)$. To this end, in this section we present estimates of the marginal effects of the covariates of the model, defined by the following vector of partial derivatives:

$$\pi_i\left(t,s \mid W_{i,t-s}\right) \equiv \frac{\partial P_{i,t}}{\partial W_{i,t-s}} = \phi\left(b' W_{i,t-s}\right) b, \tag{8.4}$$

where $\phi(.)$ is the probability density function (pdf), which corresponds to $\Phi(.)$. Note that these effects are conditional on the values of vector $W_{i,t-s}$. As Eq. (8.4) indicates, the effect of each covariate of the model on $P_{i,t}$ does not only depend on the magnitude and the sign of its slope coefficient estimates, but also on the values of all the other covariates of the model and their slope coefficient estimates. This happens through density function $\phi(.)$.

Based on the parameter estimates of the model given in the previous section, in this section we present estimates of descriptive statistics of the marginal effects $\pi_i\left(t,s \mid W_{i,t-s}\right)$ for the more important covariates of the model, in terms of their statistical significance (t-ratios). These statistics includes the mean, standard deviation and the 2.5% and 97.5% quantiles of their distribution conditional on duration time $d_i = 12$. This distribution is calculated based on the sampling method suggested by Dendramis et al. (2020). These results are presented in Tables 8.2a and 8.2b; Tables 8.2a presents results for the non-restructured loans while Table 8.2b for the restructured.

The results of the tables provide a number of interesting conclusions. First, they indicate that, among all covariates of the model, the loan-specific ones seem to have bigger marginal effects on $P_{i,t}$ and, in particular the following ratios: $\frac{\text{delinquent amount}}{\text{balance}}$, $\frac{\text{payment}}{\text{income}}$ and $\frac{\text{instalment}}{\text{income}}$. This result is consistent across the two categories of loans and the two binary functions considered. The bigger estimates of the mean of the marginal effects of the $\frac{\text{delinquent amount}}{\text{balance}}$ on $P_{i,t}$ for the restructured loans com-

Table 8.2a Descriptive statistics of marginal effects $\pi_i\left(t,s \mid W_{i,t-s}\right)$—non-restructured loans

	logit				*cloglog*			
	Mean	*Std. dev.*	*2.5%*	*97.5%*	*Mean*	*Std. dev.*	*2.5%*	*97.5%*
Car loans	-0.0018	0.0029	-0.0076	-0.0001	-0.0022	0.0032	-0.0117	-6.7e-05
Grace period	0.0047	0.0080	0.0004	0.0206	0.0046	0.0067	0.0002	0.0241
$\frac{\text{delinquent amount}}{\text{balance}}$	0.1058	0.1748	0.0090	0.4488	0.2473	0.3566	0.0083	1.2934
Delinquency buckets	0.0003	0.000	2.8e-05	0.0015	0.0004	0.0005	1.1e-05	0.0017
$\frac{\text{instalment}}{\text{income}}$	0.1375	0.2204	0.0113	0.5994	0.1754	0.2553	0.0048	0.8998
$\frac{\text{payment}}{\text{income}}$	-0.4842	0.7433	-1.9980	-0.0430	-0.2738	0.3984	-1.3965	-0.0079
$\frac{\text{payment}}{\text{balance}}$	-0.0095	0.0227	-0.0367	-0.0009	-0.0099	0.0338	-0.0549	-0.0006
$\frac{\text{balance}}{\text{instalment}}$	-3.5e-05	5e-05	-0.0001	-3e-06	4e-06	5e-06	0.0000	1.9e-05
GDP	-0.0003	0.0004	-0.0011	-2.2e-05	-0.0002	0.0003	-0.0010	-6e-06
Unemployment rate change	0.0023	0.0039	0.0002	0.0110	0.0022	0.0031	6.9e-05	0.0112
Inflation rate	0.0007	0.0011	5.5e-05	0.0028	0.0005	0.0008	1.5e-05	0.0026

Notes: The table presents values of descriptive statistics of the empirical distribution of the marginal effects $\pi_{i,t}$ (given by (8.4)), namely its mean, standard deviation (Std), and the 2.5% and 97.5% percentiles, for the non-restructured category of loans. This is done for the case that the duration time of a loan is $d_i = 12$ months and for the two binary functions considered. The empirical distribution of the marginal effects is calculated based on a resampling procedure

Table 8.2b Descriptive statistics of marginal effects $\pi_i\left(t,s\,|\,W_{i,t-s}\right)$—restructured loans

	logit				*cloglog*			
	Mean	*Std. dev.*	*2.5%*	*97.5%*	*Mean*	*Std. dev.*	*2.5%*	*97.5%*
Car loans	-0.0074	0.0075	-0.0284	-0.0006	-0.0022	0.0032	-0.0117	-6.7e-05
Grace period	0.0183	0.0185	0.00167	0.0693	0.0046	0.0067	0.0002	0.0241
delinquent amount balance	0.4007	0.3979	0.03553	1.473	0.2473	0.3566	0.0083	1.2934
Delinquency buckets	0.0014	0.0014	0.00013	0.0052	0.0004	0.0005	1.1e-05	0.0017
instalment income	0.5414	0.5354	0.053	2.0349	0.1754	0.2553	0.0048	0.8998
payment income	-1.8966	1.8037	-6.797	-0.1706	-0.2738	0.3984	-1.3965	-0.0079
payment balance	-0.0379	0.0522	-0.1481	-0.0044	-0.0099	0.0338	-0.0549	-0.0006
balance instalment	-0.0001	0.0001	-0.0005	-1.3e-05	4e-06	5e-06	0.0000	1.9e-05
GDP	-0.001	0.001	-0.0038	-9.8e-05	-0.0002	0.0003	-0.0010	-6e-06
Unemployment rate change	0.0103	0.01	0.0009	0.0369	0.0022	0.0031	6.9e-05	0.0112
Inflation rate	0.0025	0.0025	0.0002	0.0093	0.0005	0.0008	1.5e-05	0.0026

Notes: The table presents values of descriptive statistics of the empirical distribution of the marginal effects $\pi_{i,t}$ (given by (8.4)), namely its mean, standard deviation (Std), and the 2.5% and 97.5% percentiles, for the restructured category of loans. This is done for the case that the duration time of a loan is $d_i = 12$ months and for the two binary functions considered. The empirical distribution of the marginal effects is calculated based on a resampling procedure pared to the non-restructured ones, shown in the tables, can be attributed to moral hazard effects, allowing for obligors to repeatedly exploit debt payment moratorium procedures. On the other hand, the negative and larger in magnitude values of the mean of the marginal effects of $\frac{\text{payment}}{\text{income}}$ on $P_{i,t}$ for the restructured loans than the non-restructured ones can be taken as evidence of commitment of borrowers without moral hazard motives to service their debt. These results are consistent across the two different binary functions considered and are useful for credit risk mawnagement. They indicate that adjusting loan payments to borrowers' personal income levels constitutes a successful debt restructuring policy. As also noted by Dendramis et al. (2020), such a policy can help borrowers in servicing their debt and will increase the payments of consumer loans over time. By paying their debt, borrowers in the consumer loan markets may also manage to have access to credit and liquidity. To mitigate the effects of the moral hazard effects of the above policies, successful policies may be to restrict the number of times that a loan can be restructured, collateralize consumer loan obligations and/or introduce more strict foreclosure procedures (see also Artavanis and Spyropoulos 2017; Dendramis et al. 2018).

Regarding the marginal effects of the remaining covariates of the model, reported in the tables, it is worthwhile noting the following. First, the mean of the marginal effects of the qualitative dummies *grace period* and *car loans* on $P_{i,t}$ are both larger in size for the restructured loans, rather than the non-restructured, which is consistent with the hypothesis of moral hazard effects noted before. The negative and larger in size mean of the marginal effects of *car loans* on $P_{i,t}$ for the restructured loans implies that using the car as a collateral helps to mitigate possible moral hazard effects on $P_{i,t}$. Second, in terms of the mean value of their distribution, the most important marginal effects for the macroeconomic covariates are those for the unemployment rate changes followed by the GDP growth rate. This is consistent with the inability-to-pay hypothesis.

5 Conclusions

Based on a rich set of individual loan accounts data which consists of restructured and non-restructured loans, in this paper, we examine if there exist important differences between the factors determining the probability of default (PD) of these two categories of loans and if these differences can be attributed to moral hazard effects. Despite the plethora of studies investigating the factors determining the PD for other categories of loans (e.g., mortgages), there are very few studies in the literature which are focused on consumer loans. This may be attributed to the fact that consumers loans are unsecured loans and consumers' assets are difficult to be measured. Predicting the default probability for consumer loans constitutes of major interest both for households and banks, given that they constitute a large proportion of bank portfolio loans.

In answering the above questions, we rely on a panel data binary choice model which allows for duration time effects and uses as link functions the logit, or the cloglog, distribution. The cloglog distribution can capture possible asymmetries in the response of the PD to covariates of the model. The results of the paper leads to a number of interesting conclusions, with important management credit risk implications. First, we show that the cloglog link function can better describe the data, highlighting the existence of asymmetric responses of the PD to its determinants in modeling credit risk. Second, we have found that the group of the loan-specific covariates has bigger marginal effects on the PD than the macroeconomic one. Among the loan-specific covariates, we have found that the ratio of the delinquent of a loan over its total balance and the ratios of the installment and actual payments of the loan over the personal income of its obligor have the biggest marginal effects on the PD. The size of the marginal effects of these variables on the PD is bigger for the restructured than the non-restructured loans. We argue that the bigger marginal effects of the ratio of the delinquent of a loan over its total balance for the restructured loans can be attributed to moral hazard effects, arisen by the ability of borrowers to restructure their loans, repeatedly, by exploiting, for instance, a legislation framework favoring debt payment moratorium. On the other hand, the negative and larger in size effects of the ratio of the payments of a loan over the personal income of the borrower can be taken as evidence of commitment of borrowers without moral hazard motives to service their debt. These results are consistent across the two different binary functions considered. They support the view that adjusting loan payments to personal income levels may be proved a successful policy in managing consumer debt and helping borrowers to service their debt. Such a policy should be combined with appropriate measures to mitigate the effects of moral hazards on loan restructuring. A policy measure toward this direction could be a collateralization of consumer loan obligations. Finally, regarding the effects of the macroeconomic covariates on the PD of consumer loans, we show that the larger marginal effects on the PD are found for the unemployment rate changes followed by the GDP growth rate. The effects of these variables are also bigger for the group of restructured loans.

6 Appendix

In this Appendix, we present more formally the definitions of the Type I and II errors, employed to evaluate the performance of the model about default, or no-default, events.

6.1 *The Type I, II Errors and Receiver Operating Characteristic (ROC) Curve Metrics*

The Type I and II error metrics can evaluate if model (8.1) can sufficiently predict default ($Y_{i,t} = 1$) and non-default($Y_{i,t} = 0$) events, based on the estimates of the model. This can be done by calculating the type I and II errors of in-sample forecast errors of the values of the binary choice variable $Y_{i,t}$. To obtain these forecasts, we need to transform the model-predicted probabilities of default events, given by (8.1), into point forecasts based on a threshold value of probability, denoted as p^* (see Cheng et al. 2010). That is, for the in-sample forecasts, we set $Y_{i,t} = 1$, if $\Pr\left(Y_{i,t} = 1 \mid Y_{i,l} = 0; \varphi_{d_i}; \xi_i; x_{i,t-m}; z_{t-p}\right) > p^*$, $l < t$ and zero otherwise, where $0 < p^* < 1$. The Type I error is defined as

$$\alpha\left(p^*\right) = \frac{\Sigma_i \Sigma_t Y_{i,t}\left[\Pr\left(Y_{i,t} = 1 \mid Y_{i,s} = 0; \varphi_{d_i}; \xi_i; x_{i,t-m}; z_{t-p}\right) \le p^*\right]}{\Sigma_i \Sigma_t Y_{i,t}}, \ \forall l < t \quad (8.5)$$

for all i and t, and it reflects the error (in percentage terms) that a loan is predicted as non-defaulted, while it is actually defaulted. On the other hand, the Type II error is defined as

$$\beta\left(p^*\right) = \frac{\Sigma_i \Sigma_t \left(1 - Y_{i,t}\right)\left[\Pr\left(Y_{i,t} = 1 \mid Y_{i,s} = 0; \varphi_{d_i}; \xi_i; x_{i,t-m}; z_{t-p}\right) > p^*\right]}{\Sigma_i \Sigma_t \left(1 - Y_{i,t}\right)}, \ \forall l < t. \quad (8.6)$$

This reflects the error that a loan is predicted as defaulted, while it is actually non-defaulted. The threshold value p^*, above (or below) which a loan is characterized as defaulted (or non-defaulted), can be found by minimizing the sum $\alpha(p^*) + \beta(p^*)$ under the constraint that the in-sample type I error is $\alpha(p^*) < u$, where $u \in [0, 1]$. This constraint controls the size of error $\alpha(p^*)$, as this type of error is assumed that causes more severe losses for banks.

References

Andritzky, J.R. (2014). Resolving residential mortgage distress: time to modify? *IMF Working Paper* 14/226.

Alllison, P.D. (1982). Discrete-time methods for analysis of event histories. *Social Methodology*, 13, 61–98.

Artavanis, N. and I. Spyropoulos (2017). Foreclosure Moratorium and Strategic Default, *Working Paper*, Isenberg School of Management, University of Massachusetts, Amherst.

Bellotti, T. and J. Crook (2013). Forecasting and stress testing credit card default using dynamic models. *International Journal of Forecasting*, 563–574.

Chan, S., A. Haughwout, A. Hayashi and W. van der Klaauw (2016). Determinants of mortgage default and consumer credit use: The effects of foreclosure laws and foreclosure delays. *Journal of Money, Credit and Banking*, 48, 393–413.

Charalambakis, V., Y. Dendramis and E. Tzavalis (2017). On the determinants of NPLs: Lessons from Greece. In Bournakis, I., Tsoukis C., Christopoulos D.K. and Palivos T. (Eds.), *Political Economy Perspectives on the Crisis: Debt, Austerity and Unemployment* (pp. 289–309). London: Palgrave Macmillan.

Cheng, K.F., C.K. Chu and R-C Hwang (2010). Predicting bankruptcy using the discrete-time semiparametric hazard model. *Quantitative Finance*, 10, 1055–1066.

Crook, J. and T. Bellotti (2010). Time varying and dynamic models for default risk in consumer loans. *Journal of Royal Statistics Society* A, 173, 283–305.

Crook, J. and T. Bellotti (2012). Asset correlations for credit card defaults. *Applied Financial Economics*, 22, 87–95.

Dendramis, Y., E. Tzavalis and G. Adraktas (2018). Credit risk modelling under recessionary and financially distressed conditions. *Journal of Banking and Finance*, 91, 160–175.

Dendramis, Y., E. Tzavalis, P. Varthalitis and E. Athanasiou (2020). Predicting default risk under asymmetric binary link functions. *International Journal of Forecasting*, 36, 3, 1039–1056.

Deng, Y., J.M. Quigley and R. van Order (2000). Mortgage terminations, heterogeneity and the exercise of mortgage options. *Econometrica*, 68, 275–307.

Elul, R.N.S. Souleles, S. Chomsisengphet, D. Glennon, and R. Hunt (2010). What "triggers" mortgage default?, *The American Economic Review*, 100, 490–494.

Glennon, D.C., and P. Nigro (2005). Measuring the default risk of small business loans: A survival analysis approach. *Journal of Money, Credit, and Banking*, 37, 923–947.

Green, W.H (2012). *Econometric analysis*, 7th ed. New York: Pearson.

Harvey, A.C. (1990). *The econometric analysis of Time series*, 2nd ed., London: MIT Press.

Hwang, R-C (2012). A varying-coefficient default model. *International Journal of Forecasting*, 28, 675–688.

Hwang, R-C and C-K Chu (2014). Forecasting forward defaults with discrete-time hazard model. *Journal of Forecasting*, 33, 108–123.

Koenker, R. and J. Yoon (2009). Parametric links for binary choice models: A Fisherian-Bayesian colloquy. *Journal of Econometrics*, 152, 120–130.

Laeven, L. and T. Laryea (2009). Principles of household restructuring. *International Monetary Fund Staff Position Note*, SPN/09/15.

Lahiri, K., and L. Yang (2013). Forecasting binary outcomes. In A. Timmermann and G. Elliott (Eds.), *Handbook of Economic Forecasting*, Vol. 2B (pp. 1025–1106). Amsterdam: North-Holland.

Shumway, T. (2001). Forecasting bankruptcy more accurately: a simple hazard model. *Journal of Business*, 74, 101–124.

CHAPTER 9

Regime Switches in the Yield Curve-Credit Spread Relationship and the Prediction of Recessions

Dimitris A. Georgoutsos and Thomas I. Kounitis

1 Introduction

Today, there is a plethora of empirical studies that document the ability of the Treasury term spread, measured as the difference between short- and long-term Treasury rates, to forecast future economic activity (see, among others, Bordo and Haubrich, 2008; Wheelock and Wohar, 2009, Chinn and Kucko, 2010). In the present chapter, we investigate the dynamic relationship between the Treasury yield curve slope and corporate credit spreads, defined as the yield difference between corporate and Treasury bonds with similar maturity. The underlying rationale is that since the yield curve slope acts as an indicator of future economic activity, then it

D. A. Georgoutsos (✉)
Department of Accounting and Finance, Athens University of Economics and Business, Athens, Greece
e-mail: dgeorg@aueb.gr

T. I. Kounitis
eBay Analytics, Zurich, Switzerland

I. T. Kokores et al. (eds.), *Money, Trade and Finance*,
https://doi.org/10.1007/978-3-030-73219-6_9

should be closely related to corporate credit spreads, since they quantify default risks and liquidity squeezes. For example, an increase in the slope is associated, under the expectations hypothesis and neglecting term premiums, with improving economic conditions, higher expected future short rates, and, therefore, with a higher drift of the company value process, which reduces the probability of default. Equivalently, a negative slope is the outcome of a tightening monetary policy, often intended to reduce inflationary pressures, which makes a slowing-down over the subsequent months more likely and therefore increases the probability of default.

Despite the fact that structural models of corporate debt pricing do not treat the yield curve slope as a possible explanatory variable, it is nevertheless present in many empirical specifications of the stochastic behavior of credit spreads; however, no consensus has emerged on the relationship between these two variables. For example, Duffee (1998) reports a negative relationship between credit spreads and the Treasury yield curve slope, while Collin-Dufresne et al. (2001) fail to identify a statistically significant presence of the term spread among the determinants of credit spreads. Davies (2004) documents a negative long-run relationship between the Baa credit and term spreads, while within his regime switching analysis this result is confirmed only for high volatility periods. Davies (2008) treats the term spread as an exogenous variable and shows, with a longer sample period, that it is positively related in high volatility periods with the Baa credit spread. Since there are a variety of factors that are held accountable for the size of the credit spread, which range from expected default losses and the presence of liquidity and risk premiums to the asymmetric taxation of corporate and government bonds, some researchers opt for more direct measures of credit risk. Alexander and Kaeck (2008) concentrate on credit default swap (CDS) premiums, and fail to show that term spread is a significant determinant of CDS premiums in either of the two-state Markov-switching regressions.

Our study differs from previous empirical works in that we decompose the slope of the Treasury yield curve into positive and negative values, within a framework that incorporates regime shifts. In particular, this chapter focuses solely on identifying the presence of the term spread as a possible determinant of credit spreads, by estimating an asymmetric Markov-switching vector equilibrium correction model (MS-VECM), over an extensive sample period that spans from 1960 to 2010. We find that the stochastic behavior of corporate and government bond rates is better characterized by two regimes: a high and a low volatility regime. A first major result of this chapter is that the credit spread is found to be significantly related to negative realizations of the Treasury term spread, only during periods characterized by low interest rate volatility.

Although the predictive ability of the Treasury yield curve for future GDP growth is hardly disputed, there have been recent compelling arguments toward augmenting the set of yield curve variation determinants with short rates. Ang et al. (2006), among others, provide evidence by means of a principal components analysis, which is that we need at most two factors in order to capture most of the variation of yields. They further demonstrate that the first two principal components have an almost one-to-one correspondence with the short rate and the term spread.[1] In order to investigate the effect of unanticipated short interest rate changes, we implement an impulse response function analysis for each one of the two regimes of the estimated MS-VECM. The second major result of this chapter is that a positive shock in the short interest rate is associated initially, under both regimes, with a negative response of the credit spread. This response is reversed to a positive one, in the long-run, only in the case of a high volatility regime and a positively sloped yield curve. We execute the same exercise for unanticipated changes in long-term Treasury rates. The underlying rationale is that a flattening of the yield curve caused by an increase in short rates does not necessarily have the same information content when compared to a flattening of the yield curve caused by a decline in long rates (see also Wright, 2006). We provide evidence that substantiates the above argument since, in all cases, a decrease in long-term Treasury rates results in an increase in the credit spread.

The previous analysis has failed to identify an unequivocal connection between the term and credit spreads, and therefore a question arises whether credit spreads have a predicting ability for incoming recessions over and above the one that is attributed to term spreads. There are a number of empirical studies that explore the predictive ability of corporate yield spreads. For example, Gertler and Lown (1999), and Mody and Taylor (2004) show that the high yield spread (i.e. the spread between below-investment-grade corporate bonds and government bonds) has significant predictive ability for future economic activity. Chan-Lau and Ivaschenko (2001, 2002) contend that the yield spread of investment-grade corporate bonds has as well-significant predictive power for the future growth rate of industrial output. Gilchrist et al. (2009) find that credit spreads of senior unsecured corporate debt have significant predictive ability for future economic activity, while Mueller (2009) concludes that the whole term structure of credit spreads has predictive power over and above the term structure of Treasury yields.

Examining the problem from another perspective, Estrella and Trubin (2006) estimate a probit equation that translates the steepness of the yield curve, at present time, into a likelihood of an NBER recession in the future. They substantiate that the estimated probability of a recession occurring 12 months ahead exceeds 30 percent in the case of each recession in the period from January 1968 to July 2006. Wright (2006) extends this analysis by considering additional variables as predictors of NBER recessions. According to his results, probit models that control for nominal short rates produce forecasts that dominate those obtained with the use of the term spread alone. We further extend this line of research by including the credit spread as an additional predictor. We show that the estimated coefficient on the credit spread is statistically significant for predicting NBER-defined recessions over both six-month and one-year horizons and that in its presence the nominal short rate loses its predictive ability.

The plan for the remainder of this chapter is as follows. Section 2 presents the econometric methodology and the data sources. Section 3 discusses the estimation results from the Markov-switching model, and the evidence from the computed impulse response functions. Section 4 compares the predictive ability of alternative probit models for incoming recessions. Section 5 concludes.

2 Methodology and Data

2.1 *Methodology*

There is now a large volume of literature documenting empirical nonlinearities in interest rates and the suitability of regime-switching models in capturing this feature.

Ang and Bekaert (2002a, b) have illustrated the relevance of regime-switching techniques for univariate and bivariate Vector Autoregressive (VAR) models of short-term interest rates and the term spread. This relevance is attributed, at least for the US, to the smoothing actions of the Fed, which are abandoned when the focus of its policy switches to inflation fighting. Clarida et al. (2006) estimate a nonlinear VECM that is theoretically based on the expectations model of the term structure. They estimate an MS-VECM that provides good in- and out-of-sample fits, and its regimes are related to the state of the business cycle and the inflation rate. The focus of our analysis is the investigation of the short-run dynamics between corporate and government bond yields, and for that purpose we employ the MS-VECM introduced by Krolzig (1997).

In the MS-VECM, the regime generating process is assumed to be an ergodic Markov chain with a finite number of states $s_t \in \{1, \ldots, M\}$, defined by the transition probabilities:

$$p_{ij} = \Pr\left(s_{t+1} = j / s_t = i\right), \sum_{j=1}^{M} p_{ij} = 1 \quad \forall i, j \in \{1, \ldots, M\}. \tag{9.1}$$

If cointegration has been established, then the cointegrated MS-VAR(k) implies an MS-VECM (k-1) of the form:

$$\Delta z_t = \mu(s_t) + \sum_{i=1}^{k-1} \Gamma_i(s_t)\Delta z_{t-i} + \alpha(s_t)\beta' z_{t-1} + \varepsilon_t, \quad t = 1, \ldots, T, \tag{9.2}$$

where z_t is a ($n \times 1$) vector of endogenous variables, $\varepsilon_t \sim NIID(0, \Sigma(s_t))$ and β defines the cointegration space. In this chapter, we employ the most general specification that allows for regime shifts in the intercept, μ, the autoregressive terms, Γ, and the variance-covariance matrix, symbolized as MSIAH(M)-VECM(k). This model can also accommodate different speeds of adjustment to equilibrium, depending on whether there are positive or negative deviations from the equilibrium condition (Clarida et al. 2006):

$$\Delta z_t = \mu(s_t) + \sum_{i=1}^{k-1} \Gamma_t(s_t)\Delta z_{t-i} + I_t a(s_t)\beta' z_{t-1} + (1 - I_t)\bar{a}(s_t)\beta' z_{t-1} + \varepsilon_t. \tag{9.3}$$

I_t is a ($1 \times r$) vector whose j-th element at time t ($i_{j,t}$) is an indicator that takes the value one or zero according to whether the j-th cointegrating combination, $\acute{\beta} z_{jt}$, is positive or negative, that is, $i_{j,t} = 1$ ($i_{j,t} = 0$) if $\acute{\beta} z_{jt} > 0$ ($\acute{\beta} z_{jt} \leq 0$). The asymmetric MSIAH-VECM can be estimated using a two-stage procedure. In the first stage, the cointegration space is estimated by maximum likelihood cointegration technique. The second stage consists of the implementation of the Expectation-Maximization (EM) algorithm, which yields estimates of the remaining parameters of model (9.3) (Krolzig 1997).

2.2 *Data*

The data set comprises monthly data on yields of the one- and ten-year constant maturity US Treasury bonds, and the Moody's Baa-seasoned bond index. We consider the one-year Treasury rate as the short-term interest rate, and this is a compromise between the two-year Treasury rate favored by market analysts and the federal funds rate favored by academic researchers working on the yield curve's predictive power. We have selected the ten-year constant maturity Treasury bond rate, as the long-term interest rate, basically due to its relatively long history and because it is overwhelmingly adopted in related studies. The Moody's index considered in the analysis is created from an equally weighted sample of yields on 75–100-long maturity (more than 20 years) US Baa-rated bonds issued by large nonfinancial corporations. As Davies (2004) notes, the average duration of long maturity corporate bonds is expected to be close to ten years; this is justified on the grounds that due to the default risk embedded in corporate bonds, their effective duration is actually shorter compared to Treasuries of similar maturity. We choose to concentrate only on the spread of Baa bonds, since this is at the bottom of the investment-grade category and the inclusion of the Aaa spread would probably blur the stochastic properties of the model. The data set, obtained from the Federal Reserve Statistical Release H.15 (Selected Interest Rates), spans the period from January 1960 to September 2010.[2]

3 Empirical Results

In the preliminary stage of our research, we applied the Johansen (1988) methodology on the three rates and failed to reject the presence of two vectors in the cointegration space. We further failed to reject that the two vectors were identified by the credit and term spreads (see Georgoutsos and Kounitis 2014). Given that Saikkonen and Luukkonen (1997) have shown that cointegrating vectors estimated from the Johansen procedure are consistent even in the presence of regime shifts, we employ the two spreads as the equilibrium error correction terms in specification (9.3). Furthermore, we opt for an asymmetric response to the term spread, depending on its sign, since we intend to study separately the effect an inverted yield curve has on long-term rates.

The model, depicted in Eq. (9.3), is estimated with two regimes and a lag order of three, and it is denoted as MSIAH(2)-VECM(3). Specifically, we applied a bottom-up procedure that resulted in a larger log-likelihood value for the MSIAH(2)-VECM(3) than that from the corresponding linear system. The chosen three lags is the outcome of the application of the AIC, HQ and SIC model selection procedures for the lag length *k*.[3] The number of regimes is fixed a priori with the aim of capturing periods of low and high volatility. Moreover, the null hypothesis of linearity is strongly rejected according to a nonstandard likelihood ratio test suggested by Davies (1987).[4]

According to the results presented in Table 9.1, the standard errors of the three equations in regime 2 are substantially larger than those of regime 1. Therefore, we identify regime 2 as the high volatility regime that lasts approximately 6.64 months and regime 1 as the low volatility regime with an average duration of 14.17 months. The transition probabilities p_{11} and p_{22} suggest that there is an 85 percent probability that a high volatility regime will be followed by a similar one, while the corresponding probability for the low volatility period is 92 percent. Figure 9.1 provides regime classification information as this is expressed by the smoothed probabilities of being in the high and low volatility regimes for interest rates. Regime 2 covers almost all periods defined as recessions by the NBER and the estimated probability of being in that regime during recessions is close to one.

Ang and Bekaert (2002a) propose the computation of a regime classification measure, (*RCM*), so as to evaluate the quality of the regime classification produced by the regime-switching model. The *RCM* statistic is defined as $RCM(M) = 100M^{M}(1/T)\sum_{t=1}^{T}\left(\Pi_{j=1}^{M} p_{j,t}\right)$, with M denoting the number of regimes, T the number of observations, and $p_{j,t}$ the smoothed probabilities of being in regime $j = 1, \ldots M$.

They argue that if the classifying ability of the model is almost perfect, then the smoothed probabilities of observing one of the regimes ought to be close to unity and the measure close to zero. In our case, the value of the *RCM* is calculated to be 22.44, which indicates a very satisfactory regime classifying ability of our model.

Following Clarida et al. (2006), we next examine whether there is a link between the regime-switching mechanism and various macroeconomic factors. Specifically, we estimate a logit model, which involves constructing a binary dependent variable that takes on the value of one or zero depending on whether the probability of being in the high volatility period is higher or less than 0.5. The explanatory variables used are the output and inflation gap, measured as the deviations of industrial output and the inflation rate from their respective Hodrick-Prescott trends. The results of the logit estimation are reported in Table 9.2. De-trended inflation is found to be statistically significant for the regime-switching mechanism. The sign of the estimated parameter is positive, thus indicating that the probability of being in the high volatility regime is higher when inflation is above its estimated trend. This is not surprising since the two major time intervals in our estimated high volatility regime encompass the high inflation periods of 1973–1975 and 1979–1980.

From the estimated adjustment coefficients, $\alpha(s_t)$ and $\tilde{\alpha}(s_t)$ of Eq. (9.3), we find that all yields react mainly to negative values of the term spread since the point estimates, in absolute values, are larger than in the case of a positively sloped yield curve. In particular, under the high volatility period, the Baa and ten-year yields increase when the slope takes on negative values, while they are not influenced by its positive values. However, in the case of an inverted yield curve, the estimates of the adjustment coefficients, -0.158 and -0.262, are marginally not statistically different from each other, at the 95 percent level, and therefore it can be claimed that the credit spread is not affected. In contrast, during the low volatility period, a negatively sloped yield curve significantly affects all three yields, with the sign of the adjustment coefficients being positive. Furthermore, the estimates of the adjustment coefficients, 0.138 and 0.364, are statistically different from each other, at the 95 percent level, and consistent with rising credit spreads. To the extent that a negative term spread is the outcome of a change in the stance of monetary policy, its impact on credit spread is strikingly different. The evidence indicates that it is in low volatility periods only that an inverted yield curve is being interpreted by investors as a portent of a deteriorating economic climate.

Finally, positive values of the yield curve slope are not associated with any significant change of the credit spread in either regime, although their impact is statistically significant for the individual yields in the low volatility period. This evidence apparently contradicts a long-standing view that a rising slope of the Treasury yield curve signifies an improving business climate and, therefore, that it would be consistent with falling credit spreads. This makes sense theoretically as far as the expectations hypothesis components are responsible for the rising term spread. However, if instead an increase in term premiums has caused the change, then even a positive relationship between the term and credit spreads could be recorded.

Although the yield curve incorporates significant information about future economic activity, it is rather inappropriate to restrict this property to the term spread only. For instance, Ang et al. (2006) have shown that two principal components account for the 99.7 percent of the variation of zero-coupon yields over the period 1952–2001, and they go on to identify those components with the short rate and the term spread. These considerations have led us to investigate the effect that unanticipated short interest rate changes have on credit spreads. We address this issue by recovering the autoregressive representation, at levels, of the estimated MSIAH(2)-VECM(3) for each one of the four models corresponding to the two volatility regimes and the two signs of the term spread (see Ehrmann et al. 2003). Then, we calculate orthogonalized impulse response functions for each of the three yields from a Choleski factorization of the variance-covariance matrix, based on the strict exogeneity of the one-year yield shock on the one end and the full endogeneity of the corporate yield shock on the other. The cumulative response of the credit spread to a 100 basis points (*b.p.*) unanticipated change in the short rate is then calculated from the difference of the corresponding cumulative responses of the Baa corporate yield and the ten-year Treasury bond rate. This shock corresponds to a negative term spread change, that is, a flattening of the yield curve, of the first impulse response. According to the results presented in Fig. 9.2a, we observe a negative reaction of the credit spread under both regimes, which is reversed in the long run to a marginally positive one only in the specification with a high volatility regime and a positively sloped curve. However, if confidence bounds of the estimates had been taken into account, then it would be difficult to reject that the credit spread is not statistically different from zero after the initial reactions.[5,6,7]

We then proceed with the examination of the cumulative response of the credit spread to a negative 100 *b.p.* shock in the long-term Treasury rate which again corresponds to a flattening of the yield curve. This intends to examine the validity of the structural models approach to credit risk modeling which claims that there is a negative relationship between credit spreads and the long-term Treasury rates. This is confirmed from the results presented in Fig. 9.2b, since we observe an increase in the credit spread irrespective of the regime governing the behavior of interest rates and the sign of the slope of the Treasury yield curve. In this case, our results are also consistent with the expectations hypothesis that a flatter yield curve signifies a deteriorating economic climate. Overall, our results highlight the importance of the source of the yield curve shock for the dynamic behavior of the credit spread. However, in the long run both Figs. 9.2a and 9.2b suggest a slow adjustment to the long-run equilibrium where the cumulative credit spread changes tend to zero, and this is also consistent with the presence of a (1, -1) cointegrating relationship between the corporate and Treasury ten-year rates.

4 Predicting Recessions

In the previous section, we have failed to identify empirically an unambiguous relationship between the slope of the Treasury yield curve and the Baa-rated credit spread. However, we have also shown that if a relationship exists, then it must be during periods characterized by a negative yield curve. In this section, therefore, we set to examine whether credit spreads carry any additional predictive ability for incoming recessions, over and above the ability that the term spreads and short-term Treasury rates have.

Specifically, we employ various probit models, which involve constructing a binary variable that takes the value of one or zero depending on whether there is an economic recession, as defined by the NBER, over the next 6 or 12 months. The first model, hereafter Model A, incorporates the Treasury term spread as the sole indicator of future recessions. This model is then extended with the inclusion of the level of the one-year Treasury rate, and finally with the credit spread in a similar approach to that followed by Estrella and Trubin (2006), Wright (2006) and King et al. (2007). The full model, hereafter Model D, is of the following form:

$$P\left(NBER_{t+j}=1\right)=F\left(a+\beta_1 TS_t+\beta_2 RS_t+\beta_3 CS_t\right), \qquad (9.4)$$

where $NBER_{t+j}$ takes the value of one if there is an NBER recession during months $t+1$ through $t+j$, and zero otherwise, $F(.)$ is the standard cumulative normal distribution function, TS denotes the ten-year over the one-year constant maturity Treasury term spread, SR is the level of the short-term interest rate, and CS is the credit spread. The obtained evidence is presented in Table 9.3 for horizons j = 6 and 12 months, respectively.

According to the results presented in Table 9.3, the coefficient on the term spread in Model A is negative and statistically significant at both horizons. This finding is consistent with the results of previous studies that establish an inversion of the yield curve as a signal of recession. In Models B and C, the credit spread variable and the short rate appear separately, and the former only variable is statistically significant at both horizons. Finally, in Model D, which includes all three variables, the term and credit spread variables retain their significance as explanatory variables of future recessions while the same does not hold for the short rate. However, on the basis of the Bayes Information Criterion (BIC), which penalizes model size, we cannot deduce that Models B and D, which incorporate the credit spread, are the best performing models when compared to Model A. Figures 9.3a, 9.3b, 9.3c, and 9.3d demonstrate the estimated probabilities of a recession occurring six months ahead according to Models A to D. It is illustrated that the estimated probability of a recession is above 60 percent for each recession of the 1970s and 1980s, but it gets substantially smaller for the recessions of 1990–1991, 2001 and 2007–2009. However, the probability of a recession for 2001 and 2007–2009 is as high as 50 percent for Model B and D, and this is considerably higher compared to the corresponding estimate of the models without the presence of the credit spread (which hardly reaches 30 percent). Figures 9.4a, 9.4b, 9.4c, and 9.4d demonstrate the corresponding results for the 12-month horizon. Again, Models B and D illustrate a higher predictive ability for the more recent recessions, but their improvement is a marginal one over the model that includes the term spread only. However, the Bayes Information Criterion is more favorable to Models B and D since the values it takes are slightly worse than those of Model A. The general picture resembles the one provided by Estrella and Trubin (2006), where the term spread had been much more informative about future economic growth during the 1970s and 1980s, and replicates the results by King et al. (2007), who established that corporate credit spreads embed crucial information about the one-year ahead probability of a recession, for the period 1988:1–2007:12.7.

We next consider the out-of-sample predictive performance of the models previously presented, provided by recursive estimations of the probability of a recession occurring between month t and month $t + 6$ (or $t + 12$). We compute the root mean square prediction error of the fitted probability of a recession in relation to the state of the economy, as this is expressed by the NBER-defined recessions (i.e. 1 or 0). Therefore, the fitted model is penalized not only when it assigns a low probability to a realized recession, but also when it assigns a high probability to a state of the economy that is not characterized as an NBER recession. According to the results presented in Table 9.3, model B manages to outperform the others over both time horizons since it has the smallest *RMSE* and this enhances the usefulness of the credit spread variable in predicting recessions.

5 Conclusions

In this chapter, we have focused on the implications that factors accounting for the variation of the Treasury yield curve have on corporate yield spreads. An important feature of our analysis is the application of an asymmetric Markov-switching model, which facilitates the investigation of different patterns of behavior between the one-year and ten-year constant maturity Treasury rates on the one hand and the ten-year average maturity corporate rate on the other.

If the Treasury yield curve slope serves as a predictor of future economic activity, then it should also be a significant determinant of credit spreads, since they quantify default risks and liquidity squeezes. Through the estimation of our asymmetric Markov-switching model, we establish a significant relationship only during periods characterized by low interest rate volatility and inverted yield curves. By means of an impulse response function analysis, we study the reaction of the credit spread to shocks in short- and long-term Treasury rates. The obtained evidence indicates that the response of the credit spread to a given change in the term spread depends on the rate that has caused that change.

In the last part, we investigate the usefulness of the credit spread in predicting future recessions. We obtain strong evidence in support of our case, especially over a six-month horizon. Furthermore, it appears that the term spread has an enhanced predictive power for recessions in 1970s and 1980s, while the credit spread gains its strength from the most recent ones.

Notes

1. This evidence is replicated in a number of other recent studies covering different currencies and time periods. For instance, Alexander and Kaeck (2008) reached the same conclusions for Euro swap rates with maturities between 1 and 30 years. On the other hand, Diebold and Li (2006) showed that the curvature of the yield curve is an additional useful factor for the prediction of future term structures.
2. A strand of the literature relies on CDS premiums as a measure of the default component in corporate bond spreads. However, Longstaff et al. (2005) and David (2008) showed that the credit default–related component explains as much as two-thirds of the spread of investment-grade bonds relative to government bonds. Again, other researchers reported a considerably smaller percentage (see Elton et al. 2001, Driessen 2005). Since the focus of this chapter is not the identification of the determinants of corporate yield spreads, and in order to avoid any small-sample bias problems arising from the limited time coverage of other data sets, we have opted for the Baa corporate bond yield spread that provides a long and widely used time series.
3. Conventional diagnostic tests may not have their usual asymptotic distribution when residuals come from MS models, and therefore they are not reported here. However, a visual inspection of graphs of standardized smoothed residuals provides no evidence of residual serial correlation.
4. The distribution of the *LR* test is likely to be different from the adjusted χ^2 distribution proposed by Davies (1987). This is due to the violation of the regularity conditions under which this test is valid (see Hansen 1992). We have also tested for the null hypothesis that regime shifts affect separately the intercept term, the variance–covariance matrix, or the autoregressive component of the VECM. The likelihood ratio tests indicated strong rejection of the null in each case.
5. The usefulness of the inflation rate as a regime differentiating variable has been established in a number of similar studies (e.g. David 2008).
6. We choose to present cumulative responses since this provides a better understanding on the long run properties of the estimated models. Confidence bounds on the noncumulative responses are available upon request but they show, as it is common in this type of analysis, that the responses, except for the very first ones, are not statistically different from zero.
7. Ang et al. (2006) argue that the significance of the term spread in predicting future GDP growth stems from the strong positive correlation of the lagged term spread with GDP growth between 1970 and 1990. In contrast, those two variables were slightly negatively correlated during the 1990s.

Appendix

Table 9.1 Estimation results for the asymmetric MSIAH(2)-VECM(3), 1960:1–2010:09

	Asymmetric MSIAH(2)-VECM(3)		Asymmetric Linear VECM
Log-likelihood	697.579		351.240
AIC criterion	-1.989		-1.006
HQ criterion	-1.729		-0.879
SC criterion	-1.322		-0.680
LR linearity test:692.679	[0.00]		
		Regime 1	Regime 2
Duration		14.17	6.64
Unconditional probability		0.681	0.319
		p_{11} = 0.929	p_{22} = 0.849
Regime-dependent equilibrium-correction coefficient estimates			
Regime 1	ΔBaa_t	$\Delta Tcm10y_t$	$\Delta Tcm1y_t$
Constant	0.051 (2.604)	0.028 (1.043)	0.075 (2.635)
Baa spread$_{t-1}$	-0.015 (-1.187)	0.011 (0.587)	-0.015 (-0.790)
Slope+$_{t-1}$	-0.027 (-2.733)	-0.031 (-2.301)	-0.015 (-1.052)
Slope-$_{t-1}$	0.138 (3.684)	0.364 (6.961)	0.984 (17.969)
Std error	0.133	0.185	0.189
Regime 2	ΔBaa_t	$\Delta Tcm10y_t$	$\Delta Tcm1y_t$
Constant	-0.010 (-0.158)	-0.188 (-2.244)	-0.048 (-0.355)
Baa spread$_{t-1}$	0.002 (0.070)	0.062 (1.638)	-0.007 (-0.112)
Slope+$_{t-1}$	-0.022 (-0.723)	-0.023 (-0.550)	0.012 (0.192)
Slope-$_{t-1}$	-0.158 (-3.287)	-0.262 (-3.957)	-0.203 (-1.874)
Std error	0.249	0.339	0.554

LR is a test for the null hypothesis that the true model is a linear VECM(3) against the alternative hypothesis of an MSIAH-VECM with two regimes and three lags. *P*-values are calculated as in Davies 1987. p_{11} (p_{22}) stands for the transition probability of remaining in regime 1(2). To conserve space, only the estimates of the adjustment coefficients on the three error-correction terms are reported. Slope+ (Slope-) is the difference between the ten-year and the one-year Treasury rates when its value is positive (negative), and zero otherwise. *T*-values in parentheses

Table 9.2 Logit estimation results, 1960:1–2010:09

Variables	*Coefficients*	*T-Stat.*	*Sig. level*
x-x^*	-0.089	-1.166	0.243
π-π^*	0.549	5.473	0.000

Pseudo-R^2 = 0.054

The explanatory variable x-x^* denotes the output gap measured as the difference between industrial production and its Hodrick-Prescott trend. The variable π-π^* denotes the inflation gap measured as the difference between the consumer price index inflation rate and its Hodrick-Prescott trend. The dependent binary variable is defined in the text. Pseudo-R^2 denotes Estrella's (1998) measure of goodness of fit for logit models

Table 9.3 Probit results for forecasting NBER recessions, 1960:1–2010:09

Case 1 Forecasting a recession six months ahead				
Model	A	B	C	D
TS	-0.53 (0.00)	-0.79 (0.00)	-0.49 (0.00)	-0.83 (0.00)
SR	–	–	0.02 (0.32)	-0.02 (0.47)
CS	–	0.59 (0.00)	–	0.61 (0.00)
Pseudo-R^2	0.12	0.20	0.13	0.20
Bayes I.C.	-225.57	-205.335	-226.478	-206.459
RMSE	0.352087	0.339535	0.350095	0.340262
Case 2 Forecasting a recession twelve months ahead				
Model	A	B	C	D
TS	-0.75 (0.00)	-0.86 (0.00)	-0.77 (0.00)	-0.98 (0.00)
SR	–	–	-0.01 (0.69)	-0.05 (0.11)
CS	–	0.31 (0.002)	–	0.37 (0.00)
Pseudo-R^2	0.20	0.22	0.20	0.22
Bayes I.C.	-203.008	-199.862	-204.324	-199.913
RMSE	0.33887	0.337597	0.339133	0.337814

TS denotes the ten-year over the one-year constant maturity Treasury term spread, *SR* is the level of the short-term interest rate, and *CS* is the credit spread. Marginal significance levels in parentheses. Pseudo-R^2 measure of goodness of fit (does not penalize model size). Bayes Information Criterion = $\{l\text{-}klog(T)/2\}$, where l is the maximized log-likelihood, k is the number of parameters, and T the sample size. *RMSE* stands for the root mean square error of the fitted probability model over the period 1960–2010.

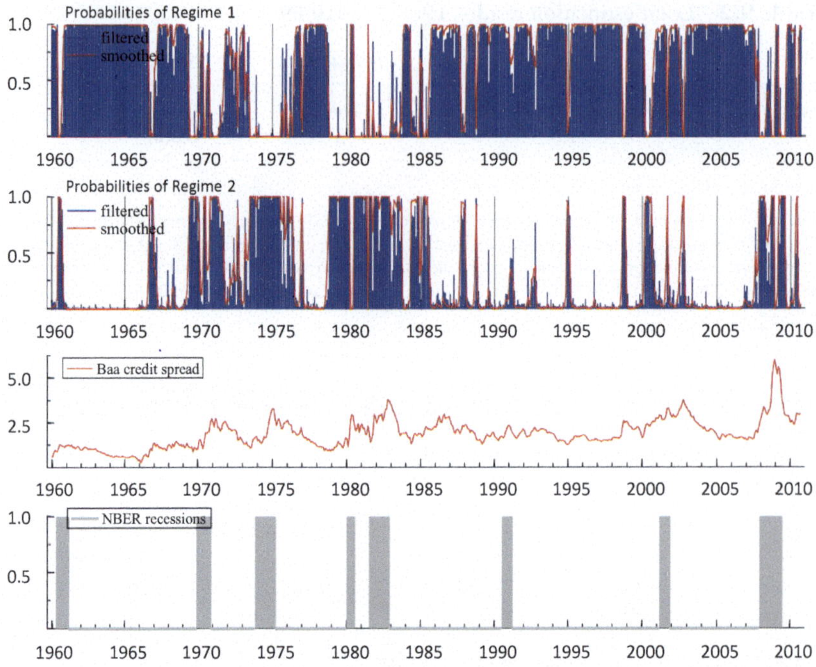

Fig. 9.1 Regime probabilities of the MSIAH(2)-VECM(3). The first figure refers to the low volatility regime, and the second one to the high volatility regime. The third panel shows Baa credit spread levels. In the lowest panel, shaded areas represent periods characterized as U.S. recessions by the NBER

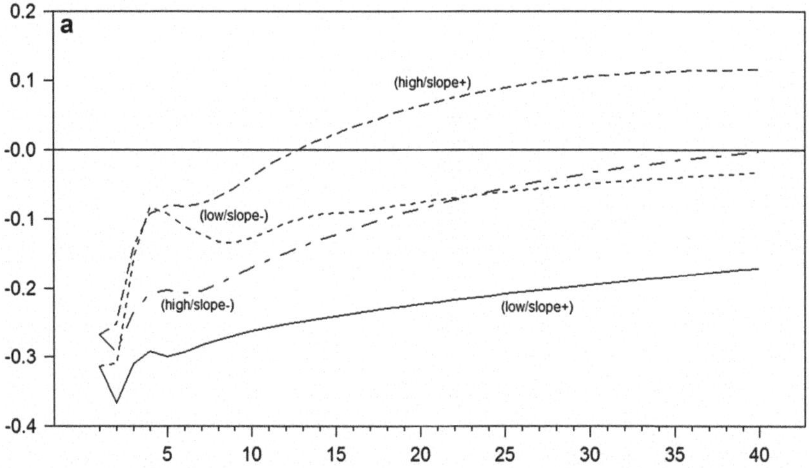

Fig. 9.2a Cumulative monthly impulse responses of the Baa credit spread to a unit positive shock in the one-year Treasury rate under a high/low volatility regime and a positive/negative slope of the yield curve

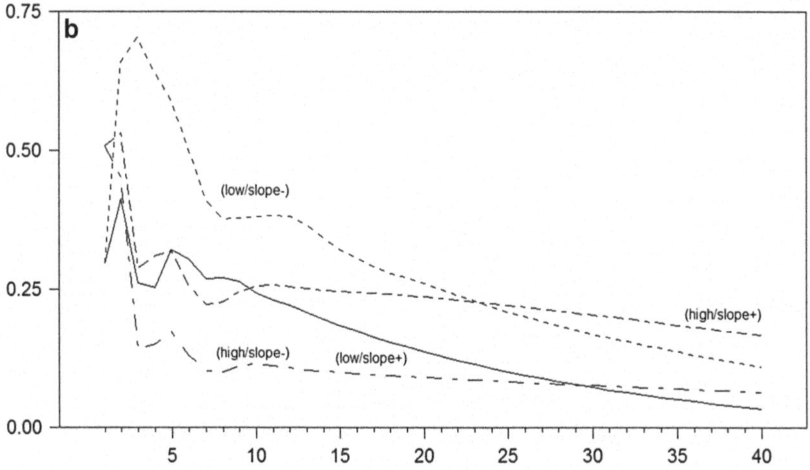

Fig. 9.2b Cumulative monthly impulse responses of the Baa credit spread to a unit negative shock in the ten-year Treasury rate under a high/low volatility regime and a positive/negative slope of the yield curve

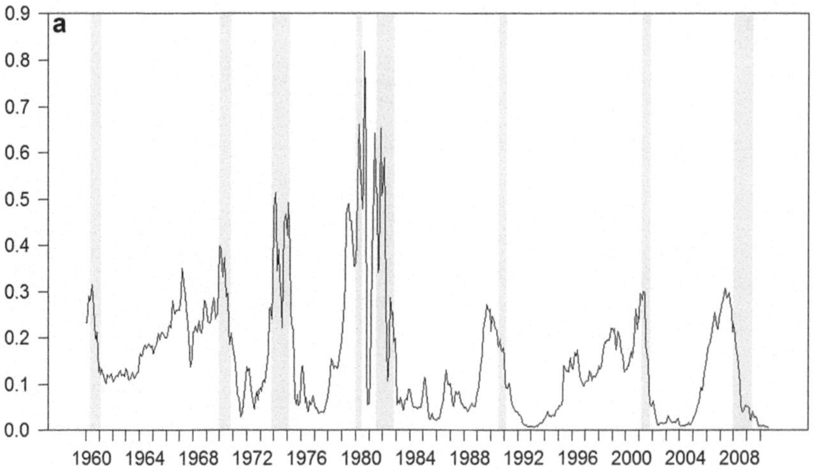

Fig. 9.3a Probability of a recession six months ahead, as predicted by model A. The shaded areas indicate periods characterized as recessions by the NBER

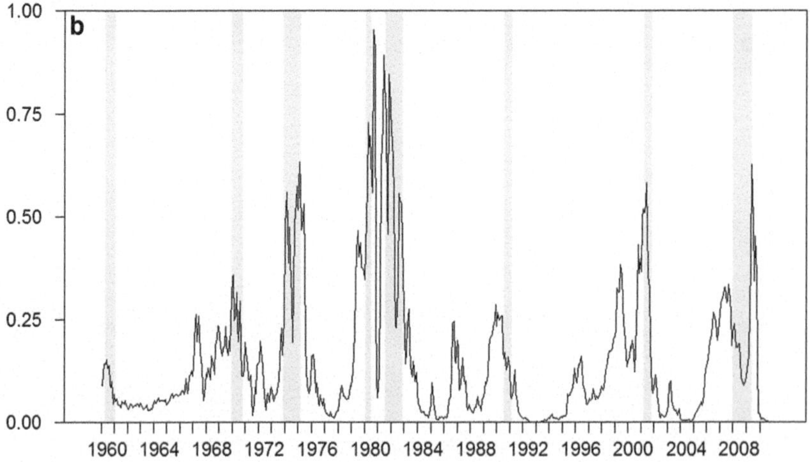

Fig. 9.3b Probability of a recession six months ahead, as predicted by model B. The shaded areas indicate periods characterized as recessions by the NBER

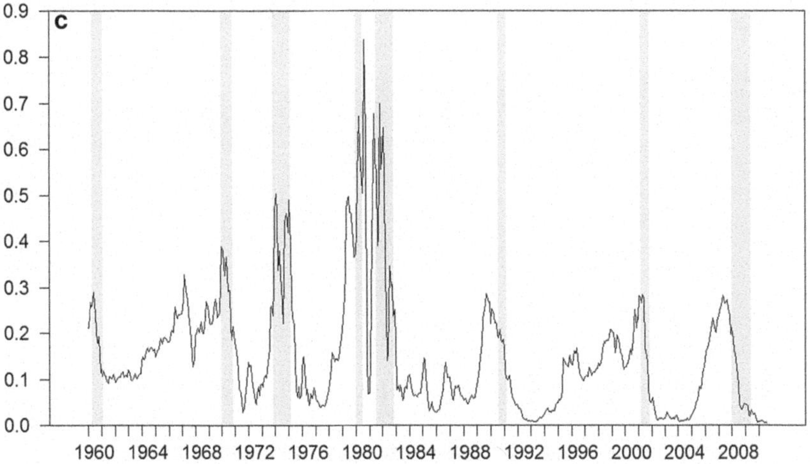

Fig. 9.3c Probability of a recession six months ahead, as predicted by model C. The shaded areas indicate periods characterized as recessions by the NBER

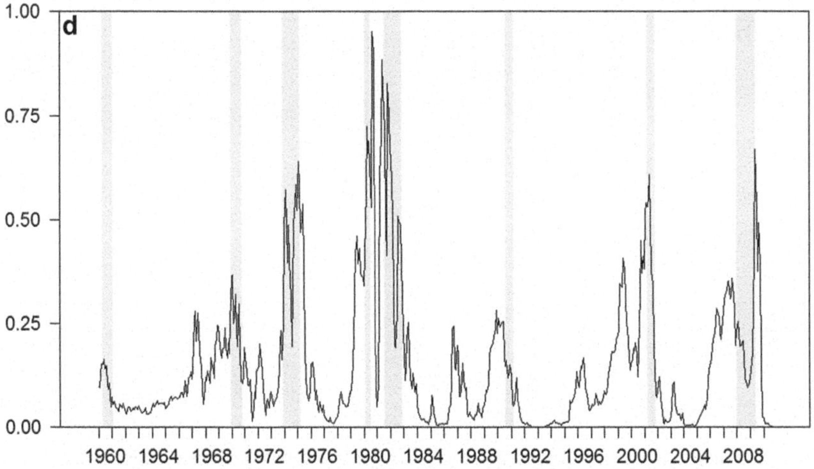

Fig. 9.3d Probability of a recession six months ahead, as predicted by model D. The shaded areas indicate periods characterized as recessions by the NBER

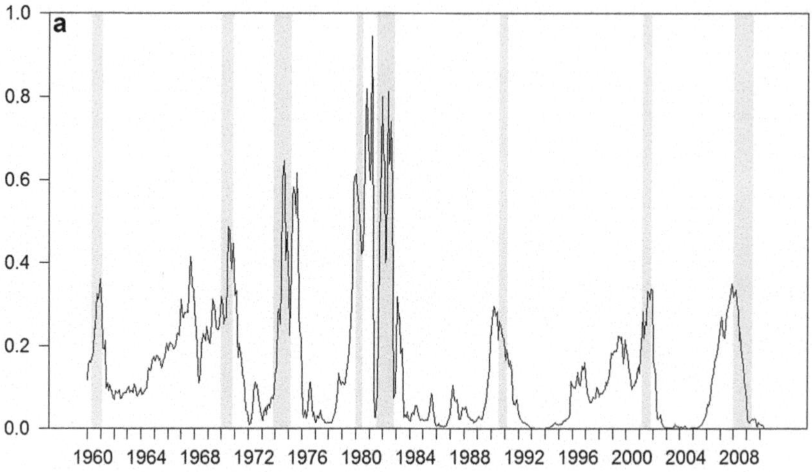

Fig. 9.4a Probability of a recession 12 months ahead, as predicted by model A. The shaded areas indicate periods characterized as recessions by the NBER

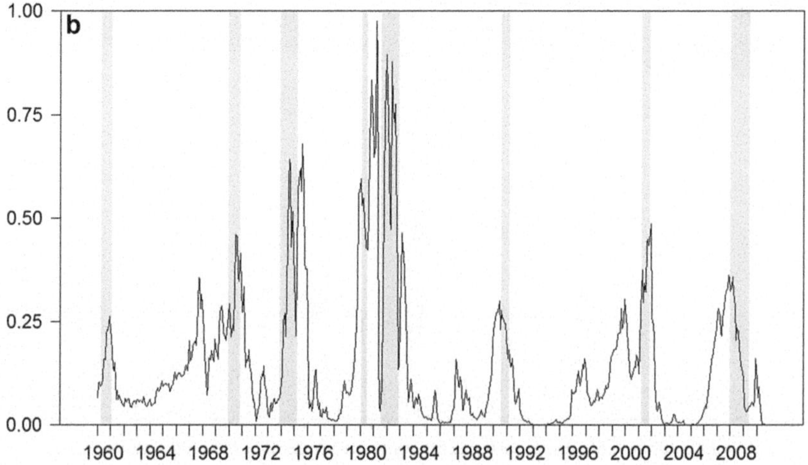

Fig. 9.4b Probability of a recession 12 months ahead, as predicted by model B. The shaded areas indicate periods characterized as recessions by the NBER

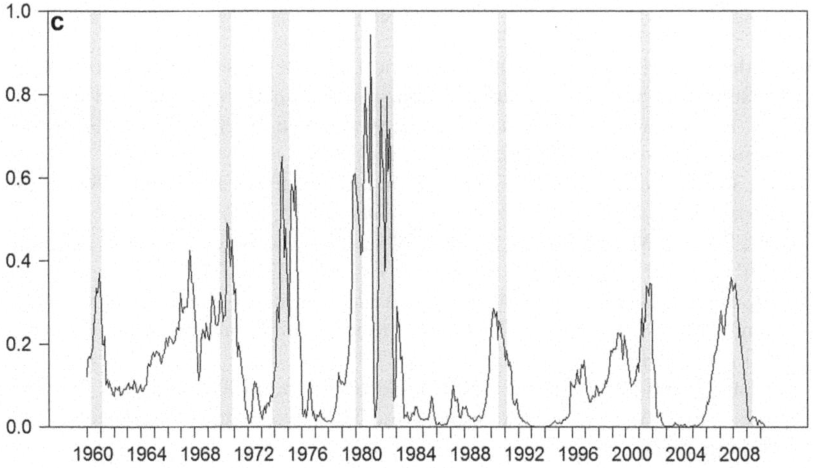

Fig. 9.4c Probability of a recession 12 months ahead, as predicted by model C. The shaded areas indicate periods characterized as recessions by the NBER

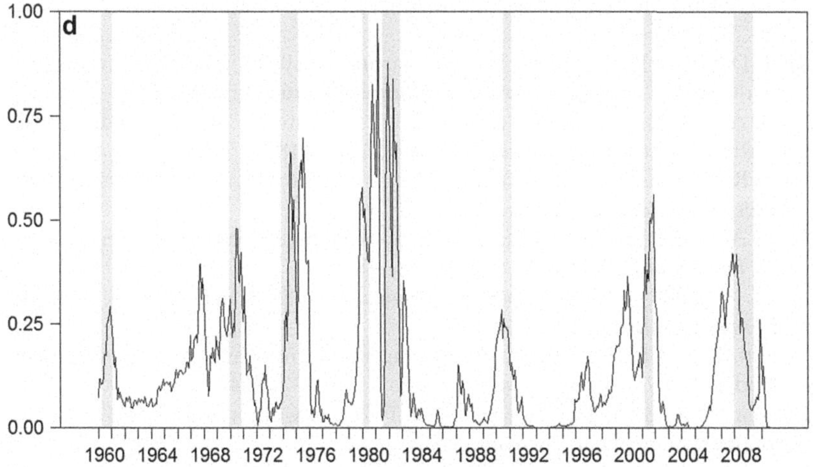

Fig. 9.4d Probability of a recession 12 months ahead, as predicted by model D. The shaded areas indicate periods characterized as recessions by the NBER

References

Alexander C. and Kaeck A. (2008). Regime Dependent Determinants of Credit Default Swap Spreads. *Journal of Banking and Finance*, vol. 32, 1008–1021.

Ang A. and Bekaert G. (2002a). Regime Switches in Interest Rates. *Journal of Business & Economic Statistics*, vol. 20, 163–82.

Ang A. and Bekaert G. (2002b). Short Rate Nonlinearities and Regime Switches. *Journal of Economic Dynamics and Control*, vol. 26, 1243–1274.

Ang A., Piazzesi M. and Wei M. (2006). What Does the Yield Curve Tell us about GDP Growth?. *Journal of Econometrics*, vol. 131, 359–403.

Bordo, M. and Haubrich, J. (2008). The Yield Curve as a Predictor of Growth: Long- Run Evidence, 1875–1997. *Review of Economics and Statistics*, 90(1), 182–185.

Chan-Lau, J. and Ivaschenko, I. (2001). Corporate Bond Risk and Real Activity: An Empirical Analysis of Yield Spreads and Their Systematic Components. IMF Working Paper.

Chan-Lau, J. and Ivaschenko, I. (2002). The Corporate Spread Curve and Industrial Production in the United States. IMF Working Paper.

Chinn, M. and Kucko, K. (2010). The Predictive Power of the Yield Curve Across Counties and Time. NBER Working Paper 16398, NBER.

Clarida R., Sarno L., Taylor M. and Valente G. (2006). The Role of Asymmetries and Regime Shifts in the Term Structure of Interest Rates. *Journal of Business*, vol. 79, 1193–1224.

Collin-Dufresne P., Goldstein R. and Martin S. (2001). The Determinants of Credit Spread Changes. *Journal of Finance*, vol. 56, 2177–2207.

David, A. (2008). Inflation Uncertainty, Asset Valuations, and the Credit Spread Puzzle. *The Review of Financial Studies*, 21(6), 2487–2534.

Davies R. (1987). Hypothesis Testing When a Nuisance Parameter is Present Only Under the Alternative. *Biometrika*, vol. 74, 33–43.

Davies A. (2004). Credit Spread Modelling with Regime-Switching Techniques. *The Journal of Fixed Income*, vol. 14, 36–48.

Davies, A. (2008). Credit Spread Determinants: An 85 Year Perspective. *Journal of Financial Markets*, 11, 180–197.

Diebold, F. and Li, C. (2006). Forecasting the Term Structure of Government Bond Yields. *Journal of Econometrics*, vol. 130, 337–364.

Driessen J. (2005). Is Default Event Risk Priced in Corporate Bonds?. *Review of Financial Studies*, vol. 18, 165–195.

Duffee G. (1998). The Relation Between Treasury Yields and Corporate Bond Yield Spreads. *Journal of Finance*, vol. 53, 2225–2241.

Ehrmann, M., Ellison, M. and Valla, N. (2003). Regime Dependent Impulse Response Functions in a Markov Switching Vector Autoregression Model. *Economics Letters*, 78(3), 295–299.

Elton E.J., Gruber M., Agrawal D. and Mann C. (2001). Explaining the Rate Spread on Corporate Bonds. *The Journal of Finance*, vol. 56, 247–277.

Estrella, A., (1998). A new measure of fit for equations with dichotomous dependent variables. *Journal of Business and Economic Statistics*, vol. 16, 198–205.

Estrella A. and Trubin M. (2006). The Yield Curve as a Leading Indicator: Some Practical Issues. *Current Issues in Economics and Finance*, Federal Reserve Bank of New York, vol. 12.

Georgoutsos D. and Kounitis T. (2014). Dynamic Relationships Between Credit Spreads and Interest Rates Using Cointegration and Regime Switching Techniques. Athens University of Economics and Business, Working Paper.

Gertler, M. and Lown, C., (1999). The Information in the High-Yield Bond Spread for the Business Cycle: Evidence and Some Implications. *Oxford Review of Economic Policy*, vol. 15, 132–50.

Gilchrist, S., Yankov, V. and Zakrajšek, E., (2009). Credit Market Shocks and Economic Fluctuations: Evidence from Corporate Bond and Stock Markets. *Journal of Monetary Economics*, vol. 56, 471–93.

Hansen, B. (1992). The Likelihood Ratio Test Under Nonstandard Conditions: Testing the Markov Switching Model of GNP. *Journal of Applied Econometrics*, vol. 7, 61–582.

Johansen, S. (1988). Statistical Analysis of Cointegration Vectors. *Journal of Economic Dynamics and Control*, vol. 12, 231–54.

King, T.B., Levin A. and Perli R. (2007). Financial Market Perceptions of Recession Risk. Board of Governors of the Federal Reserve System, Working Paper No. 2007-57.

Krolzig H.-M. (1997). *Markov-Switching Vector Autoregressions. Modelling, Statistical Inference and Application to Business Cycle Analysis*. Springer: Berlin.

Longstaff F.A., Mithal S. and Neis E. (2005). Corporate Yield Spreads: Default Risk or Liquidity? New Evidence from the Credit-Default Swap Market. *Journal of Finance*, vol. 60, 2213–2253.

Mody, A. and Taylor, M. (2004). Financial Predictors of Real Activity and the Financial Accelerator. *Economic Letters*, vol. 82, 167–72.

Mueller, P. (2009). Credit Spreads and Real Activity. London School of Economics, Working paper.

Saikkonen P. and Luukkonen R. (1997). Testing Cointegration in Infinite Order Vector Autoregressive Processes. *Journal of Econometrics*, vol. 81, 93–126.

Wheelock D. and M. Wohar (2009). Can the Term Spread Predict Output Growth and Recessions? A Survey of the Literature. *Federal Reserve of St. Louis Review*, September/October, part 1, 419–440.

Wright J.H. (2006). The Yield Curve and Predicting Recessions. Board of Governors of the Federal Reserve System, Finance and Economics Discussion Series.

PART V

Trends in Econometric Methodology

CHAPTER 10

A Comparison Study of Least Squares and Ridge Estimators in the Presence of Heteroscedasticity and Multicollinearity Under Normal and Nonnormal Disturbances

George S. Donatos and George C. Michailidis

1 Introduction

In some empirical applications, the data analyst deals with cross-sectional data that are subject to the problem of heteroscedasticity. Moreover, multivariate real data usually suffer from the problem of almost linear dependencies among the predictor variable (multicollinearity). In such applications, estimation and prediction are carried through models, and in case the data analyst is faced with the second problem, he might resort to the technique of ridge regression that offers potentially useful solutions. Moreover, the presence of small samples and the fact that in many

G. S. Donatos (✉)
Department of Economics, University of Athens, Athens, Greece
e-mail: gdonat@econ.uoa.gr

G. C. Michailidis
Department of Statistics & Informatics Institute, University of Florida, Gainesville, FL, USA

I. T. Kokores et al. (eds.), *Money, Trade and Finance*,
https://doi.org/10.1007/978-3-030-73219-6_10

situations the distribution of the disturbance term need not be normal (Fieltz and Rozelle 1983; Tucker and Pond 1988) require a thorough examination of the ridge estimators and predictors in such a setting. The purpose of this chapter is to investigate through a Monte Carlo experiment the small sample properties of ridge estimators (predictors) in the presence of heteroscedasticity and to compare with least squares (LS), under normal and nonnormal disturbances with small and large variances for varied degree of multicollinearity. The chapter is organized as follows. Section 2 gives a brief description of the ridge estimators. Section 3 contains the design of Monte Carlo experiment. In Sect. 4 the results of the simulation are presented and some concluding remarks are drawn in Sect. 5.

2 Ridge Estimators

By way of introduction, consider the standard linear regression model

$$y = X\beta + \varepsilon \tag{8.1}$$

where y is a $n \times 1$ vector of observed values of the dependent variable, X is a full column rank $n \times p$ matrix of the nonstochastic values of the explanatory variables, β is a $p \times 1$ vector of unknown coefficients and ϵ is a $n \times 1$ vector of disturbances with properties $E(\epsilon) = 0$ and $E(\epsilon\, \epsilon') = \text{diag}(\sigma_i^2)$, $i = 1,\dots, n$. The LS estimator is given by $\hat{\beta} = (X'X)^{-1}X'y$, and in the presence of heteroscedasticity is unbiased but yields inefficient parameter estimates and inconsistent estimates of the covariance matrix. The ordinary ridge estimator introduced by Hoerl and Kennard (1970) is defined as $\hat{\beta}_k = (X'X + KI_p)^{-1} X'y$, which for suitable $k > 0$ both stabilizes the estimated coefficients and improves upon the Mean Square Error (MSE) of the LS estimator (Casella 1985). In order to deal with the problem of heteroscedasticity, various approaches have been proposed in the literature. Some assume that σ_i^2's take a specific parametric form (for a survey, see Judge et al. 1985), which in turn allows their efficient estimation, while some others avoid any explicit parameterization and estimate the σ_i^2's nonparametrically (e.g. White 1982; Cragg 1983; Robinson 1987). However, all these approaches are constrained to a single regressor and do not allow the study of the combined effect of heteroscedasticity and multicollinearity that is the primary goal of this chapter. Therefore, in this chapter we only study ordinary LS and ridge estimators that do not explicitly take into account the problem of heteroscedasticity and attempt to provide a first assessment of the performance of such estimators.

Several algorithms for the biasing parameter *k* have been proposed in the literature. Hoerl et al. (1975) (HKB) proposed the following algorithm, which capitalizes on the minimization of the MSE function of the ridge estimator, for choosing k:

$$k = \mathrm{p}s^2 / \hat{\beta}'\hat{\beta} \tag{8.2}$$

where $s^2 = \left(y - X\hat{\beta}\right)'\left(y - X\hat{\beta}\right)/(n-p-1)$. McDonald and Galarneau (1975) (McDG) showed that the ridge estimator $\hat{\beta}(k)$ minimizes the residual sum of squares subject to a constraint on the length of the estimated coefficient vector. Their algorithm is implemented in the following way. First, estimate $Q = \hat{\beta}'\hat{\beta} - s^2\sum_{i=1}^{p}\lambda$, λ_i being the eigenvalues of the $X'X$ matrix. Then evaluate $\hat{\beta}'(k)\hat{\beta}(k)$ for a mesh of *k* values. Finally, choose that value of *k* which minimizes $\left|\hat{\beta}'(k)\hat{\beta}(k) - Q\right|$. This procedure defaults to the LS estimator in case Q is negative. Several authors have proposed algorithms for evaluating *k* using a Bayesian framework after an early interpretation of ridge regression provided by Lindley and Smith (1972). Dempster et al. (1977) (RIDGM) suggested to choose *k* as the value that satisfies the following equation:

$$\sum_{i=1}^{p}\hat{\gamma}_i^2 / \left(s^2 / k + s^2 / \lambda_i\right) = p \tag{8.3}$$

where $\hat{\gamma} = G'\hat{\beta}$ and G satisfies $G'X'XG = \Lambda$. Efron and Morris (1975) EB (Empirical Bayes) proposed to estimate *k* as the solution to:

$$s^2 \frac{\sum_{i=1}^{p} \frac{\lambda -}{\lambda - +k}}{\sum_{i=1}^{p}\left(\frac{\lambda -}{\lambda - +k}\right)^2 \widehat{\beta i^2}} = k \tag{8.4}$$

Finally, Golub, Heath and Wahba (1979) Generalized Cross Validation (GCV) observed the close relationship between the concept of ridge regression and the method of cross validation in solving smoothing problems and suggested the following procedure. First, estimate for a mesh of *k* values the quantity

$$V(r) = I - A(r)y^2 / \left(T(r)\left(I - A(r)\right)\right)^2 \quad (8.5)$$

where $A_{(\tau)} = X(X'X + n\tau I_p)^{-1}X'$ and $k = \tau n$. Then, choose the value of k which minimizes $V(\tau)$.

3 Design of the Experiment

We consider a design matrix X with $n = 20$ and $p = 4$. The explanatory variables are generated by

$$x_{ij} = \left(1-\alpha^2\right)^{1/2} z_{ij} + \alpha z_{i5} \qquad i = 1,\ldots,n, j = 1,\ldots,p \quad (8.6)$$

where z_{ij} are independent uniform pseudorandom numbers in the interval (0,1). The resulting correlation between any two explanatory variables is given by α^2. Properties of ridge estimators when the design matrix is of this form are discussed by McDonald (1980). Three different sets of correlation are considered, corresponding to $\alpha = 0.70$, 0.80 and 0.90 and providing to different design matrices X_1, X_2, X_3. For each set of estimators, two choices for the coefficient vector β are considered: the normalized eigenvector corresponding to the largest eigenvalue of $X'X$, denoted by β_{max}, and the normalized eigenvector corresponding to the smallest eigenvalue of $X'X$ denoted by β_{min}. The vectors β_{max} and β_{min} have the property of minimizing and maximizing the MSE function, respectively. The values of the coefficient vector β are given in Table 10.1.

The observations of the dependent variable are generated by (8.1), where the disturbance terms are generated by $\epsilon_i = \sigma_i u_i$ with the u_i^2 being

Table 10.1 Values of α and coefficient vectors

α	β_1	β_2	β_3	β_4
0.70	0.1636623	0.678855	0.6937014	0.1764905
	-0.0995342	-0.697941	0.7091283	-0.0103813
0.80	0.4970149	0.497003	0.5083127	0.4975767
	0.4179148	0.139671	-0.8441387	0.3054
0.90	0.5014548	0.498993	0.5005008	0.4991051
	-0.7153518	-0.115042	0.6699431	0.1619057

Note: The upper entry is β_{max} and the lower β_{min}

independent and identically distributed pseudorandom numbers with zero mean and variance $\sigma_u^2 = 0.1$ and 0.5, drawn from various members of Box and Tiao's (1962) family of symmetric power-exponential distributions. For different values of a specific parameter, this family of distributions generates as special cases normal, uniform and double exponential (Laplace) random variables. The nonnormal disturbances are generated following the methods suggested in Knuth (1968). For this study, we implemented in C language the portable random number generator proposed by L'Ecuyer (1988, 1989) with 32-bit integer arithmetic.

Three different functional forms are considered for σ_i^2's in this experiment:

$$F_1 : \sigma_i^2 = c + d\left(\beta x_i\right)^2, c = 0.5, d = 0.5 \tag{8.7}$$

$$F_2 : \sigma_i^2 = c\exp\left(d\left|\beta x_i\right|\right), c = 1.2, d = 0.6 \tag{8.8}$$

$$F_3 : \sigma_i^2 = c\exp\left(d\beta x_i\right)^2, c = 0.1, d = 0.2 \tag{8.9}$$

The first functional form was used in Jobson and Fuller (1980), the second in Bickel (1978) and the third in Caroll (1982). The true model was replicated 5000 times, and the following summary statistics were calculated: bias, MSE, Predictive Mean Square Error (PMSE) and the multiple correlation coefficient (R^2) (see Donatos (1989)).

4 Evaluation of Results

In this section, we summarize the main results of the Monte Carlo experiment. These results reflect the information in Tables 10.2a, 10.2b and 10.2c, which reports regarding the statistics of bias, MSE and PMSE, the ratio of every ridge estimator to the LS estimator as well as the R^2 statistic of every ridge estimator, for various forms of heteroscedasticity, levels of multicollinearity and distributions of the error time.

We can summarize the main findings regarding the various heteroskedastic models, levels of multicollinearity and distributions of the disturbance term as follows:

(a) *Case* $\beta = \beta_{max}$

With respect to the different functional forms of heteroscedasticity and levels of multicollinearity, the LS estimator dominates the other estimators for the criterion of R^2. On the contrary, it performs poorly overall for the criteria of bias, MSE and PMSE for all levels of multicollinearity and the different forms of heteroscedasticity. With respect to the criteria of bias and dispersion, the GCV estimator exhibits the best results with the sole exception of the F_2 form of heteroscedasticity regarding the PMSE criterion for $\sigma_u^2 = 0.1$ and for the criteria of bias and MSE for $\sigma_u^2 = 0.5$, in which case the ranking is not clear. It should be noted that the GCV estimator performs best for the criteria of bias MSE and PMSE for all levels of multicollinearity. Moreover, the EB and HKB estimators give satisfactory results in the considered settings.

(b) *Case* $\beta = \beta_{\min}$

The LS estimator dominates all the ridge estimators for the criterion of R^2. Moreover, it exhibits a very good performance for the F_1 form of heteroscedasticity, as well as for the F_3 form for the PMSE criterion. It should be noted that for all the other settings the ranking of the examined estimators does not exhibit a clear pattern.

Specifically, for the various levels of multicollinearity and regardless of the form of heteroscedasticity, the following conclusions are apparent. For low levels of multicollinearity, the LS estimator is superior to the ridge estimators with the EB and HKB estimators performing poorly. For high levels of multicollinearity, the EB and HKB estimators perform better, while the GCV and LS estimators fall behind. Finally, for very high levels of multicollinearity the GCV and HKB estimators perform well, while the EB and LS estimators exhibit a poor behavior.

Regarding the performance of the various estimators considered in the study for the different forms of the error distribution, the following remarks can be made.

Under all examined settings, the estimators have highest R^2 under normal disturbances. For the other criteria and for F_1 form of heteroscedasticity, regardless of the level of multicollinearity, the best results come under normal disturbances. For the F_2 form, satisfactory results come under uniform disturbances, while for the F_3 form the pattern is not clear. Finally, in the majority of the settings the worst results come under Laplace disturbances.

Estimation and prediction should not be evaluated with the same standards as seemingly trivially increases in predictive accuracy can result in substantial benefits (see Rubin (1980)). Therefore, in the problem of prediction the goodness of fit of the model plays a central role. Also, there are no striking differences between the different functional forms of heteroscedasticity. However, when $\beta = \beta_{min}$ and especially under very high levels of multicollinearity, all the examined predictors (including LS) exhibited very poor results. A data analyst would not probably rely on any of the examined predictors if such a low R^2 statistic were observed in a real data set.

No other study has been undertaken to compare LS to ridge estimators. Therefore, it is not possible to make comparisons with previous work. However, we establish for heteroscedasticity disturbances the good overall performance of the GCV estimator, a finding also reported in Golub et al. (1970) and Gibbons (1981). In the present study, the HKB estimator performed well in many settings. A result is also reported in Donatos and Michailidis (1993) for normal and nonnormal autocorrelated disturbances. However, the RIDGM and McDG estimators that have performed well in other settings (see Gibbons 1981; Donatos and Michailidis 1990, 1993) did not exhibit analogous results under heteroscedasticity disturbances. Finally, it seems that the results reported in Gibbons (1981) regarding the good performance of LS when the parameter vector is aligned to the smallest eigenvalue of the *X'X* matrix cannot be extended in the presence of heteroscedasticity, in accordance with the case of autocorrelated disturbances (see Donatos and Michailidis (1993)).

5 Conclusion Remarks

In the present simulation study, we studied the small sample behavior of the LS and some ridge estimators in the presence of heteroscedasticity and multicollinearity for normal and nonnormal disturbances. In case $\beta = \beta_{max}$, the GCV estimator exhibited the best results for the criteria of bias and dispersion, for all examined settings. On the contrary, the LS estimator gave the poorest results. For both coefficient vectors considered ($\beta = \beta_{max}$ and $\beta = \beta_{min}$), the LS estimator dominates the other ones with respect to the R^2 criterion. In case $\beta = \beta_{min}$, and for the F_1 form of heteroscedasticity, the LS estimator dominates the other ones with respect to the R^2 criterion. In case $\beta = \beta_{min}$, and for the F_1 form of heteroscedasticity the LS estimator is superior to the other estimators, while for the F_2 and F_3 forms of heteroscedasticity the ranking of the estimators does not follow a clear pattern. It is worth noting that R^2 statistic takes its maximum value under normal disturbances and its minimum one under Laplace disturbances. Moreover, for the F_1 and F_2 forms of heteroscedasticity, the best estimates corresponded to normal and uniform disturbances respectively, while for the F_3 form none of the two distributions gave overall better results.

Appendix

Table 10.2a Ordinary estimators

Normal errors	*Low Multicollinearity*				*High Multicollinearity*				*Very high Multicollinearity*			
	Bias	*MwSE*	*PMSE*	R^2	*Bias*	*MSE*	*PMSE*	R^2	*Bias*	*MSE*	*PMSE*	R^2
	F_1											
	$\sigma_u^2 = .1, \beta_{\max}$											
OLS	0.482	0.077	0.864	0.881	0.857	0.249	1.128	0.949	2.237	1.806	1.398	0.949
HKB	0.468	0.073	0.870	0.881	0.759	0.191	1.084	0.948	1.415	0.765	1.176	0.948
McDG	0.474	0.075	0.872	0.881	0.716	0.174	1.138	0.947	1.392	0.945	1.364	0.944
RIDGM	0.482	0.078	0.868	0.881	0.852	0.247	1.128	0.948	2.180	1.750	1.392	0.949
EB	0.474	0.075	0.872	0.881	0.772	0.197	1.072	0.948	1.259	0.671	1.175	0.946
GCV	0.469	0.073	0.899	0.879	0.668	0.147	1.099	0.946	1.079	0.563	1.157	0.945
	$\sigma_u^2 = .1, \beta_{\min}$											
OLS	0.377	0.046	0.480	0.816	0.669	0.151	0.556	0.590	1.301	0.610	0.502	0.314
HKB	0.389	0.049	0.505	0.814	0.665	0.146	0.588	0.582	1.190	0.500	0.571	0.290
McDG	0.378	0.046	0.482	0.816	0.670	0.153	0.589	0.587	1.311	0.609	1.191	0.250
RIDGM	0.378	0.046	0.482	0.816	0.669	0.151	0.558	0.589	1.303	0.610	0.510	0.313
EB	0.378	0.046	0.482	0.816	0.652	0.144	0.607	0.571	1.496	0.737	1.177	0.203
GCV	0.385	0.048	0.496	0.815	0.679	0.157	0.642	0.577	1.308	0.593	0.855	0.261

	$\sigma_u^2 = .5, \beta_{max}$											
OLS	1.068	0.377	4.303	0.618	1.879	1.203	5.491	0.784	4.898	8.847	6.721	0.797
HKB	0.987	0.312	4.659	0.606	1.344	0.622	5.129	0.775	2.515	2.783	5.270	0.785
McDG	1.003	0.325	4.507	0.610	1.327	0.656	5.095	0.772	3.544	5.389	5.755	0.789
RIDGM	1.039	0.349	4.644	0.610	1.262	0.539	4.876	0.773	2.776	4.112	5.275	0.783
EB	1.003	0.326	4.507	0.610	1.262	0.539	4.876	0.773	2.776	4.112	5.275	0.783
GCV	0.969	0.304	4.225	0.604	1.304	0.612	4.892	0.771	2.258	3.005	5.106	0.778
	$\sigma_u^2 = .5, \beta_{min}$											
OLS	0.841	0.230	2.443	0.520	1.469	0.741	2.679	0.332	2.857	2.965	2.448	0.223
HKB	0.912	0.267	3.039	0.500	1.291	0.544	2.985	0.301	1.928	1.293	2.591	0.182
McDG	0.869	0.246	2.670	0.516	1.380	0.626	3.179	0.304	2.336	1.999	2.509	0.194
RIDGM	0.927	0.277	3.032	0.506	1.449	0.697	3.267	0.308	2.507	2.372	3.139	0.187
EB	0.868	0.246	2.670	0.516	1.246	0.496	3.101	0.271	2.395	2.068	3.213	0.173
GCV	0.900	0.259	2.853	0.505	1.319	0.564	3.123	0.285	1.939	1.302	3.200	0.150

(continued)

Table 10.2a (continued)

Normal errors	*Low Multicollinearity*				*High Multicollinearity*				*Very high Multicollinearity*			
	Bias	*MwSE*	*PMSE*	R^2	*Bias*	*MSE*	*PMSE*	R^2	*Bias*	*MSE*	*PMSE*	R^2
	F_2											
	$\sigma_u^2 = .1, \beta_{max}$											
OLS	0.638	0.134	1.480	0.809	1.166	0.453	1.999	0.909	2.841	3.016	2.297	0.917
HKB	0.628	0.128	1.621	0.806	0.964	0.305	1.923	0.907	1.666	1.162	1.880	0.914
McDG	0.639	0.132	1.632	0.806	0.904	0.285	2.047	0.904	1.787	1.653	2.050	0.911
RIDGM	0.654	0.139	1.619	0.808	1.135	0.429	2.020	0.908	2.627	2.747	2.264	0.916
EB	0.639	0.132	1.632	0.807	0.972	0.306	1.875	0.907	1.453	1.025	1.833	0.911
GCV	0.627	0.127	1.698	0.802	0.841	0.213	1.983	0.903	1.311	0.956	1.881	0.910
	$\sigma_u^2 = .1, \beta_{min}$											
OLS	0.541	0.095	1.002	0.687	0.968	0.315	1.160	0.451	1.948	1.390	1.134	0.264
HKB	0.576	0.109	1.162	0.683	0.936	0.284	1.265	0.434	1.544	0.824	1.213	0.231
McDG	0.563	0.102	1.088	0.689	0.979	0.313	1.334	0.439	1.717	1.026	1.749	0.208
RIDGM	0.569	0.105	1.109	0.689	0.977	0.318	1.220	0.447	1.925	1.351	1.266	0.256
EB	0.563	0.102	1.088	0.689	0.915	0.270	1.311	0.416	1.861	1.142	2.021	0.172
GCV	0.573	0.108	1.146	0.686	0.983	0.310	1.471	0.421	1.616	0.878	1.656	0.197

	$\sigma_u^2 = .5, \beta_{max}$											
OLS	1.414	0.652	7.389	0.500	2.623	2.351	10.209	0.705	6.227	14.222	10.866	0.698
HKB	1.253	0.507	8.326	0.487	1.744	1.074	9.074	0.673	3.032	4.145	8.186	0.680
McDG	1.281	0.539	7.617	0.497	1.851	1.281	8.466	0.676	4.807	9.229	9.497	0.690
RIDGM	1.323	0.576	7.539	0.497	2.104	1.655	9.396	0.677	4.062	8.684	9.032	0.678
EB	1.281	0.539	7.617	0.497	1.698	1.070	8.359	0.668	4.023	8.283	8.693	0.679
GCV	1.289	0.552	7.047	0.499	1.886	1.254	8.153	0.676	3.509	6.367	8.101	0.678
	$\sigma_u^2 = .5, \beta_{min}$											
OLS	1.206	0.472	5.084	0.390	2.182	1.645	6.041	0.269	4.217	4.000	5.364	0.215
HKB	1.296	0.530	7.409	0.351	1.722	0.963	6.623	0.226	2.388	2.110	4.812	0.169
McDG	1.271	0.506	5.804	0.377	1.839	1.151	5.935	0.239	3.331	4.123	4.835	0.193
RIDGM	1.269	0.501	5.779	0.363	1.955	1.336	6.122	0.238	3.028	3.799	5.360	0.158
EB	1.272	0.506	5.805	0.377	1.688	0.969	6.096	0.200	3.377	4.389	5.435	0.179
GCV	1.177	0.445	5.179	0.369	1.771	1.081	5.492	0.233	2.633	2.670	4.876	0.151

(continued)

Table 10.2a (continued)

Normal errors	*Low Multicollinearity*				*High Multicollinearity*				*Very high Multicollinearity*			
	Bias	*MSE*	*PMSE*	R^2	*Bias*	*MSE*	*PMSE*	R^2	*Bias*	*MSE*	*PMSE*	R^2
	F_3											
	$\sigma_u^2 = .1, \beta_{\max}$											
OLS	0.507	0.085	0.941	0.869	1.103	0.405	2.084	0.926	3.010	3.429	2.230	0.936
HKB	0.483	0.076	0.924	0.872	0.927	0.277	1.966	0.925	1.900	1.486	1.821	0.933
McDG	0.489	0.078	0.928	0.873	0.864	0.253	1.977	0.922	2.101	2.161	2.024	0.931
RIDGM	0.495	0.080	0.919	0.873	1.076	0.386	2.113	0.925	2.915	3.292	2.209	0.935
EB	0.489	0.078	0.928	0.873	0.932	0.276	1.908	0.925	1.799	1.632	1.875	0.931
GCV	0.485	0.077	0.956	0.871	0.809	0.217	1.902	0.922	1.590	1.346	1.795	0.930
	$\sigma_u^2 = .1, \beta_{\min}$											
OLS	0.416	0.056	0.597	0.779	0.710	0.170	0.628	0.566	1.434	0.760	0.612	0.308
HKB	0.423	0.058	0.620	0.782	0.695	0.163	0.663	0.557	1.261	0.566	0.675	0.282
McDG	0.410	0.054	0.591	0.785	0.712	0.172	0.671	0.562	1.394	0.690	1.331	0.243
RIDGM	0.411	0.054	0.590	0.785	0.713	0.172	0.634	0.565	1.432	0.758	0.624	0.306
EB	0.410	0.054	0.592	0.786	0.691	0.159	0.683	0.545	1.589	0.837	1.350	0.198
GCV	0.418	0.056	0.608	0.783	0.723	0.177	0.731	0.551	1.369	0.653	0.977	0.254

	$\sigma_u^2 = .5, \beta_{\max}$											
OLS	1.122	0.413	4.685	0.591	2.604	2.302	11.990	0.705	6.814	18.540	11.437	0.753
HKB	1.062	0.359	5.356	0.587	1.781	1.071	11.276	0.690	3.776	6.867	8.714	0.738
McDG	1.084	0.376	5.155	0.592	1.885	1.301	10.379	0.693	5.173	12.452	9.905	0.745
RIDGM	1.121	0.406	5.233	0.593	2.258	1.815	11.304	0.697	5.019	13.634	10.098	0.738
EB	1.084	0.376	5.153	0.592	1.770	1.203	10.385	0.687	4.181	10.015	8.680	0.734
GCV	1.040	0.348	4.750	0.587	1.865	1.283	9.989	0.692	3.852	8.868	8.760	0.733
	$\sigma_u^2 = .5, \beta_{\min}$											
OLS	0.924	0.277	3.013	0.474	1.695	0.979	3.521	0.325	3.344	4.058	3.246	0.233
HKB	1.016	0.334	4.001	0.447	1.441	0.673	3.749	0.292	2.120	1.608	3.136	0.197
McDG	0.991	0.316	3.555	0.465	1.544	0.782	3.883	0.297	2.903	3.280	3.962	0.196
RIDGM	1.050	0.348	3.951	0.452	1.621	0.876	4.065	0.298	2.903	3.280	3.962	0.196
EB	0.991	0.316	3.554	0.466	1.330	0.567	3.788	0.257	2.681	2.677	3.719	0.180
GCV	0.995	0.316	3.617	0.453	1.440	0.677	3.788	0.278	2.129	1.662	3.648	0.167

(continued)

Table 10.2b Ordinary estimators

Uniform errors	*Low Multicollinearity*				*High Multicollinearity*				*Very high Multicollinearity*			
	Bias	*MSE*	*PMSE*	R^2	*Bias*	*MSE*	*PMSE*	R^2	*Bias*	*MSE*	*PMSE*	R^2
	F_1											
	$\sigma_u^2 = .1, \beta_{max}$											
OLS	0.489	0.078	0.879	0.880	0.897	0.264	1.163	0.948	2.229	1.769	1.336	0.948
HKB	0.479	0.074	0.896	0.880	0.793	0.204	1.119	0.947	1.396	0.748	1.111	0.947
McDG	0.485	0.076	0.898	0.880	0.746	0.186	1.159	0.946	1.348	0.902	1.297	0.943
RIDGM	0.489	0.074	0.882	0.880	0.893	0.262	1.166	0.948	2.181	1.721	1.329	0.948
EB	0.478	0.074	0.882	0.880	0.809	0.212	1.111	0.948	1.148	0.541	1.105	0.944
GCV	0.481	0.075	0.931	0.878	0.695	0.157	1.134	0.945	1.059	0.541	1.077	0.944
	$\sigma_u^2 = .1, \beta_{min}$											
OLS	0.387	0.047	0.499	0.815	0.699	0.161	0.572	0.580	1.299	0.611	0.507	0.314
HKB	0.398	0.050	0.519	0.813	0.689	0.156	0.607	0.572	1.196	0.497	0.565	0.289
McDG	0.387	0.047	0.500	0.815	0.703	0.163	0.607	0.577	1.315	0.607	1.123	0.256
RIDGM	0.388	0.048	0.501	0.815	0.699	0.160	0.572	0.580	1.299	0.611	0.513	0.313
EB	0.428	0.059	0.589	0.804	0.686	0.153	0.626	0.561	1.497	0.735	1.280	0.186
GCV	0.394	0.049	0.515	0.814	0.714	0.169	0.667	0.567	1.309	0.588	0.835	0.260

	$\sigma_u^2 = .5, \beta_{max}$											
OLS	1.123	0.412	4.645	0.619	2.001	1.331	5.866	0.783	5.151	9.326	7.221	0.787
HKB	1.028	0.339	4.887	0.607	1.445	0.703	5.433	0.774	2.646	2.922	5.631	0.774
McDG	1.051	0.357	4.843	0.610	1.414	0.731	5.282	0.771	3.737	5.639	6.144	0.779
RIDGM	1.101	0.393	5.054	0.611	1.736	1.057	5.947	0.776	3.588	6.068	6.537	0.773
EB	1.013	0.330	4.678	0.609	1.310	0.551	5.019	0.770	3.030	4.520	5.655	0.772
GCV	0.995	0.322	4.446	0.605	1.355	0.633	4.983	0.769	2.356	2.962	5.401	0.766
	$\sigma_u^2 = .5, \beta_{min}$											
OLS	0.872	0.246	2.546	0.509	1.532	0.787	2.825	0.269	2.947	3.095	2.613	0.230
HKB	0.930	0.281	3.106	0.489	1.344	0.580	3.183	0.295	1.979	1.341	2.651	0.188
McDG	0.896	0.262	2.759	0.505	1.447	0.669	3.388	0.300	2.343	1.983	2.642	0.171
RIDGM	0.943	0.290	3.116	0.495	1.543	0.770	3.491	0.302	2.497	2.392	3.318	0.189
EB	0.984	0.300	3.449	0.451	1.266	0.504	3.211	0.263	2.375	1.992	3.258	0.172
GCV	0.926	0.278	2.993	0.493	1.347	0.584	3.306	281	1.948	1.310	3.325	0.155

(continued)

Table 10.2b (continued)

Uniform errors	*Low Multicollinearity*				*High Multicollinearity*				*Very high Multicollinearity*			
	Bias	*MSE*	*PMSE*	R^2	*Bias*	*MSE*	*PMSE*	R^2	*Bias*	*MSE*	*PMSE*	R^2
	F_2											
	$\sigma_u^2 = .1, \beta_{\max}$											
OLS	0.655	0.137	1.526	0.809	1.141	0.430	1.868	0.908	2.833	2.874	2.284	0.919
HKB	0.625	0.124	1.526	0.807	0.938	0.289	1.776	0.906	1.650	1.076	1.792	0.915
McDG	0.637	0.129	1.537	0.808	0.877	0.266	1.913	0.902	1.700	1.457	1.927	0.911
RIDGM	0.653	0.136	1.533	0.809	1.118	0.416	1.884	0.907	2.610	2.592	2.172	0.918
EB	0.625	0.124	1.498	0.808	0.949	0.293	1.737	0.906	1.476	1.054	1.799	0.912
GCV	0.625	0.124	1.586	0.803	0.815	0.221	1.834	0.902	1.269	0.816	1.725	0.911
	$\sigma_u^2 = .1, \beta_{\min}$											
OLS	0.560	0.099	1.046	0.686	0.945	0.299	1.094	0.444	1.983	1.392	1.129	0.264
HKB	0.576	0.106	1.124	0.680	0.896	0.266	1.172	0.427	1.555	0.832	1.203	0.231
McDG	0.565	0.100	1.064	0.685	0.941	0.294	1.238	0.433	1.740	1.039	1.795	0.207
RIDGM	0.568	0.102	1.075	0.685	0.957	0.304	1.139	0.441	1.939	1.336	1.225	0.255
EB	0.637	0.132	1.379	0.653	0.850	0.255	1.221	0.408	1.846	1.148	1.967	0.174
GCV	0.573	0.104	1.105	0.682	0.940	0.290	1.352	0.414	1.620	0.888	1.626	0.199

	$\sigma_u^2 = .5, \beta_{max}$											
OLS	1.453	0.679	7.570	0.502	2.595	2.233	9.387	0.683	6.373	14.395	10.923	0.714
HKB	1.277	0.513	8.228	0.480	1.720	1.020	8.338	0.667	3.194	4.331	8.278	0.698
McDG	1.295	0.535	7.470	0.489	1.801	1.185	7.837	0.669	4.848	8.987	9.411	0.707
RIDGM	1.323	0.569	7.418	0.488	2.075	1.584	8.684	0.670	4.250	8.895	9.135	0.696
EB	1.244	0.491	7.281	0.482	1.606	0.943	7.662	0.660	3.871	7.465	8.362	0.694
GCV	1.279	0.525	6.763	0.490	1.855	1.175	7.523	0.669	3.536	5.923	7.961	0.694
	$\sigma_u^2 = .5, \beta_{min}$											
OLS	1.257	0.505	5.313	0.391	2.164	1.569	5.631	0.269	4.317	6.621	5.450	0.226
HKB	1.315	0.544	7.025	0.356	1.736	0.957	6.128	0.226	2.467	2.217	4.931	0.181
McDG	1.290	0.526	5.943	0.380	1.825	1.119	5.548	0.241	3.348	4.181	4.883	0.201
RIDGM	1.289	0.512	5.785	0.368	1.910	1.232	5.912	0.232	3.144	4.129	5.593	0.170
EB	1.213	0.468	5.310	0.366	1.633	0.878	5.819	0.195	3.317	4.211	5.491	0.184
GCV	1.204	0.458	5.245	0.373	1.752	1.003	5.115	0.234	2.612	2.603	5.028	0.161

(continued)

Table 10.2b (continued)

Uniform errors	*Low Multicollinearity*				*High Multicollinearity*				*Very high Multicollinearity*			
	Bias	*MSE*	*PMSE*	R^2	*Bias*	*MSE*	*PMSE*	R^2	*Bias*	*MSE*	*PMSE*	R^2
	F_3											
	$\sigma_u^2 = .1, \beta_{\max}$											
OLS	0.516	0.085	0.943	0.867	1.111	0.404	2.102	0.921	3.036	3.346	2.159	0.933
HKB	0.500	0.074	0.951	0.866	0.934	0.280	2.036	0.919	1.892	1.412	1.752	0.930
McDG	0.507	0.082	0.956	0.866	0.875	0.259	2.094	0.917	2.093	2.039	1.969	0.928
RIDGM	0.515	0.084	0.946	0.867	1.087	0.387	2.135	0.920	2.908	3.171	2.129	0.932
EB	0.500	0.079	0.937	0.866	0.943	0.283	1.974	0.920	1.796	1.582	1.826	0.927
GCV	0.500	0.080	0.986	0.864	0.811	0.216	2.046	0.916	1.564	1.234	1.726	0.927
	$\sigma_u^2 = .1, \beta_{\min}$											
OLS	0.420	0.055	0.592	0.777	0.713	0.171	0.630	0.552	1.466	0.771	0.615	0.302
HKB	0.429	0.058	0.620	0.774	0.699	0.164	0.665	0.543	1.291	0.578	0.676	0.275
McDG	0.418	0.055	0.591	0.777	0.717	0.173	0.668	0.548	1.436	0.708	1.360	0.237
RIDGM	0.422	0.055	0.595	0.777	0.714	0.171	0.634	0.552	1.469	0.770	0.627	0.300
EB	0.470	0.070	0.722	0.761	0.697	0.162	0.693	0.530	1.596	0.837	1.322	0.197
GCV	0.426	0.057	0.608	0.775	0.729	0.178	0.732	0.536	1.397	0.667	0.991	0.244

	$\sigma_u^2 = .5, \beta_{\max}$											
OLS	1.128	0.411	4.667	0.589	2.564	2.070	10.890	0.698	6.825	16.990	11.239	0.747
HKB	1.035	0.337	5.019	0.576	1.748	0.970	10.412	0.682	3.724	5.960	8.728	0.731
McDG	1.053	0.352	4.870	0.580	1.813	1.119	9.272	0.686	5.325	11.354	9.902	0.741
RIDGM	1.091	0.379	5.094	0.579	2.192	1.599	10.295	0.690	4.895	11.604	9.913	0.729
EB	1.018	0.325	4.737	0.578	1.600	0.832	8.948	0.678	4.244	9.356	8.801	0.728
GCV	1.002	0.318	4.405	0.575	1.821	1.118	8.832	0.685	3.834	7.512	8.524	0.727
	$\sigma_u^2 = .5, \beta_{\min}$											
OLS	0.935	0.278	3.054	0.462	1.630	0.873	3.264	0.309	3.270	3.853	3.189	0.236
HKB	1.012	0.324	3.832	0.437	1.414	0.623	3.649	0.275	2.131	1.595	3.173	0.194
McDG	0.969	0.299	3.354	0.457	1.499	0.707	3.734	0.279	2.634	2.542	3.109	0.209
RIDGM	1.032	0.336	3.846	0.443	1.587	0.805	3.962	0.280	2.718	2.869	4.046	0.189
EB	1.012	0.319	3.838	0.410	1.342	0.554	3.807	0.241	2.658	2.605	3.784	0.188
GCV	0.991	0.308	3.547	0.442	1.400	0.621	3.594	0.262	2.105	1.597	3.824	0.164

Table 10.2c Ordinary estimators

Laplace errors	*Low Multicollinearity*				*High Multicollinearity*				*Very high Multicollinearity*			
	Bias	*MSE*	*PMSE*	R^2	*Bias*	*MSE*	*PMSE*	R^2	*Bias*	*MSE*	*PMSE*	R^2
	F_1											
	$\sigma_u^2 = .1, \beta_{max}$											
OLS	0.558	0.110	0.378	0.830	1.135	0.467	1.631	0.899	2.441	2.490	1.928	0.911
HKB	0.503	0.086	1.171	0.827	0.898	0.269	1.551	0.896	1.267	0.767	1.366	0.907
McDG	0.516	0.092	1.211	0.828	0.841	0.251	1.649	0.893	1.449	1.306	1.545	0.904
RIDGM	0.547	0.105	1.344	0.829	1.064	0.406	1.686	0.897	2.144	2.100	1.770	0.909
EB	0.506	0.088	1.179	0.828	0.856	0.247	1.635	0.894	1.057	0.442	1.219	0.905
GCV	0.491	0.081	1.115	0.824	0.801	0.225	1.610	0.892	0.906	0.576	1.218	0.903
	$\sigma_u^2 = .1, \beta_{min}$											
OLS	0.478	0.075	0.903	0.714	1.015	0.351	0.983	0.563	1.513	0.876	0.672	0.179
HKB	0.503	0.087	0.907	0.716	0.757	0.198	0.754	0.548	1.468	0.752	1.055	0.149
McDG	0.480	0.075	0.917	0.714	0.902	0.283	0.885	0.559	1.513	0.806	1.928	0.089
RIDGM	0.490	0.075	0.917	0.714	0.927	0.246	0.845	0.548	1.525	0.878	0.894	0.169
EB	0.547	0.093	1.100	0.695	0.792	0.231	0.823	0.536	1.566	0.857	1.657	0.108
GCV	0.491	0.079	0.966	0.710	0.777	0.210	0.789	0.547	1.520	0.803	1.697	0.111

	$\sigma_u^2 = .5, \beta_{max}$											
OLS	1.287	0.598	7.390	0.595	2.514	2.323	8.206	0.678	6.192	17.296	11.556	0.721
HKB	1.023	0.358	5.690	0.579	1.498	0.803	6.968	0.661	2.755	4.564	7.771	0.706
McDG	1.065	0.400	5.755	0.585	1.710	1.116	6.774	0.665	4.759	11.333	9.962	0.715
RIDGM	1.162	0.483	6.419	0.586	2.047	1.671	7.375	0.668	3.924	10.630	8.787	0.705
EB	1.056	0.393	5.608	0.583	1.940	1.247	6.105	0.654	2.003	2.081	6.171	0.694
GCV	1.093	0.425	5.823	0.583	1.973	1.555	7.036	0.668	3.333	8.272	8.115	0.703
	$\sigma_u^2 = .5, \beta_{min}$											
OLS	1.095	0.400	4.834	0.424	2.274	1.824	5.104	0.349	3.638	5.119	3.556	0.137
HKB	1.026	0.362	5.473	0.421	1.424	0.730	3.514	0.310	2.167	1.698	4.084	0.094
McDG	1.103	0.388	4.968	0.416	1.763	1.149	4.183	0.331	3.193	3.897	3.400	0.121
RIDGM	1.151	0.408	5.202	0.401	1.835	1.150	4.235	0.308	2.808	3.250	4.216	0.091
EB	1.176	0.400	5.337	0.378	1.671	0.892	3.961	0.291	2.210	1.772	4.168	0.086
GCV	1.078	0.359	4.763	0.406	1.503	0.835	3.654	0.304	2.518	2.557	4.197	0.083

(continued)

Table 10.2c (continued)

Laplace errors	*Low Multicollinearity*				*High Multicollinearity*				*Very high Multicollinearity*			
	Bias	*MSE*	*PMSE*	R^2	*Bias*	*MSE*	*PMSE*	R^2	*Bias*	*MSE*	*PMSE*	R^2
	F_2											
	$\sigma_u^2 = .1, \beta_{\max}$											
OLS	0.741	0.189	2.349	0.747	1.576	0.883	2.849	0.838	3.190	4.126	3.134	0.864
HKB	0.667	0.153	2.128	0.745	1.100	0.416	2.637	0.827	1.681	1.409	2.296	0.856
McDG	0.685	0.165	2.189	0.746	1.083	0.426	3.076	0.833	2.336	2.860	2.805	0.857
RIDGM	0.727	0.187	2.384	0.748	1.371	0.686	2.868	0.829	2.644	3.599	2.922	0.858
EB	0.667	0.152	2.093	0.746	1.143	0.538	2.375	0.829	1.249	0.631	1.934	0.905
GCV	0.651	0.145	2.031	0.40	1.065	0.425	2.614	0.823	1.237	1.220	2.067	0.850
	$\sigma_u^2 = .1, \beta_{\min}$											
OLS	0.672	0.148	1.788	0.567	1.457	0.721	2.013	0.453	2.262	1.958	1.469	0.150
HKB	0.683	0.173	2.135	0.573	0.973	0.26	1.453	0.413	1.797	1.102	2.099	0.111
McDG	0.698	0.163	2.003	0.562	1.173	0.481	1.690	0.429	2.056	1.563	2.000	0.107
RIDGM	0.740	0.181	2.174	0.555	1.271	0.657	2.764	0.412	2.034	1.525	2.413	0.113
EB	0.839	0.208	2.367	0.522	1.164	0.583	1.936	0.423	1.823	1.140	2.703	0.086
GCV	0.727	0.170	2.094	0.553	1.003	0.350	1.538	0.406	1.761	1.079	2.939	0.077

	$\sigma_u^2 = .5, \beta_{max}$											
OLS	1.703	1.018	12.567	0.494	3.508	4.426	14.468	0.567	8.042	18.735	18.655	0.630
HKB	1.237	0.519	9.104	0.484	1.853	1.250	9.801	0.555	3.055	5.454	9.545	0.613
McDG	1.319	0.608	9.126	0.496	2.497	2.398	14.968	0.553	5.847	14.846	12.844	0.627
RIDGM	1.451	0.748	10.136	0.498	2.751	2.944	10.914	0.567	4.632	12.502	10.986	0.613
EB	1.395	0.704	9.805	0.495	2.487	2.856	9.054	0.551	2.398	3.205	9.200	0.650
GCV	1.481	0.765	10.350	0.500	2.897	3.108	11.274	0.571	4.792	12.228	11.105	0.617
	$\sigma_u^2 = .5, \beta_{min}$											
OLS	1.537	0.786	9.542	0.319	3.258	3.726	10.438	0.293	3.638	5.119	3.556	0.137
HKB	1.428	0.743	8.913	0.316	1.771	1.146	6.199	0.242	2.617	2.560	6.893	0.085
McDG	1.429	0.635	8.649	0.321	2.260	1.930	7.155	0.267	4.552	7.723	6.419	0.120
RIDGM	1.417	0.638	8.515	0.311	2.356	1.944	7.102	0.254	4.206	7.169	6.662	0.101
EB	1.487	0.702	8.879	0.315	2.273	1.864	6.938	0.262	2.890	3.343	6.668	0.082
GCV	1.370	0.611	8.287	0.319	2.157	1.719	6.636	0.251	3.981	6.663	6.435	0.098

(continued)

Table 10.2c (continued)

Laplace errors	*Low Multicollinearity*				*High Multicollinearity*				*Very high Multicollinearity*			
	Bias	*MSE*	*PMSE*	R^2	*Bias*	*MSE*	*PMSE*	R^2	*Bias*	*MSE*	*PMSE*	R^2
	F_3											
	$\sigma_u^2 = .1, \beta_{\max}$											
OLS	0.558	0.110	1.378	0.830	1.545	0.872	3.148	0.838	3.307	4.978	3.319	0.892
HKB	0.553	0.105	1.382	0.814	1.103	0.396	2.973	0.835	1.971	2.177	2.578	0.886
McDG	0.568	0.112	1.427	0.815	1.083	0.426	3.076	0.833	2.500	3.902	3.042	0.886
RIDGM	0.597	0.126	1.585	0.816	1.353	0.670	3.127	0.838	3.156	5.201	3.323	0.889
EB	0.556	0.106	1.387	0.815	1.378	0.771	1.985	0.881	1.843	4.107	3.214	0.881
GCV	0.542	0.089	1.318	0.810	1.108	0.491	3.023	0.833	1.594	2.170	2.348	0.882
	$\sigma_u^2 = .1, \beta_{\min}$											
OLS	0.503	0.083	1.008	0.658	1.098	0.410	1.135	0.539	1705	1.113	0.825	0.170
HKB	0.563	0.118	1.453	0.624	0.803	0.229	0.874	0.516	1.605	0.905	1.270	0.130
McDG	0.524	0.091	1.094	0.660	0.948	0.321	1.012	0.538	1.720	1.070	2.038	0.077
RIDGM	0.540	0.098	1.160	0.658	0.956	0.342	0.947	0.526	1.731	1.131	1.146	0.147
EB	0.629	0.119	1.400	0.634	0.876	0.259	0.926	0.521	1.668	0.965	1.838	0.098
GCV	0.545	0.097	1.167	0.656	0.827	0.244	0.913	0.513	1.613	0.907	1.977	0.092

	$\sigma_u^2 = .5, \beta_{max}$											
OLS	1.283	0.598	7.340	0.595	3.469	4.475	16.597	0.569	8.493	36.390	21.560	0.692
HKB	1.049	0.362	6.205	0.554	1.964	1.376	15.178	0.542	3.647	8.245	11.810	0.667
McDG	1.086	0.395	5.880	0.561	2.497	2.398	14.968	0.553	6.268	18.691	15.210	0.679
RIDGM	1.116	0.473	6.473	0.561	2.948	3.645	16.301	556	5.410	19.221	13.997	0.668
EB	1.073	0.397	5.769	0.559	2.398	3.205	9.200	0.650	5.325	17.256	13.847	0.665
GCV	1.150	0.456	6.251	0.562	2.999	3.746	16.249	0.559	5.050	15.230	13.356	0.670
	$\sigma_u^2 = .5, \beta_{min}$											
OLS	1.150	0.439	5.351	0.367	2.452	2.112	5.882	0.376	4.103	1.113	4.825	0.173
HKB	1.149	0.462	5.723	0.347	1.508	0.784	4.134	0.294	2.265	1.805	4.913	0.088
McDG	1.173	0.421	5.472	0.353	1.877	1.267	4.755	0.315	3.439	4.502	4.042	0.120
RIDGM	1.168	0.416	5.405	0.340	1.745	1.154	4.643	0.321	3.086	4.029	4.717	0.094
EB	1.206	0.433	5.613	0.329	1.693	1.053	4.543	0.318	2.304	1.994	4.935	0.081
GCV	1.111	0.383	5.075	0.347	1.619	0.948	4.109	0.293	2.740	3.191	4.653	0.084

References

Bickel, P.J. (1978). Using Residuals Robustly I: Test for Heteroscedasticity, Nonlinearity. *The Annuals of Statistics,* 6: 266–291.

Box, G.E.P. and G.C.Tiao (1962). A Further Look at Robustness via Bayes's Theorem. *Biometrica,* 49: 419–432.

Caroll, R.J. (1982). Adapting for Heteroscedasticity in Linear Models. *The Annuals of Statistics,* 10: 1224–1233.

Casella, G. (1985). Condition Numbers and Minimax Ridge Regression Estimators. *Journal of the American Statistical Association,* 80: 753–758.

Cragg, J.G. (1983). More Efficient Estimation in the Presence of Heteroscedasticity of Unknown Form. *Econometrica,* 51: 751–764.

Dempster, A.P., Schatzoff, M. and N.Wermuth (1977). A Simulation Study of Alternatives to Ordinary Least Squares. *Journal of the American Statistical Association,* 72: 77–106.

Donatos, G.S. (1989). A Monte Carlo Study of k-class Estimators for Small Samples with Normal and Non-normal Disturbances. *The Statistician,* 38: 11–20.

Donatos, G.S. and G.C. Michailidis (1990). Small Sample Properties of Ridge Estimators with Normal and Non-normal Disturbances. *Communications in Statistics, Simulation and Computation,* 19: 935–950.

——— (1993). A Simulation Study of Least Squares and Ridge Estimators for Normal and Non-normal Autocorrelated Disturbances. *Journal of Statistical Simulation and Computation,* 47: 49–68.

Efron, B. and C. Morris (1975). Data Analysis Using Stein's Estimator and its Generalization. *Journal of the American Statistical Association,* 70: 311–319.

Fieltz, B. and J. Rozelle (1983). Stable Distributions and Mixture of Distributions Hypothesis for Common Stock Returns. *Journal of the American Statistical Association,* 78: 28–36.

Gibbons, D.G. (1981). A Simulation Study of Some Ridge Estimators. *Journal of the American Statistical Association,* 76: 131–139.

Golub, G.H., Health M., and G. Wahba (1970). Generalized Cross Validation as a Method for Choosing a Good Ridge Parameter. *Technometrics,* 21: 215–223.

Hoerl, A.E. and R.W. Kennard (1970). Ridge Regression: Biased Estimation for Non-orthogonal Problems. *Technometrics,* 12: 56–67.

Hoerl, A.E., Kennard, R.W. and K.F. Baldwin (1975). Ridge Regression: Some Simulations. *Communications in Statistics, Theory and Methods,* 4: 104–123.

Jobson, J.D. and W.A. Fuller (1980). Least Squares Estimation when the Covariance Matrix and Parameter Vector are Functionally Related. *Journal of the American Statistical Association* 75: 176–181.

Judge G.C., Griffiths, W.E., Hill, R.C., Lutkepohl, H. and T.C. Lee (1985). *The Theory and Practice of Econometrics*, Second Edition. New York: John Wiley & Sons.

Knuth, D.E. (1968). *The Art of Computer Programming 2, Seminumerical Algorithms*. Addison – Wesley, Reading, Mass.

L'Ecuyer, P. (1988). Efficient and Portable Combined Random Number Generators. *Communication of the ACM*, 31: 742–749.

______. (1989). Efficient and Portable Combined Random Number Generators. *Communication of the ACM* 32: 1019–1020.

Lindley, D.V. and A.F.M. Smith (1972). Bayes Estimates for the Linear Model. *Journal of the Royal Statistical Society*, Ser. B. 34.1: 1–41.

McDonald, G.C. (1980). Some Algebraic Properties of Ridge Coefficients. *Journal of Royal Statistical Society*, B, 42: 31–34.

McDonald, G.C. and D.I. Galarneau (1975). A Monte Carlo Evaluation of Some Ridge Type Estimators. *Journal of the American Statistical Association*, 70: 407–416.

Robinson, P. (1987). Asymptotically Efficient Estimation in the Presence of Heteroscedasticity of Unknown Form. *Econometrica* 55: 875–891.

Rubin, D.B. (1980). Using Empirical Bayes Techniques in the Law School Validity Studies, *Journal of the American Statistical Association*, 75: 801–816.

Tucker, A. and L. Pond. (1988). The Probability Distribution of Foreign Exchange Price Changes. *Review of Economics and Statistics*, 70: 638–647.

White, H. (1982). Instrumental Variables Regression with Independent Observations. *Econometrica*, 50: 483–499.

CHAPTER 11

The Effects of Temporal Aggregation and Random Sampling on the Power of the Augmented Dickey Fuller Stationarity Test: A Monte Carlo Study

Dikaios Tserkezos

1 Introduction

Temporal aggregation poses many interesting questions which have been explored in time series analysis and which yet remain to be explored. An early example of research in this area is Quenouille (1957), where the temporal aggregation of $ARMA(p, d, q)$ processes is studied. Amemiya and Wu (1972) and Brewer (1973) review and generalize Quenouille's result by including exogenous variables. Zellner and Montmarquette (1971) discuss the effects of temporal aggregation on estimation and testing. Engle (1969) and Wei (1978) analyze the effects of temporal aggregation on parameter estimation in a distributed lag model. Granger and Lee (1999) discuss the implications of aggregation on the nonlinearity. Other

D. Tserkezos (✉)
Department of Economics and Business, Neapolis University Paphos, Paphos, Cyprus
e-mail: d.tserkezos@nup.ac.cy

I. T. Kokores et al. (eds.), *Money, Trade and Finance*,
https://doi.org/10.1007/978-3-030-73219-6_11

contributions in this area include Tiao (1972), Stram and Wei (1986), Weiss (1984), Rossana R.J. and Seater, J.J. (1995), and Marcellino (1999), Granger C.W.J. and Siklos, P.L (1995), Tommaso Di Fonzo (2003), Tserkezos et al. (1998) and Tserkezos D. (1992), only to name but a few.

In this short chapter, via Monte Carlo techniques we examine the impact of temporal aggregation and random sampling on the power of the Augmented Dickey Fuller t-test (hereafter ADF) stationarity test developed by Dickey, D.A. and W.A. Fuller (1979).[1] This test is a very popular test in testing stationarity of a time series. According to our results, temporal aggregation and random sampling affect quite seriously the power of the above test. Our results are in line with the more general findings of previous studies.[2]For the first time we present Monte Carlo experiments under different random sampling.

This chapter is organized as follows. Section 2 presents the simulation experiment. Section 3 is referring to the simulation results, and conclusions are presented in the final section.

2 Design of the Experiments

For our simulation experiment,[3] we used the following specification[4]:

$$y_t = ay_{t-1} + \left(\sqrt{(1-a^2)}\right)\varepsilon_t \qquad (11.1)$$

$$\varepsilon_t \approx NID\left(0, \sigma_e^2 = 1\right) \qquad (11.2)$$

Where y_t is the simulated variable,
ε_t is the disturbance term with variance $\sigma_e^2 = 1$,a is a parameter
The ADF t-test is calculated by using the specification:

$$z_t = \hat{\mu} + \hat{\beta}t + \hat{a}z_{t-1} + \sum_{k=1}^{l} \hat{\gamma}_K \Delta z_{t-1} + \hat{w}_t$$

[1] Dickey and Fuller (1979), 'Distribution of the Estimators for Time Series Regressions with a Unit Root', J.A.S.A., pp. 427–431.

[2] We are referring to the papers Lahiri, K. and Mamingi, N. (1995), Pierce and Snell (1995), Choi, I. and Chung, B.S. (1995) and Haug Al. (2002). Of course, there are the opposite opinions, including the research of Granger and Siklos (1995) and Rossana and Seater (1995) and Giles D (2014), in which unit root findings are invariant to the degree of temporal aggregation and the choice of systematic sampling level.

[3] The computations were performed with RATS 8.00 (www.estima.com) with a program written by the author. This RATS code program is available on request.

[4] $Var(y_t) = \frac{\sigma^2}{1-\rho^2}$.

with $z_t = y_t$ or the corresponding aggregated data.

The reader is refereed to Said and Dickey (1984)[5] for the definitions of the test.

In order to test the performance of the ADF t-test, we use the simulated data under two data 'transformations' approaches, say Temporally Aggregated and Randomly Sampled data.

Temporal aggregates are formed by averaging basic observations over nonoverlapping intervals. Let y_T^A represent the temporally aggregated data:

$$y_T^A = Cy_t \tag{11.3}$$

Where y_T^A is the temporal aggregated data, m is the time aggregation level and C is a time aggregation[6] matrix of the form:

$$C = \begin{bmatrix} 11\ 1100000000000000000000 \\ 00000011\ 11000\ 0000000000 \\ 0000000000 \quad 0011 \quad 1100000 \\ \ldots \\ 0000 \quad 0000000000 \quad 111 \quad 11 \end{bmatrix} \tag{11.4}$$

In the random sampled approach, temporally aggregated data were obtained at each iteration, using a random starting period in the whole sample data and averaging the selected observations using the C matrix at 20 different time aggregation levels.

The sampling intervals examined are 1 to 20 observations of the basic time series. Under the null hypothesis n of stationarity, 5000 replications of the basic time series (1)–(2) are generated and time aggregated for each sampling interval. The ADF t-test was used to test the stationary of the 20 times aggregated values of variable y_t.

[5] Said and Dickey (1984) 'Testing for Unit Root in Autoregressive Moving Average Models of Unknown Order', Biometrica 71: 599–607; Fuller(1976) Introduction to Statistical Time Series, New York, Wiley; Dickey and Fuller (1979). Distribution of the Estimators for Time Series Regressions with a Unit Root, J.A.S.A., pp. 427–431. The (approximate) critical values for t-test are from: MacKinnon (1991) 'Critical Values for Cointegration Tests'. in R.F. Engle and C.W.J. Granger (eds). *Long-Run Economic Relationships*, London, Oxford, pp. 267–276.

[6] For more about these Time-Aggregation relations using matrix approach, see: Gilbert (1977, 223–225). A similar aggregation formulation is $\tilde{r}_T = \frac{1}{m}\left(\sum_{j=o}^{m-1} L^j\right) r_t$, where L is the backshift operator on t.

3 Results

Some of the results of our Monte Carlo experiments are summarized in Figs. 11.1 and 11.2 and Tables 11.1 and 11.2 in the Appendix.

The following conclusions regarding the effects of time aggregation on the reliability of the ADF test can be drawn from an analysis of the data in Tables 11.1 and 11.2.

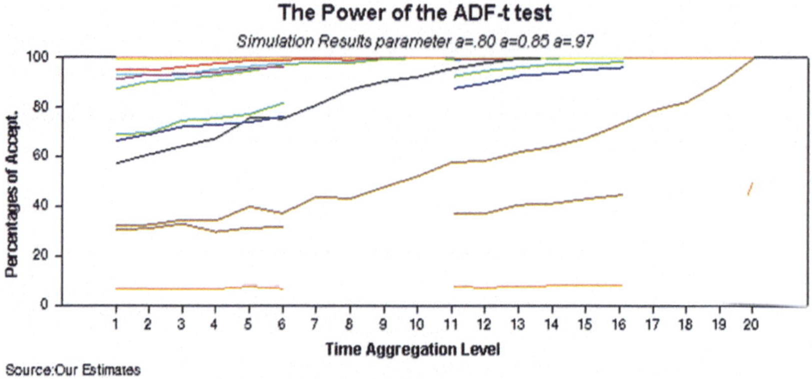

Fig. 11.1 The power of the ADF t-test in relation to different number of available data, different temporal disaggregation level at 0.025 significance level and the parameter $a = 0.8$, $a = 0.9$ and $a = 0.98$

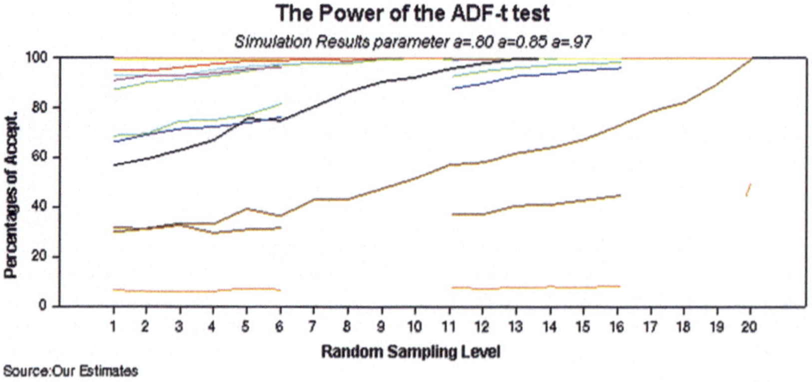

Fig. 11.2 The power of the ADF t-test in relation to different number of available data, different time disaggregation random sampling level at 0.025 significance level and the parameter $a = 0.8$, $a = 0.9$ and $a = 0.98$

In Fig. 11.1, we present graphically the power of the ADF t-test for testing stationarity, under different number of available data, different temporal aggregation level and different values of the parameter a (0.8, 0.9, 0.98) at a 0.025 significance level for testing stationarity.

An arithmetic presentation of the results of Fig. 11.1 is given in Table 11.1 in the Appendix.

Figure 11.2 and Table 11.2 present similar results for the case of random sampling.

According to the above results, we may conclude that in general there are negative implications of the power of the ADF t-test due to different levels of temporal aggregation. These effects are getting smaller as the number of the available data is increasing, but this improvement is weakening as the number of the parameter a is getting near number 1.

4 Conclusions

The results of this note show the importance of temporal aggregation and random sampling in applied time series work. Using Monte Carlo simulation techniques, we found that by using temporally aggregated and randomly sampled data, the use of the ADF t-test could lead to wrong conclusions about the stationarity characteristics of a time series.

As the span of disaggregation widens, the time series properties are distorted, leading to wrong conclusions about the stationary characteristics of a time series. Using time aggregated or randomly sampled data and the ADF t-test for testing stationarity, the power of this test is distorted dramatically.

The method of temporal aggregation of the data does not play a crucial role. On the basis of our Monte Carlo results, it emerges that on all the levels of disaggregation (aggregation) use of temporally aggregated or randomly sampled data leads to quit similar results.

Lastly, the conclusions of this short chapter are in line with the more general findings[7] of similar studies on the negative effects of time aggregation and systematic sampling on the effectiveness of the ADF t-test. On the contrary, we extend these results using randomly sampled data.

[7] We are referring to the papers Lahiri, K. and Mamingi, N. (1995), Pierce and Snell (1995), Choi, I. and Chung, B.S. (1995) and Haug Al. (2002).

Appendix

Table 11.1 Accepted frequencies of the power of the ADF stationarity t-test at different number of observations, **temporal aggregation** level, 0.025 significance level and the parameter a

	Parameter a = 0.8								
Temporal aggregation level	Available data								
	400			600			800		
1	100	100	100	100	100	100	100	100	100
2	100	100	100	100	100	100	100	100	100
3	100	100	100	100	100	100	100	100	100
4	100	100	100	100	100	100	100	100	100
5	100	100	100	100	100	100	100	100	100
6	100	100	100	100	100	100	100	100	100
7	100	100	100	100	100	100	100	100	100
8	99.6	100	100	100	100	100	100	100	100
9	97.8	100	100	100	100	100	100	10s0	100
10	95.6	99.8	99.8	100	100	100	100	100	100
11	92.2	100	100	100	100	100	100	100	100
12	90.4	99.6	99.6	100	100	100	100	100	100
13	87	98	98	99.2	100	100	100	100	100
14	80.8	98.2	98.2	99.6	100	100	100	100	100
15	75.4	97.2	97.2	99.2	100	100	100	100	100
16	75.6	94.8	94.8	99	100	100	100	100	100
17	67.4	93	93	97.8	100	100	100	100	100
18	64.2	91.4	91.4	96.4	99.8	99.8	100	100	100
19	60.8	90.4	90.4	95	99.6	99.6	99.6	100	100
20	57	87.4	87.4	95	99.8	99.8	100	100	100
	Parameter a = 0.9								
Temporal aggregation level	Available data								
	400			600			800		
1	99.6	100	100	100	100	100	100	100	100
2	89.8	99.8	99.8	100	100	100	100	100	100
3	82.2	99	99	100	100	100	100	100	100
4	78.8	98	98	99.4	100	100	100	100	100
5	73	96	96	98.4	100	100	100	100	100
6	67.6	95.2	95.2	97.8	100	100	100	100	100
7	64.2	93.6	93.6	97.4	99.8	99.8	100	100	100
8	62	92.8	92.8	96.2	100	100	100	100	100
9	58.4	89.8	89.8	94.8	99.6	99.6	99.6	100	100
10	57.8	87.6	87.6	92.6	99.2	99.2	99.4	100	100

(continued)

Table 11.1 (continued)

11	52.2	87.4	87.4	90.6	99.2	99.2	99	100	100
12	47.8	82.2	82.2	89	98.4	98.4	98.4	100	100
13	43.2	80.6	80.6	87.4	98	98	97.4	100	100
14	43.8	79.8	79.8	83.6	97.8	97.8	98	100	100
15	37.2	76.4	76.4	81.8	97.6	97.6	96.4	99.8	99.8
16	40	74	74	77.4	96.6	96.6	95.6	99.8	99.8
17	34.2	73	73	75.6	95.4	95.4	94.2	99.6	99.6
18	34.6	72.2	72.2	74.8	93	93	93.4	99.6	99.6
19	32.6	69.2	69.2	69.8	93.2	93.2	93.2	99.6	99.6
20	32.2	66.4	66.4	69	92.8	92.8	91.2	99.6	99.6
	Parameter a = 0.98								
Temporal aggregation level	Available data								
1	50	87.2	87.2	92.4	99.8	99.8	99.6	100	100
2	14.6	59	59	57.2	94.6	94.6	93	99.6	99.6
3	11	51	51	46.2	90.4	90.4	85.4	99.2	99.2
4	9.6	46.4	46.4	38.4	87	87	81.8	98.8	98.8
5	8.4	44.6	44.6	37	84.8	84.8	78.6	98.6	98.6
6	8.2	43	43	35.4	82.6	82.6	74.8	97.6	97.6
7	8.2	41.2	41.2	31.4	79.8	79.8	71.8	97.4	97.4
8	8	40.6	40.6	31.4	79.6	79.6	70.4	96.6	96.6
9	7.4	37.2	37.2	29.4	78	78	68.2	95.2	95.2
10	8	37.2	37.2	29.6	77.8	77.8	67.8	95.4	95.4
11	7.8	36.2	36.2	28.6	73.8	73.8	63.8	94.2	94.2
12	6.8	34.8	34.8	28.8	76.2	76.2	62.8	95	95
13	6.6	33.8	33.8	27.2	72.4	72.4	61.6	92.2	92.2
14	7.2	31.2	31.2	26	69	69	61.2	91.8	91.8
15	7	31.6	31.6	26.8	68.8	68.8	58.6	91.2	91.2
16	7.8	31.4	31.4	24.4	66.4	66.4	59.6	90.4	90.4
17	6.8	29.8	29.8	22.8	66.4	66.4	56.8	89.2	89.2
18	6.6	33	33	24.2	64.8	64.8	54.4	87.4	87.4
19	6.6	31.2	31.2	22.4	63.8	63.8	52.6	86.6	86.6
20	7	30.4	30.4	24	65.2	65.2	51.2	88	88

Source: Empirical probabilities of acceptance stationarity using the ADF t-test. Results based on 5000 replications

Table 11.2 Accepted frequencies of the power of the ADF stationarity t-test at different number of observations, **random sampling** level, 0.025 significance level and the parameter *a*

	Parameter $a = 0.8$								
Temporal aggregation level	Available data								
	400			600				800	
1	100	100	100	100	100	100	100	100	100
2	100	100	100	100	100	100	100	100	100
3	100	100	100	100	100	100	100	100	100
4	100	100	100	100	100	100	100	100	100
5	100	100	100	100	100	100	100	100	100
6	100	100	100	100	100	100	100	100	100
7	100	100	100	100	100	100	100	100	100
8	99.6	100	100	100	100	100	100	100	100
9	97.8	100	100	100	100	100	100	100	100
10	95.6	99.8	99.8	100	100	100	100	100	100
11	92.2	100	100	100	100	100	100	100	100
12	90.4	99.6	99.6	100	100	100	100	100	100
13	86.4	98	98	99.2	100	100	100	100	100
14	80.4	98	98	99.6	100	100	100	100	100
15	74.8	97.2	97.2	99.2	100	100	100	100	100
16	75.6	94.8	94.8	99	100	100	100	100	100
17	67	93	93	97.8	100	100	100	100	100
18	63	91.4	91.4	96.4	99.8	99.8	100	100	100
19	59.4	90.2	90.2	95	99.6	99.6	99.6	100	100
20	56.6	87.4	87.4	95	99.8	99.8	100	100	100
	Parameter $a = 0.9$								
Temporal aggregation level	Available data								
	400			600				800	
					0.8				
		400			600			800	
1	99.6	100	100	100	100	100	100	100	100
2	89.8	99.8	99.8	100	100	100	100	100	100
3	82.2	99	99	100	100	100	100	100	100
4	78.6	98	98	99.4	100	100	100	100	100
5	72.8	96	96	98.4	100	100	100	100	100
6	67.4	95.2	95.2	97.8	100	100	100	100	100
7	64	93.6	93.6	97.2	99.8	99.8	100	100	100
8	61.8	92.8	92.8	96.2	100	100	100	100	100

(*continued*)

Table 11.2 (continued)

9	58.2	89.8	89.8	94.8	99.6	99.6	99.6	100	100
10	57.2	87.6	87.6	92.6	99.2	99.2	99.4	100	100
11	51.6	87.2	87.2	90.6	99.2	99.2	99	100	100
12	47.4	82.2	82.2	88.8	98.4	98.4	98.4	100	100
13	43.2	80	80	87.4	98	98	97.4	100	100
14	43	79	79	83.4	97.8	97.8	98	100	100
15	36.4	76.2	76.2	81.6	97.4	97.4	96.4	99.8	99.8
16	39.4	74	74	77.2	96.6	96.6	95.6	99.8	99.8
17	33.2	72.4	72.4	75.2	95.4	95.4	94	99.6	99.6
18	33.6	71.6	71.6	74.8	93	93	93.2	99.6	99.6
19	31.4	69.2	69.2	69.6	93.2	93.2	93	99.6	99.6
20	31.6	66.2	66.2	68.8	92.8	92.8	91	99.6	99.6
	Parameter a = 0.98								
Temporal aggregation level	Available data								
	400			600				800	
					0.8				
		400			600			800	
1	50	87.2	87.2	92.4	99.8	99.8	99.6	100	100
2	14.6	59	59	57.2	94.6	94.6	93	99.6	99.6
3	11	51	51	46	90.4	90.4	85.4	99.2	99.2
4	9.6	46.4	46.4	38.4	87	87	81.8	98.8	98.8
5	8.4	44.6	44.6	37	84.8	84.8	78.6	98.6	98.6
6	8	42.8	42.8	35.4	82.6	82.6	74.8	97.6	97.6
7	8.2	41	41	31.4	79.8	79.8	71.8	97.4	97.4
8	7.8	40.6	40.6	31.4	79.4	79.4	70.2	96.6	96.6
9	7.4	37.2	37.2	29.4	77.8	77.8	68.2	95.2	95.2
10	8	37.2	37.2	29.6	77.6	77.6	67.8	95.4	95.4
11	7.6	36	36	28.6	73.8	73.8	63.6	94.2	94.2
12	6.6	34.6	34.6	28.6	76	76	62.8	95	95
13	6.2	33.8	33.8	27	72.4	72.4	61.6	92.2	92.2
14	6.8	31.2	31.2	25.8	68.8	68.8	61.2	91.8	91.8
15	7	31.6	31.6	26.6	68.6	68.6	58.6	91.2	91.2
16	7.6	31	31	24.2	66.4	66.4	59.2	90.4	90.4
17	6.4	29.6	29.6	22.4	66.4	66.4	56.6	89.2	89.2
18	6.4	32.8	32.8	23.6	64.8	64.8	54.2	87.4	87.4
19	6.4	31.2	31.2	22	63.8	63.8	52.6	86.6	86.6
20	6.6	30	30	23.2	65.2	65.2	50.4	88	88

Source: Empirical probabilities of acceptance stationarity using the ADF t-test. Results based on 5000 replications

References

Amemiya, T. and R.Y. Wu (1972). The Effect of Aggregation on Prediction in the Autoregressive Model. *Journal of the American Statistical Association*, No. 339, 628–632.

Brewer K.R.W. (1973). Some Consequences of Temporal Aggregation and Systematic Sampling for ARIMA and ARIMAX Models. *Journal of Econometrics*, 1, 133–154.

Choi, I. and Chung, B.S. (1995). Sampling Frequency and The Power of Tests for a Unit Root: A Simulation Study. *Economics Letters,* 49, 131–136.

Dickey, D. A. and W. A. Fuller (1979). Distribution of the Estimators for Autoregressive Time Series with a Unit Root. *Journal of the American Statistical Association*, 74, 427–431.

Di Fonzo, Tommaso (2003). Introduction to the Principles of Benchmarking and Temporal Dissagregation for Economic Series. *OECD/Eurostat Workshop* in "Application of Advanced Temporal Dissagregation Techniques to Economic Statistics". OECD Tour Europe, November 23. Available online: https://www.oecd.org/sdd/21783043.pdf.

Engle, R.F. (1969). *Biases from Time-Aggregation of Distributed Lag Models.* Ph.D. Dissertation, Cornell University.

Fuller (1976). *Introduction to Statistical Time Series.* New York: Wiley.

Gilbert, C.L., (1977). Estimation of Regression Equations Using Mixed Annual and Quarterly Data. *Journal of Econometrics*, 221–239.

Giles, David C. (2014). *Advanced Research Methods in Psychology.* London: Routledge.

Granger, C.W.J. and T.-H. Lee (1999). The Effect of Aggregation on Nonlinearity. *Econometric Reviews*, 18, 259–269.

Granger C.W.J. and Siklos, P.L. (1995). Systematic Sampling, Temporal Aggregation, Seasonal Adjustment and Cointegration: Theory and Evidence. *Journal of Econometrics*, 66, 357–369.

Haug, Alfred (2002). Temporal Aggregation and the Power of Cointegration Tests: A Monte Carlo Study. *Oxford Bulletin of Economics and Statistics* 64(4), 399–12.

Lahiri, K. and Mamingi, N. (1995). Testing for Cointegration: Power versus Frequency of Observation – Another View. *Economics Letters,* 49, 121–124.

Marcellino, M. (1999). Some Consequences of Temporal Aggregation in Empirical Analysis. *Journal of Economic and Business Statistics*, 17, 129–136.

MacKinnon, J.G. (1991). Critical Values for Cointegration Tests. In R.F. Engle and C.W.J. Granger (Eds.), *Long-Run Economic Relationships* (pp. 267–276). London: Oxford UP.

Quenouille, M.H. (1957). *The Analysis of Multiple Time Series.* London: Griffin.

Pierce R.G. and Snell, A. J. (1995). Temporal Aggregation and the Power of Tests for a Unit Root. *Journal of Econometrics*, 65, 333–345.

Rossana R. J. and Seater, J.J. (1995). Temporal Aggregation and Economic Time Series. *Journal of Business and Economic Statistics*, 13, 441–451.

Said and Dickey (1984). Testing for Unit Root in Autoregressive Moving Average Models of Unknown Order. *Biometrica*, 71, 599–607.

Stram, D.O. and W.W.S. Wei (1986). Temporal Aggregation in the ARIMA Process. *Journal of Time Series Analysis*, 7, 279–292.

Tiao, G.C. (1972). Asymptotic Behaviour of Temporal Aggregates of Time Series. *Biometrika*, 59, 525–531.

Tserkezos D. (1992). Forecasting Residential Electricity Consumption in Greece Using Monthly and Quarterly Data. *Energy Economics*. July 1992, 14(3) 226–232.

Tserkezos D., Georgoutsos D. and Kouretas G. (1998). Temporal Aggregation in Structure VAR Models. *Applied Stochastic Models and Data Analysis*, 14, 19–34.

Weiss, A. A. (1984). Systematic Sampling and Temporal Aggregation in Time Series Models. *Journal of Econometrics*, 26, 271–281.

Wei, W.W.S. (1978). The Effect of Temporal Aggregation on Parameter Estimation in Distributed Lag Models. *Journal of Econometrics*, 8, 237–246.

Zellner A. and Montmarquette C. (1971). A Study of Some Aspects of Temporal Aggregation Problems in Econometric Analyses. *Review of Economics and Statistics*, 63, 335–342.

PART VI

International Business: Expansion and Environmental Issues

CHAPTER 12

Revisiting the Environmental Kuznets Curve Hypothesis: A Dynamic Panel VAR Analysis

Michael L. Polemis

1 Introduction

Going back to the seminal paper of Grossman and Krueger (1995), we examine herein the Environmental Kuznets Curve (EKC) hypothesis using a dynamic Panel VAR approach to reveal the true covariates of environmental pollution. This approach allows a flexible way to analyse correlations of the underlying environmental Kuznets curve based on transmission pathways and micro-foundations.

Since then there are hundreds of academic papers on the examination of the EKC hypothesis. Even though the topic might be considered narrow, the literature on it is broad in its relevance, being pertinent to theory (Smulders et al. 2011; Cassou and Hamilton 2004), total factor productivity (Chimeli and Braden 2005), growth, market concentration (Gillanders and Whelan 2014; Polemis 2017b), among others. The topic has become of interest to economists in a number of fields such as

M. L. Polemis (✉)
Department of Economics, University of Piraeus, Piraeus, Greece

Hellenic Competition Commission, Athens, Greece
e-mail: mpolemis@unipi.gr

I. T. Kokores et al. (eds.), *Money, Trade and Finance*,
https://doi.org/10.1007/978-3-030-73219-6_12

Environmental Economics, Industrial Organization and Applied Econometrics *inter alia* which, along with the availability of data, helped spawn a large empirical literature and also several important empirical contributions.

This literature spans more than 20 years and dozens of countries, uses data at various levels of spatial aggregation, from individual countries to continent-sized countries, like the US or economic blocks such as the EU, the OECD, or the BRICS countries (see, among others, Azevedo et al. 2018; Polemis and Stengos 2018a; Rasli et al. 2018; Sephton and Mann 2016; Galeotti et al. 2009), covers periods of less than one year to longer than a decade and ranges in frequency from a single day to one month, considers both macroeconomic and microeconomic variables (see, for example, Zambrano-Monserrate et al. 2018), which are sometimes in logs and sometimes in levels.

One would expect that this volume of work would have led to some robust conclusions on the existence of the EKC hypothesis, and on what factors this magnitude depends on. Though many important contributions have been made, the basic question of how large and non-transitory is the existence of the EKC hypothesis has drawn widely different answers. Part of the reason is that different markets exhibit different dynamics because they differ along with relevant characteristics, such as competitiveness. But part of the reason may simply come down to differences in the data structure, for example data frequency, spatial aggregation and price definition, or to minor differences in specification, for example lag structure. If different data structures tend to provide different patterns of pollution–growth nexus, then much of what seems like divergence in point estimates across studies might disappear if the underlying data were similarly configured. In addition to this, there seems to be a tendency for some recent contributions finding alternative patterns of this relationship (N-shaped curves). This might be because they are becoming less important over time, but could also be because researchers look at new research directions (López Menéndez et al. 2014; Halkos and Polemis 2018), our results are more likely to be considered a publishable contribution when they differ from prior findings.

Our study contributes to the literature on many fronts. First and foremost, we test the validity of the EKC hypothesis when global (CO_2 emissions) and local pollutants (SO_2 and NO_X emissions) are taken into account. Second, unlike traditional panel data approaches which provide a specific functional form for the entire panel, our approach allows us to identify whether the EKC hypothesis holds across the 51 states even in a panel set-up. Third, we examine underlying short-run dynamics within a panel-VAR. Fourth, the empirical findings will assist government officials and policymakers in their effort to design and implement a blend of policy measures targeted at the limitation of environmental degradation in the electricity US sector across the regions (states).

The rest of this chapter is structured as follows: Sect. 2 surveys the literature, while Sect. 3 performs the necessary preliminary panel unit root and cointegration testing. Section 4 discusses the Panel-VAR methodology and the empirical findings. Finally, Sect. 5 concludes the chapter and provides some policy implications.

2 Literature Review

The literature examining the existence of the EKC using panel data techniques has steered some debates as empirical results demonstrate considerable variability (see, for example, Özokcu and Özdemir 2017; Halkos and Managi 2017; Desbordes and Verardi 2012; Bertinelli and Strobl, 2005; Millimet et al. 2003; Taskin and Zaim, 2000). However, it is widely regarded that there should be a non-linear relationship between the level of pollution and economic growth as proxied by GDP/capita in most studies.[1]

Specifically, the EKC hypothesis has primarily concentrated on time series studies for individual countries or panel data analyses of a set of countries, often clubbed together, based on their level of development (Carson 2010). The varied evidence on the EKC hypothesis witnessed in the literature, especially that from panel data estimates, could be the result of different methodologies and procedures used across countries to measure emissions (Apergis et al. 2017).

The parametric reduced-form equations (Hsueh 2015; Figueroa and Pasten 2013; Halkos and Tzeremes 2009) assume a unique response coefficient for the covariates in environmental pollution regressions. We argue herein that this assumption is too strong and thereby not plausible. The empirical evidence emphasizes the existence of multiple regimes (i.e.

[1] Most studies estimate reduced-form equations using parametric (e.g. piecewise linear, quadratic, cubic models) methods (see, for example, Hsueh 2015; Figueroa and Pasten 2013; Halkos and Tzeremes 2009). But non-parametric methods are also applied whether semiparametric, or partially linear models, or spline specifications (Desbordes and Verardi 2012; Bertinelli and Strobl 2005).

threshold effects) followed by strong non-linear effects (see Halkos and Polemis 2018; Millimet et al. 2003). Along these lines, Narayan and Narayan (2010), test the EKC hypothesis for 43 developing countries based on the short-run and long-run income elasticities. They argue that only for the Middle Eastern and South Asian panels the income elasticity in the long run is smaller than in the short run, implying that carbon dioxide emission has fallen with a rise in income. Halkos and Tzeremes (Halkos and Tzeremes 2009) claim that some global pollutants such as CO_2 emissions exhibit an N shape, implying that the environmental damage starts rising again after a fall to a specific point. On the other hand, relatively few empirical studies adopt a simultaneous equations system to address the impact of economic growth on environmental degradation.

Apergis (2016) tests the validity of the EKC hypothesis using both panel and time series standard cointegration techniques utilizing data from fifteen countries, spanning the period 1960–2013. The empirical findings indicate that the EKC hypothesis holds in 12 out of the 15 countries, while the evidence from panel cointegration methodologies is mixed. However, as suggested by Hong and Wagner (2008), the empirical EKC literature fails to acknowledge the presence of non-linear panel cointegration testing since all of the empirical studies apply linear cointegration tests along the lines of Pedroni (1999) and Westerlund (2007). We must argue though that the use of traditional linear panel cointegration tests in non-linear relationships is strongly biased (see, for example, Enders and Siklos 2001; Enders and Granger 1998).

In a more recent study, Apergis et al. (2017) assess the validity of the hypothesis across the US states, over the period 1960–2010 using the common correlated effects estimation. In their study, they find that the EKC hypothesis holds in only ten states, while the remaining 38 states should be reforming their environmental regulatory policies to prevent environmental degradation coming only at the expense of production and economic growth.

Moreover, Halkos and Polemis (2017) examine the validity of the EKC hypothesis when financial development is taking into consideration. The empirical findings do indicate that local and global pollutants redefine the EKC hypothesis uncovering an N-shape relationship in both static and dynamic framework with a very slow adjustment. Similarly, Ozturk and Acaravci (2013) investigate the impact of financial development on the EKC nexus. Their results indicate the existence of a neutral effect between financial development proxied by variables such as treasury bonds, non-performing loans, credit risk, stocks and the level of environmental awareness.

Lastly, Polemis (2017b) employed a semiparametric fixed effects estimator to examine the impact of market structure on the level of toxic chemical releases to a sample of four-digit industrial sectors among the US states. Contrary to the parametric results, the study uncovers an inverted "*U-shaped*" relationship between industrial output and toxic chemical releases when market concentration is present.

3 Data and Preliminary Testing

3.1 Sample Variables and Unit Root Testing

Our empirical application is based on a panel of 51 US regions covering the period from 1990 to 2012. The environmental variables (CO_2, SO_2 and NOx emissions per capita) are obtained by the Energy Information Administration (EIA), while logged values of per capita real GDP (in 2009 $US) by the state are drawn from the Regional Economic Accounts of the Bureau of Economic Analysis. Table 12.1 depicts the main descriptive statistics from the model variables.

Before testing for non-stationarity in the underlying data generating process of our panel data set, we opt to examine any cross-section dependence. We use the cross-section dependence tests proposed by Breusch

Table 12.1 Descriptive statistics

Variables	*Obs*	*Mean*	*St. dev*	*Min*	*Max*
log(GDP)	1173	4.578	20.985	96.291	442.339
$\log(GDP)^2$	1173	0.152	1.404	9.774	60.674
$\log(GDP)^3$	1173	4.240	17.981	76.244	323.301
$\log(GDP)^4$	1173	5.238	27.435	143.700	752.676
SO_2	1173	0.047	0.063	0.011	0.554
NO_X	1173	0.028	0.041	0.015	0.419
CO_2	1173	11.370	14.030	0.011	95.130

Notes: NOx stands for the NOx per capita emissions, SO_2 stands for the SO_2 per capita emissions, CO_2 stands for the CO_2 per capita emissions (metric tonnes/capita) and $lgdp^2$ is the squared logged real GDP per capita in constant 2009 USD dollar prices. Standard errors are 5% on each side generated by Monte-Carlo with 500 repetitions and Pagan (1980) and Pesaran (2006). Both tests strongly reject the null hypothesis (p-value = 0.000) of cross-section independence for all the models.

Next we employ the second-generation unit root test proposed by Pesaran (2007) denoted as *CIPS* properly accounting for cross-section dependence. Similarly, to Breitung and Das (2005), the Pesaran test is based on OLS regressions. However, the former breaks down if it is assumed that cross-correlation is due to common factors while the latter remains valid (Polemis and Stengos 2018b). The CIPS panel unit root test does not require the estimation of factor loading to eliminate cross-sectional dependence. According to Apergis et al. (2017), "the usual ADF regression is augmented to include the lagged cross-sectional mean and its first difference to capture the cross-sectional dependence that arises through a single-factor model." As it is evident, the test results strongly suggest that except for the CO_2 variable, the rest of the sample variables are integrated of order one (I-1), supporting the presence of a unit root (see Table 12.2).

Table 12.2 Second generation panel unit root test results

Test	CO_2	SO_2	NO_x	*GDP*	GDP^2	GDP^3	GDP^4
Levels							
CIPS with an intercept	-2.358***	-2.049	-2.028	-1.714	-1.654	-1.761	-1.832
CIPS with an intercept and a trend	-3.313***	-2.314	-2.105	-2.070	-1.931	-1.629	-1.590
First differences							
CIPS with an intercept	–	-4.386***	-4.915***	-3.644***	-3.545***	-3.320***	-3.115***
CIPS with an intercept and a trend	–	-4.620***	-4.979***	-3.889***	-3.758***	-3.393***	-3.202***

Notes: CIPS stands for the cross-sectionally augmented IPS (CIPS) panel unit root test. The null hypothesis assumes stationarity. Significant at ***1%

3.2 Cointegration Testing

In order to investigate whether a long-run equilibrium relationship exists among the variables in both models, we implement two cointegration tests proposed by Westerlund (2007) that allow for cross-section dependence. The results of the tests are presented in Table 12.3; the critical values were created using a bootstrapping method. The results clearly indicate that the four tests reject the null hypothesis of no cointegration for both models.

The existence of cointegration among the model variables is also evident if we perform Pedroni's (1999) panel cointegration test statistics. From Table 12.3, we argue that nearly all tests reject the null hypothesis of no cointegration in the SO_2 and the NO_X model, respectively. The results clearly indicate that the first and the second test reject the null hypothesis of no cointegration for both models (Table 12.4).

Table 12.3 Westerlund ECM panel cointegration tests

Equation	*Statistic*			
	G_τ	G_α	P_τ	P_α
SO_2 = f(GDP)	-3.049***	-15.449***	-17.690***	-17.457***
	(0.000)	(0.000)	(0.001)	(0.000)
SO_2 = f(GDP)^2	-3.003***	-14.973***	-18.085***	-18.331***
	(0.000)	(0.001)	(0.001)	(0.000)
SO_2 = f(GDP)^3	-2.997***	-14.896***	-17.672***	-18.803***
	(0.000)	(0.001)	(0.001)	(0.000)
SO_2 = f(GDP)^4	-2.963***	-14.734***	-17.635***	-19.328***
	(0.000)	(0.001)	(0.002)	(0.000)
NO_X = f(GDP)	-2.566**	-16.381***	-25.759***	-16.722***
	(0.031)	(0.000)	(0.000)	(0.000)
NO_X = f(GDP)^2	-2.552**	-17.221***	-25.758***	-21.524***
	(0.041)	(0.000)	(0.000)	(0.000)
NO_X = f(GDP)^3	-2.584**	-17.546***	-22.800***	-18.517***
	(0.021)	(0.000)	(0.000)	(0.000)
NO_X = f(GDP)^4	-2.662***	-18.300***	-21.241***	-16.558***
	(0.003)	(0.000)	(0.000)	(0.000)

Notes: The test regression was fitted with a constant and trend and one lag and lead. The kernel bandwidth was set according to the rule $4(T/100)^{2/9}$. The null hypothesis assumes that there is no cointegration. The numbers in parentheses denote the p-values. Significant at ***1% and **5%, respectively

Table 12.4 Pedroni panel cointegration tests

Model 1: Dependent variable SO_2 *(with trend)*			
Within dimension test statistics		*Between dimension test statistics*	
Panel v-statistic	4.109***	Group ρ-statistic	5.276***
	(0.000)		(0.000)
Panel ρ-statistic	2.489**	Group PP-statistic	-10.180***
	(0.012)		(0.000)
Panel PP-statistic	-9.202***	Group ADF-statistic	-3.945***
	(0.000)		(0.000)
Panel ADF-statistic	-7.606***		
	(0.000)		
Model 2: Dependent variable NO_X *(with trend)*			
Within dimension test statistics		*Between dimension test statistics*	
Panel v-statistic	-0.008	Group ρ-statistic	2.012**
	(0.990)		(0.044)
Panel ρ-statistic	-0.197	Group PP-statistic	-6.699***
	(0.847)		(0.000)
Panel PP-statistic	-6.731***	Group ADF-statistic	-4.487***
	(0.000)		(0.000)
Panel ADF-statistic	-5.740***		
	(0.000)		

Notes: Of the seven tests, the panel v-statistic is a one-sided test where large positive values reject the null hypothesis of no cointegration, whereas large negative values for the remaining test statistics reject the null hypothesis of no cointegration. Significant at ***1% and **5%, respectively

4 Empirical Methodology and Results

Having derived the long-run relationship, we turn next to the underlying short-run dynamics. We opt for a panel-VAR analysis. For each estimated group, all variables within the panel VAR enter as endogenous.

For exposition purposes, we present a first-order 4 × 4 panel-VAR model:

$$X_{it} = \mu_i + \Phi X_{it-1} + \gamma_t + u_i + e_{it}, i = 1,\ldots,N, t = 1,\ldots,T. \quad (12.1)$$

where X_{it} is a vector of four random variables, that is logged GDP per capita ($lgdp_{it}$) and its powers (i.e. $lgdp_{it}^2$, $lgdp_{it}^3$, $lgdp_{it}^4$), the level of per capita CO_2 emissions (CO_{2it}), the level of per capita SO_2 emissions (SO_{2it}) and, finally, the level of per capita NO_X emissions (NO_{Xit}). Thus, Φ is a 4 × 4 matrix of coefficients, and μ_i is a vector of μ individual effects. The γ_t stands for the time fixed effects and u_i are the state fixed effects that control for differences across regions (e.g. differences in technology used in the production process, economic conditions, environmental legislation, etc.). Finally, e_{it} is the idiosyncratic error term that is assumed to be i.i.d.

The panel-VAR takes the following form[2]:

$$q_{it} = a_{10} + \sum_{J}^{j=1} \beta_{11j} q_{it-j} + \sum_{J}^{j=1} \beta_{12j} k_{it-j} + \sum_{J}^{j=1} \beta_{13j} h_{it-j} + \sum_{J}^{j=1} \beta_{14j} ex_{it-j} + e_{1it} \tag{12.2}$$

$$k_{it} = a_{20} + \sum_{J}^{j=1} \beta_{21j} q_{it-j} + \sum_{J}^{j=1} \beta_{22j} k_{it-j} + \sum_{J}^{j=1} \beta_{23j} h_{it-j} + \sum_{J}^{j=1} \beta_{24j} ex_{it-j} + e_{2it} \tag{12.3}$$

$$h_{it} = a_{30} + \sum_{J}^{j=1} \beta_{31j} q_{it-j} + \sum_{J}^{j=1} \beta_{32j} k_{it-j} + \sum_{J}^{j=1} \beta_{33j} h_{it-j} + \sum_{J}^{j=1} \beta_{34j} ex_{it-j} + e_{3it} \tag{12.4}$$

$$ex_{it} = a_{40} + \sum_{J}^{j=1} \beta_{41j} q_{it-j} + \sum_{J}^{j=1} \beta_{42j} k_{it-j} + \sum_{J}^{j=1} \beta_{43j} h_{it-j} + \sum_{J}^{j=1} \beta_{44j} ex_{it-j} + e_{4it} \tag{12.5}$$

The moving averages (MA) form of the model sets q_{it}, k_{it}, h_{it} and ex_{it}, equal to a set of present and past residuals e_1, e_2, e_3 and e_4 from the panel-VAR estimation:

$$q_{it} = \mu_{10} + \sum_{J}^{j=1} b_{11j} e_{1it-j} + \sum_{J}^{j=1} b_{12j} e_{2it-j} + \sum_{J}^{j=1} b_{13j} e_{3it-j} + \sum_{J}^{j=1} b_{14j} e_{4it-j} + e_{1it} \tag{12.6}$$

$$k_{it} = \mu_{20} + \sum_{J}^{j=1} b_{21j} e_{1it-j} + \sum_{J}^{j=1} b_{22j} e_{2it-j} + \sum_{J}^{j=1} b_{23j} e_{3it-j} + \sum_{J}^{j=1} b_{24j} e_{4it-j} + e_{2it} \tag{12.7}$$

$$h_{it} = \mu_{30} + \sum_{J}^{j=1} b_{31j} e_{1it-j} + \sum_{J}^{j=1} b_{32j} e_{2it-j} + \sum_{J}^{j=1} b_{33j} e_{3it-j} + \sum_{J}^{j=1} b_{34j} e_{4it-j} + e_{3it} \tag{12.8}$$

$$ex_{it} = \mu_{40} + \sum_{J}^{j=1} b_{41j} e_{1it-j} + \sum_{J}^{j=1} b_{42j} e_{2it-j} + \sum_{J}^{j=1} b_{43j} e_{3it-j} + \sum_{J}^{j=1} b_{44j} e_{4it-j} + e_{4it} \tag{12.9}$$

[2] For the sake of concreteness, we omit the fixed effects from the relevant equations.

We orthogonalize the residuals by multiplying the MA representation with the Cholesky decomposition of the covariance matrix of the residuals. Using the above panel-VAR individual heterogeneity in the levels is ensured by introducing fixed effects in the model, denoted μ_i, and the data are forward mean-differenced using the Helmert procedure (Arellano and Bover, 1995). Standard errors of the impulse response functions are calculated and confidence intervals are generated with Monte Carlo simulations.

As a first step in the panel VAR estimation, we shall choose the optimal lag order j for the right-hand variables in the system of equations (Lütkepohl, 2006).[3] In addition, normality tests for the residuals use the Sahpiro-Francia W-test.[4] Last we employ Monte Carlo simulations to estimate standard errors for the Impulse Response Functions (IRFs).

4.1 Impulse Response Functions

Having identified the existence of a structural relationship between the sample variables through the cointegration testing, we move to the next step of our analysis which is the GMM estimation of the panel-VAR and the extraction of the IRFs and VDC since the estimated coefficients of the panel-VAR do not have an economic interpretation (Polemis 2017a). It is worth mentioning that a more appropriate analysis in order to capture the dynamic relationships between the sample variables is to utilize a panel Vector Error Correction Model (PVECM) instead. However, the curvatures of the IRFs and the results of the VDC extracted by the PVECM did not display significant differences making our analysis rather robust.

More specifically, the IRFs derived from the unrestricted panel-VAR in the case of per capita NO_X emissions (NO_X), per capita SO_2 emissions (SO_2), per capita CO_2 emissions (CO_2) and real logged GDP per capita (lgdp) are reported in Fig. 12.1. This diagram plots the response of each variable in the Panel-VAR (NO_X, SO_2, CO_2 and lgdp) to its own innovation and the

[3]The Arellano-Bond GMM estimator is used for the lags of j = 1, 2 and 3 (see next subsection). Results are available upon request. Optimal lag order of one is based on the Akaike Information Criterion (AIC), confirmed by Arellano-Bond AR tests. To test for autocorrelation, more lags are added. The Sargan tests show that for lag ordered one, the null hypothesis cannot be rejected, and thus the VAR model is of order one. The lag order of one preserves the degrees of freedom and information, given the low time frequency of the data.

[4]The results do not show violation of the normality. Panel VAR results are available under request.

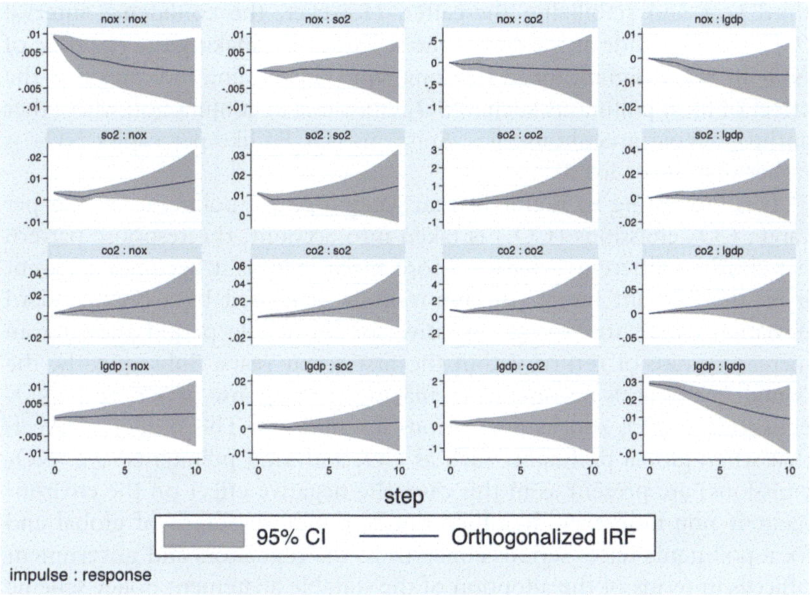

Fig. 12.1 Impulse Response Functions (IRFs) for per capita NO_X emissions (NO_X), per capita SO_2 emissions (SO_2), per capita CO_2 emissions (CO_2) and real logged GDP per capita (lgdp). Note: Each row of the diagram shows the response of each variable to a one standard deviation shock of the other variables entered in Panel-VAR. The ordering of the variables entered the panel-VAR is as follows: NO_X, SO_2, CO_2 and lGDP. In order to estimate the IRFs, we use the Cholesky decomposition method adjusted by the degrees of freedom. NOx stands for the NOx per capita emissions, SO_2 stands for the SO_2 per capita emissions, CO_2 stands for the CO_2 per capita emissions and lgdp is the real logged GDP per capita in constant 2009 USD dollar prices. Standard errors are 5% on each side generated by Monte-Carlo with 500 repetitions

innovations of the other variables within a confidence interval. The first column shows the response of per capita NO_X emissions (NOx) to a one standard deviation shock in the NO_X, SO_2, CO_2 and lgdp variables.

The response of NO_X to its own innovations is downward sloping but positive across the whole simulated time period (ten years) turning into negative after the ninth year of the analysis. In addition, the response of per capita NO_X emissions (NO_X) to innovations generated by the per capita SO_2 emissions (SO_2) is negative in the short run (e.g. for the first three simulated years), where it reaches its low turning into positive after the third year and stabilizing thereafter. However, the confidence interval (CI) becomes wide at the end of the seventh year, making the response of NO_X to SO_2 insignificant in the long run. This finding indicates that the effect of local pollutants such as SO_2 emissions in conjunction with other anthropogenic greenhouse gas emissions (GCE) like per capita NOx is rather than short-lived.

It is interesting to highlight that when a global pollutant such as per capita CO_2 emissions (CO_2) is taken into account, the response pattern has clearly a different behavior. More specifically, as it becomes apparent from the relevant figure, the innovations generated by a one standard deviation shock are strongly positive for the whole period showing an increasing rate of return within the first seven years. Subsequently, the confidence bounds become wide, making the response of per capita NO_X emissions to CO_2 shocks fluctuations insignificant. This outcome reveals that when global pollutants such as CO_2 and local pollutants (e.g. NO_X emissions) are present as in this case, the negative effect on the environment is non-transitory. In other words, the co-existence of global and local pollutants raises serious concerns to the regulators and government officials in terms of the adoption of the suitable abatement policy scheme (i.e. green taxes, tradable permits, voluntary schemes, etc.) since environmental degradation is time invariant.

Lastly, the response of NO_X to one standard innovation of per capita GDP (lgdp) follows a slightly positive but stable statistically significant relationship until the first five years of the simulated period. Thereafter, confidence bands become wide, making the response of NO_X to income shocks (lgdp) insignificant. This means that in the short run the effect of growth on the environmental degradation when a local pollutant such as NO_X is taken into consideration is strongly positive and reversed when the economy reaches its peak indicating a non-linear relationship between economic growth and environmental pollution. This outcome lends support to the "*EKC hypothesis*", although the exact pattern of this relationship is unknown (i.e. inverted U). This finding is in alignment with other similar studies (see, for example, Millimet et al. 2003; Halkos and Tzeremes 2009; Apergis 2016).

The discussion now turns to the investigation of the response pattern of per capita SO_2 emissions (SO_2) to its own innovations and the one standard deviation shocks in the NO_X, CO_2 and lgdp variables. As it is clear from Fig. 12.3, the response of SO_2 is negative in the very short-run period (almost one year after the initial shock), turning into positive henceforth. The peak response occurs ten years after the initial shock, indicating that the impact of the local pollutant to its own innovations is non-transitory. However, the confidence bands become wide at the end of the eighth year, making the response of SO_2 to its own innovations insignificant. Taken together, this set of findings points out that the responses last at least eight years after the initial shock.

It is noteworthy that the response of SO_2 to innovations of NO_X reveals a non-linear relationship starting from negative (for the first two years after the initial shock) to positive (at the end of the fourth year) and declining thereafter. This is consistent with an inverted N-shaped curve and the existence of two turning points (low and high, respectively). Moreover, the response of per capita SO_2 emissions (SO_2) to innovations, generated by the increase of per capita CO_2 emissions (CO_2), are strongly positive and statistically significant since the responses are captured around a narrow CI, for the whole simulated period showing an increasing rate of return within the first ten years of after the initial shock. Similarly, with the previous findings, this pattern is consistent with the notion that CO_2 emissions generated mostly by industrial activities in the energy sector (i.e. generation of electricity, natural gas and oil extraction, etc.) are most evident in the long run since the response of per capita SO_2 to innovations generated by the CO_2 variable exceed 2% at the end of the simulated period (ten years after the shock). As in the case of NO_X emissions, the response of SO_2 to a one standard innovation of per capita GDP (lgdp) follows a positively stable and statistically significant path until the first five years of the simulated period. Thereafter, confidence bands become wide, making the response of SO_2 to growth shocks not statistically significant. In other words, in the short run the effect of growth on environmental degradation, when a local pollutant such as SO_2 is taken into account, is strongly positive and reversed when the economy reaches its peak. This behavior is consistent with a non-linear relationship between economic growth and environmental degradation.

The discussion now turns to the examination of the response of per capita CO_2 emissions (CO_2) to its own innovations, and the one standard deviation shocks of the rest (endogenous) variables (e.g. NO_X, SO_2 and lgdp) is taken into account. More specifically, the response of a global pollutant to one standard deviation shock of NO_X is negative throughout the ten-year simulated period. On the contrary, the response of CO_2 to innovations of SO_2 reveals a positive and stable linear relationship lasting nearly more than six years after the initial shock. Within the next simulated period, the confidence bands become wide, making the response insignificant. Lastly, the response of CO_2 to its own innovations follows a similar plot, while in the short run the effect of growth on the environmental degradation, when a global pollutant (CO_2) is taken into account, is positive and reversed when the economy reaches its peak, indicating a non-linear relationship between economic growth and environmental pollution.

The above findings do not drastically change when the extra polynomial powers of lgdp are taken into consideration (lgdp2, lgdp3 and lgdp4). As a general statement, we argue that non-linearities are present in most of the cases regarding the responses of global (CO_2) and local pollutants (NO_X and SO_2) to their own innovations and the other variables as well. These empirical findings do confirm the previous cointegration analysis highlighting the existence of non-linear relationships when all the sample variables are endogenous as in the case of Panel-VAR analysis (Figs. 12.2, 12.3 and 12.4).

Lastly, if we try to compare the IRF curvatures between the four relevant figures, some important results emerge. First, the response of SO_2 to a one standard innovation shock of the other local pollutant (i.e. per capita NO_X emissions in the energy sector) is more abrupt in the fourth model (i.e. when quartic GDP enters the Panel-VAR) than in the other three Panel-VARs since the relevant peak response within the short-run time span is greater in the former model than in the other three.

Second, in all of the estimated Panel-VARs, the income growth's shocks are positive and short-lived, lasting for almost five years. This finding reveals the absence of a sluggish adjustment mechanism, which may reflect weak competition and significant market power (SMP) by the incumbents in the US energy sector (Polemis 2017a).

Third and foremost, the rate of response of the global pollutant (CO_2) to income and environmental shocks (i.e. NO_X and SO_2 per capita emissions) differs significantly between the four Panel-VAR_S, indicating that combating CO_2 emissions requires the implementation of a mixture of environmental policy measures (i.e. market based instruments, command and control measures).

4.2 *Variance Decomposition Analysis*

These results are further confirmed by the variance decompositions estimations (VDCs) of the sample variables entering the Panel-VARs. More specifically, it becomes apparent from Table 12.5 (see Panel A) that in a

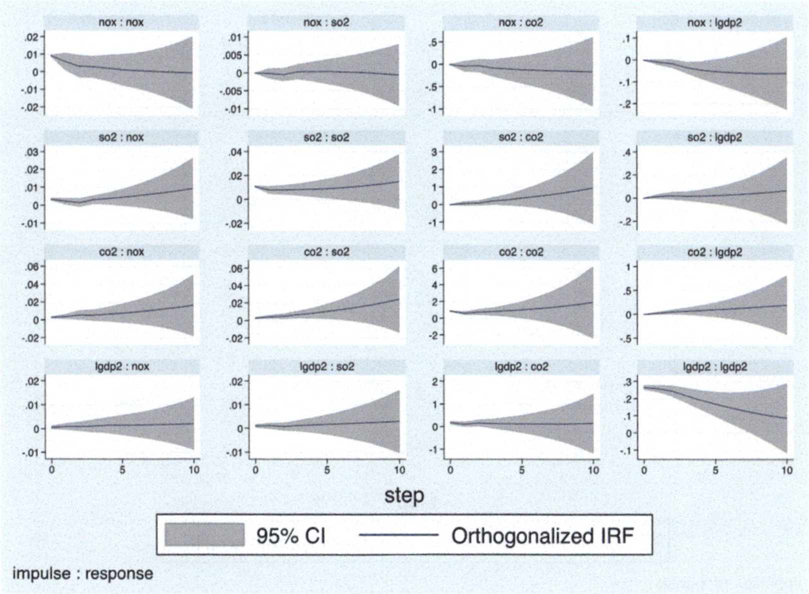

Fig. 12.2 Impulse Response Functions (IRFs) for per capita NO_X emissions (NO_X), per capita SO_2 emissions (SO_2), per capita CO_2 emissions (CO_2) and real squared logged GDP per capita (lgdp2). Note: Each row of the diagram shows the response of each variable to a one standard deviation shock of the other variables entered in Panel-VAR. The ordering of the variables entered the panel-VAR is as follows: NO_X, SO_2, CO_2 and lGDP. In order to estimate the IRFs, we use the Cholesky decomposition method adjusted by the degrees of freedom. NOx stands for the NOx per capita emissions, SO_2 stands for the SO_2 per capita emissions, CO_2 stands for the CO_2 per capita emissions and $lgdp^2$ is the squared logged real GDP per capita in constant 2009 USD dollar prices. Standard errors are 5% on each side generated by Monte-Carlo with 500 repetitions

simulated ten-year time frame from the initial shock, around 21.5% of the forecast error variance of per capita real logged GDP (lgdp) can be explained by disturbances in the global pollutant (CO_2), while around 4.1% from disturbances in one of the local pollutants such as per capita NO_X emissions (NO_X). Moreover, disturbances in the other local pollutant (per capita SO_2 emissions) appear to have minimal impact (1.6%) on growth (lgdp). This finding is also evident in the IRFs presented before. In addition, per capita CO_2 emissions (CO_2) are also confirmed to be

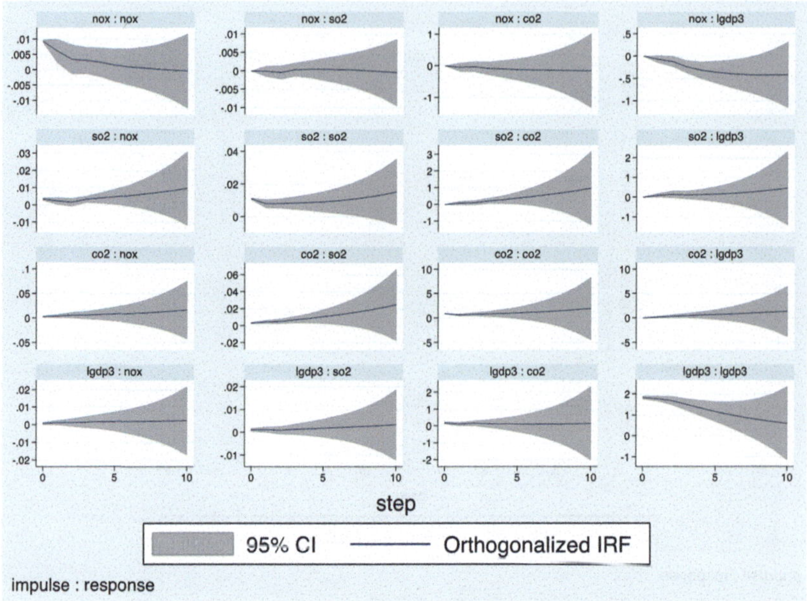

Fig. 12.3 Impulse Response Functions (IRFs) for per capita NO_X emissions (NO_X), per capita SO_2 emissions (SO_2), per capita CO_2 emissions (CO_2) and real cubed logged GDP per capita (lgdp3). Note: Each row of the diagram shows the response of each variable to a one standard deviation shock of the other variables entered in Panel-VAR. The ordering of the variables entered the panel-VAR is as follows: NO_X, SO_2, CO_2 and lGDP. In order to estimate the IRFs, we use the Cholesky decomposition method adjusted by the degrees of freedom. NOx stands for the NOx per capita emissions, SO_2 stands for the SO_2 per capita emissions, CO_2 stands for the CO_2 per capita emissions and $lgdp^3$ is the cubed logged real GDP per capita in constant 2009 USD dollar prices. Standard errors are 5% on each side generated by Monte-Carlo with 500 repetitions

important determinants of local pollutants as 63.5% and 57.7% of the forecast error variance of per capita NO_X emissions (NO_X) and per capita SO_2 emissions (SO_2) after ten years is explained by shocks in the CO_2 variable. Finally, disturbances in the growth variable (lgdp) appear to have minimal impact in forecasting error variance of the local pollutants (NO_X and SO_2) confirming the results of the fixed effects and dynamic panel analysis.

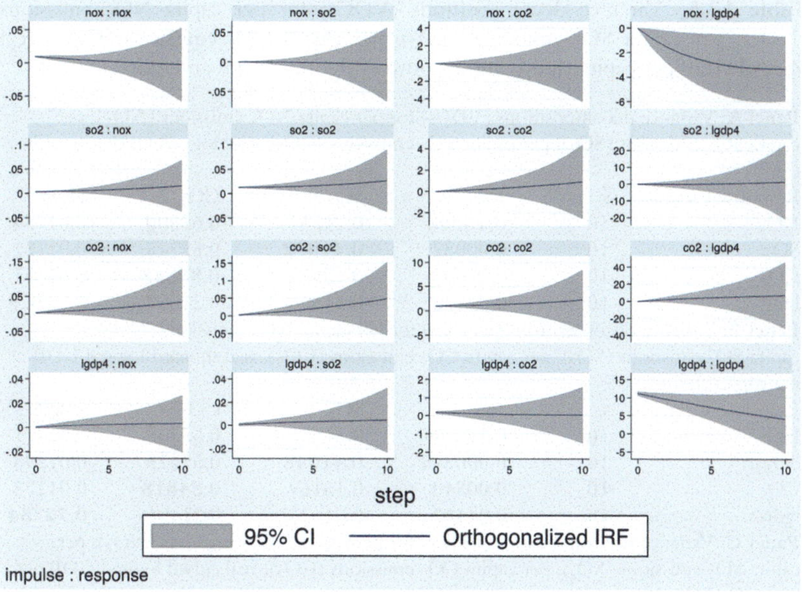

Fig. 12.4 Impulse Response Functions (IRFs) for per capita NO_X emissions (NO_X), per capita SO_2 emissions (SO_2), per capita CO_2 emissions (CO_2) and real quartic logged GDP per capita (lgdp4). Note: Each row of the diagram shows the response of each variable to a one standard deviation shock of the other variables entered in Panel-VAR. The ordering of the variables entered the panel-VAR is as follows: NO_X, SO_2, CO_2 and lGDP. In order to estimate the IRFs, we use the Cholesky decomposition method adjusted by the degrees of freedom. NOx stands for the NOx per capita emissions, SO_2 stands for the SO_2 per capita emissions, CO_2 stands for the CO_2 per capita emissions and $lgdp^4$ is the quartic logged real GDP per capita in constant 2009 USD dollar prices. Standard errors are 5% on each side generated by Monte-Carlo with 500 repetitions

Similar findings are provided in the other three Panel-VARs (see Panels B, C and D), where polynomial powers of real logged per capita GDP are taken into account. The most striking finding is the increased forecast error variance that exhibits the global pollutant (CO_2) in explaining many fraction of the response of the other local pollutants. More specifically, when the fourth power of per capita GDP enters the model (see

Table 12.5 Variance decompositions (VDCs) for per capita NO_X emissions (NO_X), per capita SO_2 emissions (SO_2), per capita CO_2 emissions (CO_2), real logged GDP per capita (lgdp) and its powers (lgdp2, lgdp3 and lgdp4)

Panel A: Variance decompositions (VDCs) for per capita NO_X emissions (NO_X), per capita SO_2 emissions (SO_2), per capita CO_2 emissions (CO_2), real logged GDP per capita (lgdp)					
Response variable	s	NO_X	SO_2	CO_2	Lgdp
NO_X	10	**0.13398**	0.21367	0.63500	0.01734
SO_2	10	0.00032	**0.41072**	0.57745	0.01151
CO_2	10	0.00892	0.12951	**0.85048**	0.01151
lgdp	10	0.04176	0.01596	0.21553	**0.72673**
Panel B: Variance decompositions (VDCs) for per capita NO_X emissions (NO_X), per capita SO_2 emissions (SO_2), per capita CO_2 emissions (CO_2), real squared logged GDP per capita (lgdp2)					
Response variable	s	NO_X	SO_2	CO_2	lgdp2
NO_X	10	**0.13178**	0.21553	0.63298	0.01971
SO_2	10	0.000345	**0.41048**	0.57625	0.01293
CO_2	10	0.00840	0.13169	**0.84818**	0.01173
lgdp2	10	0.04102	0.01623	0.21491	**0.72784**
Panel C: Variance decompositions (VDCs) for per capita NO_X emissions (NO_X), per capita SO_2 emissions (SO_2), per capita CO_2 emissions (CO_2), real cubed logged GDP per capita (lgdp3)					
Response variable	s	NO_X	SO_2	CO_2	lgdp3
NO_X	10	**0.12936**	0.21710	0.63159	0.02194
SO_2	10	0.00038	**0.40965**	0.57582	0.01415
CO_2	10	0.00785	0.13390	**0.84607**	0.01217
lgdp3	10	0.04068	0.01650	0.21362	**0.72919**
Panel D: Variance decompositions (VDCs) for per capita NO_X emissions (NO_X), per capita SO_2 emissions (SO_2), per capita CO_2 emissions (CO_2), real quartic logged GDP per capita (lgdp4)					
Response variable	s	NO_X	SO_2	CO_2	lgdp4
NO_X	10	**0.06258**	0.17161	0.75207	0.01373
SO_2	10	0.00298	**0.33645**	0.64957	0.01099
CO_2	10	0.00993	0.08019	**0.90518**	0.00468
lgdp4	10	0.06938	0.00196	0.20618	**0.72247**

Notes: s defines the periods ahead of VDCs. The numbers in bold of the main diagonal explain the forecast error variance of the variable to its own innovations. NO_x stands for the NO_x per capita emissions, SO_2 stands for the SO_2 per capita emissions, CO_2 stands for the CO_2 per capita emissions, lgdp is the real logged GDP per capita in constant 2009 USD dollar prices, lgdp2 is the squared real logged GDP per capita in constant 2009 USD dollar prices, lgdp3 is the cubed real logged GDP per capita in constant 2009 USD dollar prices and lgdp4 is the quartic real logged GDP per capita in constant 2009 USD dollar prices

Panel D), around 75% of the forecast error variance of per capita NO_X emissions (NO_X) after ten years is explained by shocks in the CO_2 variable. Similarly, 64.9% of the forecast error variance of per capita SO_2 emissions (SO_2) at the end of the simulated period can be explained by disturbances in the CO_2 variable. These results are in alignment with the (IRFs), presented above highlighting the importance of CO_2 emissions on the evolution of the other local pollutants and economic growth.

5 Concluding Remarks

In this chapter, we employ a panel data framework with general cross-sectional dependence. Our empirical application is based on a balanced panel of pollutants (CO_2, SO_2 and NOx emissions per capita) from the energy sector of 51 US regions covering the period 1990–2012.

From the econometric standpoint, we argue that the co-existence of global and local pollutants (CO_2 and NO_X, respectively) raises serious concerns to the policymakers in terms of the adoption of the suitable abatement policy scheme such as green taxes, tradable permits and voluntary schemes since environmental degradation is time invariant. Regarding NO_X emissions, we argue that one standard innovation of per capita GDP follows a slightly positive but stable statistically significant relationship until the first five years of the simulated period. Moreover, we find that in the short run the effect of growth on environmental degradation is strongly positive and reversed when the economy reaches its peak, indicating a non-linear relationship between economic growth and environmental pollution. This outcome lends support to the "*EKC hypothesis*", which is in alignment with other related studies (Millimet et al. 2003; Halkos and Tzeremes 2009; Apergis 2016).

These results could be important for policymakers and government officials. More specifically, they call for the need to strengthen the effectiveness of environmental degradation policies by ensuring sustainability of the electricity sector in order to drastically reduce emissions. Lastly, when interpreting our empirical findings, some limitations have to be taken into consideration. Although we used several polynomial powers of GDP to address the impact of growth on environmental degradation and test the EKC hypothesis, special attention should be given to the use of additional macroeconomic indicators (i.e. unemployment rate, debt/GDP ratio, level of the public deficit, etc.). Moreover, another alley for future research may be to include spatial or threshold aspects such as geographical proximity or terms of trade among the US states, in order to unveil possible state differences and the sources of these different patterns.

Finally, when interpreting our empirical findings, some limitations have to be taken into account. Although we used fourth order polynomials of logged GDP to examine the EKC hypothesis, special attention should be given to the use of additional macroeconomic indicators including inter alia as the level of unemployment, the debt/GDP ratio, the level of public deficit, and so on. These measures affect the causality driven by the inclusion of financial indicators and reduce the possibility of endogeneity bias between the sample variables. Another limitation is the small sample size due to data restrictions. To make valid inferences about the non-linear relationship between economic growth and pollution for the US, a much larger time span is needed, starting before the oil crises until recent years. Lastly, another alley for future research may be to include spatial aspects (i.e. proximity, terms of trade across states, etc.) in order to unmask possible regional differences and the sources of these different patterns.

Acknowledgments The author wishes to express his gratitude to the Organizational Committee of the 5th Environmental Economics and Natural Resources Conference (ENVECON) organized by the University of Thessaly, in Volos, Greece (November 1–3, 2018). Special thanks should be given to Professor George Halkos and the participants of the conference for their fruitful comments and suggestions that enhance the merit of the text. All remaining errors belong to the author. The usual disclaimer applies.

References

Apergis, N., Christou, C., and Gupta, R (2017). Are There Environmental Kuznets Curves for US State-Level CO2 Emissions?. *Renewable and Sustainable Energy Reviews*, 69, 551–558.

Apergis N. (2016). Environmental Kuznets Curves: New Evidence on Both Panel and Country Level CO2 Emissions. *Energy Economics*, 54, 263–271.

Arellano, M., and Bover, O. (1995). Another look at the instrumental variable estimation of error-components models. *Journal of Econometrics*, 68(1), 29–51.

Azevedo, V.G., Sartori, S., Campos, L. (2018). CO_2 Emissions: A Quantitative Analysis Among the BRICS Nations. *Renewable and Sustainable Energy Reviews*, 81, Part 1, 107–115.

Bertinelli, L., and Strobl, E. (2005). The Environmental Kuznets Curve semiparametrically revisited. *Economics Letters*, 88(3), 350–357.

Breitung, J., and Das, S. (2005). Panel unit root tests under cross-sectional dependence. *Statistica Neerlandica*, 59, 414–433.

Breusch, S. A., and Pagan, R. (1980). The Lagrange Multiplier Test and its Applications to Model Specification in Econometrics. *The Review of Economic Studies*, 47(1), 239–253.

Carson RT. (2010). The Environmental Kuznets Curve: Seeking Empirical Regularity and Theoretical Structure. *Review of Environmental Economic Policy*, 4, 3–23.

Cassou, S.P., and Hamilton, S.F., (2004). The Transition from Dirty to Clean Industries: Optimal Fiscal Policy and the Environmental Kuznets Curve. *Journal of Environmental Economics and Management*, 48(3), 1050–1077.

Chimeli, A.B., Braden, J.B. (2005). Total Factor Productivity and the Environmental Kuznets Curve. *Journal of Environmental Economics and Management*,49, 366–380.

Desbordes, R., Verardi, V., (2012). Refitting the Kuznets Curve. *Economics Letters*, 116, 258–261.

Enders, W., and Granger, C.W. J. (1998). Unit-Root Tests and Asymmetric Adjustment with an Example Using the Term Structure of Interest Rates. *Journal of Business and Economic Statistics*, 16, 304–312.

Enders, W., and Siklos, P. L. (2001). Cointegration and Threshold Adjustment. *Journal of Business and Economic Statistics*, 19, 166–177.

Figueroa E., and Pasten R. (2013). A Tale of Two Elasticities: A General Theoretical Framework for the Environmental Kuznets Curve Analysis. *Economics Letters*, 119 (1), 85–88.

Galeotti, M., Manera, M., Lanza, A. (2009). On the Robustness of Robustness Checks of the Environmental Kuznets Curve Hypothesis. *Environmental and Resource Economics*, 42, 551.

Gillanders R., and Whelan K (2014). *Open For Business? Institutions, Business Environment and Economic Development*. Kyklos, 67(4), 535–568.

Grossman G.M. and Krueger A.B. (1995). Economic Growth and the Environment. *Quarterly Journal of Economics*, 110(2), 353–377.

Halkos G. and Managi, S. (2017). Measuring the Effect of Economic Growth on Countries' Environmental Efficiency: A Conditional Directional Distance Function Approach. *Environmental and Resource Economics*, 68(3), 753–775.

Halkos, G. and Polemis, M. (2017). Does Financial Development Affect Environmental Degradation? Evidence from the OECD Countries, *Business Strategy and the Environment*, 26(8), 1162–1180.

Halkos G. and Polemis M. (2018). The Impact of Economic Growth on Environmental Efficiency of the Electricity Sector: A Hybrid Window DEA Methodology for the USA. *Journal of Environmental Management*, 211, 334–346.

Halkos, G. and Tzeremes, N. (2009). Exploring the Existence of Kuznets Curve in Countries' Environmental Efficiency Using DEA Window Analysis. *Ecological Economics*, 68(7), 2168–2176.

Hong, S. H. and Wagner, M. (2008). Nonlinear Cointegration Analysis and The Environmental Kuznets Curve. Institute for Advanced Studies, Economics Series No. 224.

Hsueh L. (2015). Regulatory Effectiveness and the Long-run Policy Horizon: The Case of U.S. Toxic Chemical Use. *Environmental Science and Policy*, 52, 6–22.

López Menéndez, A.J., Perez, R. and Moreno, B. (2014). Environmental Costs and Renewable Energy: Re-visiting the Environmental Kuznets Curve. *Journal of Environmental Management*, 145, 368–373.

Lütkepohl, H. (2006). Structural Vector Autoregressive Analysis for Cointegrated Variables, Springer Books. In Olaf Hübler & Jachim Frohn (eds.), *Modern Econometric Analysis*, 6, 73–86, Springer.

Millimet D., List J. and Stengos T., (2003). The Environmental Kuznets Curve: Real Progress or Misspecified Models?. *The Review of Economics and Statistics*, 85(4), 1038–1047.

Zambrano-Monserrate, M.A., Silva-Zambrano, C., Davalos-Penafiel J., Zambrano-Monserrate, A., Ruano, M.A. (2018). Testing Environmental Kuznets Curve Hypothesis in Peru: The Role of Renewable Electricity, Petroleum and Dry Natural Gas, *Renewable and Sustainable Energy Reviews*, 82 (Part 3), 4170–4178.

Narayan P.K. and Narayan S. (2010). Carbon Dioxide Emissions and Economic Growth: Panel Data Evidence from Developing Countries, *Energy Policy*, 38(1), 661–666.

Özokcu, S., Özdemir, O. (2017). Economic Growth, Energy, and Environmental Kuznets Curve. *Renewable and Sustainable Energy Reviews*, 72, 639–647.

Ozturk I. and Acaravci A. (2013). The Long-Run and Causal Analysis of Energy, Growth, Openness and Financial Development on Carbon Emissions in Turkey. *Energy Economics*, 36(C), 262– 267.

Pedroni, P. (1999). Critical Values for Cointegration Tests in Heterogeneous Panels with Multiple Regressors. *Oxford Bulletin of Economics and Statistics*, 61, 653–670.

Pesaran, M. H. (2006). Estimation and Inference in Large Heterogeneous Panels with a Multifactor Error Structure. *Econometrica*, 74(4), 967–1012.

Pesaran, M. H. (2007). A simple panel unit root test in the presence of cross-section dependence, *Journal of Applied Econometrics*, 22(2), 265–312.

Polemis, M., and Stengos, T. (2018a). Taming the SO_2 and NO_x Emissions: Evidence from a SUR Model for the US. In Michael Polemis and Thanasis Stengos, *Letters in Spatial and Resource Sciences*. https://doi.org/10.1007/s12076-018-0203-8.

Polemis, M. and Stengos, T. (2018b). Does Competition Prevent Industrial Pollution? Evidence from a Panel Threshold Model, *Business Strategy and the Environment*, 1–13. https://doi.org/10.1002/bse.2212.

Polemis, M., (2017a). Capturing the Impact of Shocks on the Electricity Sector Performance in the OECD. *Energy Economics* 66, 99–107.

Polemis, M., (2017b). Revisiting the Environmental Kuznets Curve: A Semi-Parametric Analysis on the Role of Market Structure on Environmental Pollution, *Letters in Spatial and Resource Sciences.* https://doi.org/10.1007/s12076-017-0195-9.

Rasli, A.M., Qureshi, M.I., Chikaji, A.I., Zaman, K., Ahmad, M. (2018). New Toxics, Race to the Bottom and Revised Environmental Kuznets Curve: The Case of Local and Global Pollutants, *Renewable and Sustainable Energy Reviews*, 81(Part 2), 3120–3130.

Sephton, P. and Mann J. (2016). Compelling Evidence of an Environmental Kuznets Curve in the United Kingdom. *Environmental and Resource Economics*, 64(2), 301–315.

Smulders, S., Bretschger, L. and Egli, H. (2011). Economic Growth and the Diffusion of Clean Technologies: Explaining Environmental Kuznets Curves. *Environmental and Resource Economics*, 49(1), 79–99.

Taskin, F. and Zaim, O. (2000). Searching for a Kuznets curve in environmental efficiency using kernel estimation. *Economics Letters*, 68, 217–223.

Westerlund, J., (2007). Testing for Error Correction in Panel Data. *Oxford Bulletin of Economics and Statistics,* 69, 709–748.

CHAPTER 13

International Expansion Strategies: Developing Some Research Propositions on the Scope and Speed of the Path of Internationalization

Marina Kyriakou and Markos Tsogas

1 Introduction

The selection of a suitable expansion strategy is the most crucial decision a company takes during the process of internationalization (Cavusgil and Zou 1994). Two critical questions have to be answered in order for an expansion strategy to be designed: (a) Will entry be concentrated or diversified across international markets? and (b) Will entry be incrementally or simultaneously to various markets? (Hollensen 2011). Although these strategies have been studied in pairs in the past, no evidence has been found supporting their strategic consideration as a set.

The main objective of this study is to investigate the evaluation of these strategies by marketing managers, during their strategic selection of

M. Kyriakou (✉) • M. Tsogas
Department of Business Administration, University of Piraeus, Piraeus, Greece
e-mail: mtsogas@unipi.gr

I. T. Kokores et al. (eds.), *Money, Trade and Finance*,
https://doi.org/10.1007/978-3-030-73219-6_13

international markets. We examine whether marketing managers make concurrent decisions about the number of countries and the speed of international expansion, that is, selecting between one of the four targeting strategies which emerge by this combination.

An extensive list of items, grounded in literature and related to company, product, technology, market, and competition characteristics (Katsikeas and Leonidou 1996; Kalish et al. 1995) act as antecedents of such options, and can be used in order to explain and predict successfully the reported adopted strategy. Although these items have been previously examined as antecedents of each strategic dilemma (Katsikeas and Leonidou 1996; Katsikea et al. 2005; Kalish et al. 1995), in this study we attempt to contribute to the literature by suggesting the investigation of their explanatory power for the complete set of options, as derived by the combinations of strategic alternatives. In addition, while a number of studies have investigated the relationship between the adopted market expansion strategy and company's international performance (Cieślik et al. 2012), emphasis was placed only on the number of markets entered, partially ignoring the speed of internationalization. The chapter is structured around a novel but solid conceptual framework, which is grounded on a brief literature review and encompasses all facets of the decision-making dilemmas. At the end, the relevant research prepositions are formed and presented, in order to guide the future researcher in his or her efforts to empirically validate the proposed model.

2 Typology Dimensions

During a company's internalization process, the market selection stage is followed by the selection of the expansion strategy (Hollensen 2011). In particular, it is supported that a company has to take two major decisions in order to design its expansion strategy to international markets. The first one is related to the number of international markets the company targets, whereas the second is associated with the time frame of internationalization.

The first dimension, which is related to the number of international markets, identifies two alternatives along a concentration–diversification continuum (Ayal and Zif 1979; Katsikeas and Leonidou 1996; Katsikea et al. 2003). Companies following a strategy closely to the one end, focus their efforts and resources on few, carefully chosen, foreign markets. In contrast, companies which adopt the strategy at the other end of the spectrum, disperse efforts and resources in as many as possible foreign markets.

At the same time, companies have to decide along a timing dimension from incremental to simultaneous entry. These strategies have been named "waterfall" and "sprinkler / shower", respectively (Kalish et al. 1995). In the first option, the company chooses to enter all foreign markets gradually, while in the second case the company chooses to enter the same number of market, simultaneously (Keegan and Green 2000).

2.1 Expansion Strategy Based on the Number of New Markets

The selection between a wider diversification or a concentration on core foreign markets has been the object of study in numerous empirical papers (for a recent review see Cieślik et al. 2012). The aforementioned deliberation is referred in the literature as "the concentration versus spreading debate" (Crick and Jones 2000; Katsikea et al. 2003; Cieślik et al. 2012). Trying to conclude upon normative guidelines, researchers investigated the relationship between the expansion strategy and a company's performance but evidence is still broadly inconclusive (Ayal and Zif 1979; Cooper and Kleinschmidt 1985; Fenwick and Amine 1979; Piercy 1981; Tessler 1977; Leonidou et al. 2010).

More specifically, several studies propose the adoption of a market concentration strategy, arguing that the fewer the markets that an export company focuses, the higher the realized market share (Tessler 1977; Tookey 1975). Evidently, this strategy seems to enhance the company's profitability in the long term, as it is positively correlated to sales increases (Leonidou et al. 2002). In contrast, the implementation of the market spreading strategy, whereas a less risky alternative with lower overall sales volume, achieves a similar performance result through claiming a relatively lower market share, but on a much larger number of disparate foreign markets (Hammermesh et al. 1978; Hirsch and Lev 1973; Lee and Yang 1990; Katsikea et al. 2003; Lages et al. 2006; Lu and Beamish 2006; Pangarkar 2008).

Although it is not possible to conclude on the superiority of one strategy over the other, there are specific and well-defined reasons why companies follow a particular approach to their expansion in foreign markets (Piercy 1982). Mostly market and company-specific characteristics determine to a large extent the nature of the focal strategy (Ayal and Zif 1979; Fenwick and Amine 1979; Piercy 1982). These characteristics presented in Table 13.1 are clear antecedents of the strategic dilemma and in no case performance or success criteria.

Table 13.1 Antecedents of diversification versus market concentration strategies

International market diversification versus market concentration	
Factors favoring country diversification	*Factors favoring country concentration*
Company factors	
High management risk consciousness (accept risk)	Low management risk consciousness (risk-averse)
Objective of growth through market development	Objective of growth through market penetration
Little market knowledge	Ability to pick "best" markets
Product factors	
Limited specialist uses	General uses
Low volume	High volume
Nonrepeat	Repeat-purchase product
Early or late in product life cycle	Middle of product life cycle
Standard product saleable in many markets	Product requires adaptation to different markets
Radical innovation can trigger new global customer solutions	Incremental innovation—narrow market scope
Market factors	
Small markets—specialized segments	Large markets—high-volume segments
Unstable markets	Stable markets
Many similar markets	Limited number of markets
New or declining markets	Mature markets
Low growth rate in each market	High growth rate in each market
Large markets are very competitive	Large markets are not excessively competitive
Established competitors have large share of key markets	Key markets are divided among many competitors
Low customer loyalty	High customer loyalty
High synergy effects between countries	Low synergy effect between countries
Learning can be transferred across markets	Lack of awareness of global opportunities and threats
Short competitive lead time	Long competitive lead time
Marketing factors	
Low communication costs for additional markets	High communication costs for additional markets
Low order-handling costs for additional markets	High order-handling costs for additional markets
Low physical distribution costs for additional markets	High physical distribution costs for additional markets

(*continued*)

Table 13.1 (continued)

International market diversification versus market concentration	
Factors favoring country diversification	*Factors favoring country concentration*
Standardized communication in many markets	Communication requires adaptation to different markets

Source: Ayal and Zif (1979), Piercy (1981), Da Rocha et al. (1990), Katsikeas and Leonidou (1996), Barkema and Vermeulen (1998), and Albaum et al. (2002), Katsikea et al. (2005), and Hollensen (2011)

However, large multinational companies have adopted a dual strategy using both expansion paths simultaneously (Aspelund et al. 2007; Crick and Jones 2000; Morgan-Thomas and Jones 2009), developing thus ambidextrous capabilities. Ambidexterity provides the global firm with the opportunity to deploy an exploratory and innovative new market strategy, milking at the same time its presence in a variety of international markets (March 1991; Barkema and Drogendijk 2007; Cellard and Prange 2008).

2.2 Expansion Strategy Based on Time Frame of Internationalization

The traditional internationalization models place emphasis to an incremental learning process which favors gradual expansion into international markets, initiating firms entry into psychic close and usually neighboring markets (Eriksson et al. 1997; Johanson and Vahlne 1977). More recently, the development of the strategic paradigm and approach, added into the modeling efforts, variables of the competitive environment of the firm and variables relating to the totality of its resources and placed them as the main reasons explaining the adoption of a waterfall or sprinkler approach (Sleuwaegen and Onkelinx 2014). The former is associated with a small initial investment and the gradual penetration into new international markets, allowing thus the firm to reap the benefits from the lead and spillover effects. The latter entails the simultaneous entrance to a considerable number of foreign markets with a systematic way, conquering thus a prominent competitive position in the global market place (Kalish et al. 1995; Keegan and Green 2000).

The traditional approach has been challenged by new models of international businesses, like the born-global firm and the globally savvy ones (Chetty and Campbell-Hunt 2004; Knight and Cavusgil 2004; Preece et al. 1999). In addition, a company's desire to have a large dispersion of international markets stems from the need to ensure the further development and exploitation of critical resources, like patents or brand names (Knight et al. 2004; Madsen and Servais 1997; Oviatt and McDougall 1994, 1995).

According to Kalish et al.'s (1995) theoretical framework about the introduction of a new product into global markets, an effort is made to (a) investigate the optimal timing and scope (number of countries) of new product introduction and (b) identify alternative strategies to maximize profits. In such an occasion, companies are able to select the most suitable expansion strategy, taking into consideration environmental factors of the industrial sector they operate in, the domestic and foreign markets' conditions, and of course the cost of entry to foreign markets.

After taking into account the trade-off which is interwoven into the nature of international expansion strategic decision making, that is, the trade-off between the maximization of internationalization revenues and the minimization of expansion risks (Stremersch and Tellis 2004), the current study adopts and adapts the work of Kalish et al. (1995), as a suitable research framework (Table 13.2).

Table 13.2 Antecedents of waterfall versus sprinkler strategies

Market conditions favoring waterfall over sprinkler strategy
Conditions favoring waterfall strategies
1. Very long life cycle of the product
2. Nonfavorable conditions in the foreign market
2a. Small foreign market (vs. home market)
2b. Slow growth in the foreign market (vs. home market)
2c. Low innovativeness in the foreign market
2d. High fixed cost of entry into the foreign market
3. 3. Weak competitiveness of the foreign market
3a. Very weak competitors in the foreign market
3b. Cooperative behavior among competitors
3c. No competitors in the foreign market

Source: Kalish et al. (1995)

3 Typology Framework and Conceptual Model

The literature provides seminal efforts in developing typologies of internationalization strategies, which thought focus either on the time dimension of expansion (e.g. Kuivalainen et al. 2012; Vissak and Masso 2015; Oviatt and McDougall 1994) or at the number of markets penetrated or targeted (Rugman and Verbeke 2004). The authors have failed to pinpoint published research that investigates concurrent decision-making along the dimensions of time and number of markets entered.

3.1 Typology Framework

Following the stream of previous research which identifies two separate strategies for the number of foreign markets (concentration vs. diversification) and two similarly separate strategies for the timing of entry (waterfall vs. sprinkler), it is evident that the combination of these produces for distinctive strategic options among which companies can select. Therefore, companies can either (a) focus resources on few international markets, in which they expand gradually, or (b) diversify efforts and resources among many markets in which again choose to expand incrementally. In addition, firms can (c) either expand in many global markets simultaneously, a strategy that requires the deployment of the greatest amount of resources, or (d) expand at the same time but to a limited number of carefully chosen markets.

The strategic expansion options in this chapter are conceptualized, for the first time, along a continuum of varying degrees of involvement. This is achieved through the measurement approach of the firms' adopted strategy and by the construction of a latent formative variable which is comprised by the two distinct options of expansion (Hollensen 2011; Katsikea et al. 2005; Kalish et al. 1995). The use of a more complex construct, which depicts the adopted strategy, necessitates the reshuffling of the proposed in the literature antecedent variables. The resulting constructs are thus formed by items which have previously been used for the modeling of either the degree of diversification or the speed of expansion are deployed concurrently in one model for the first time (Fig. 13.1).

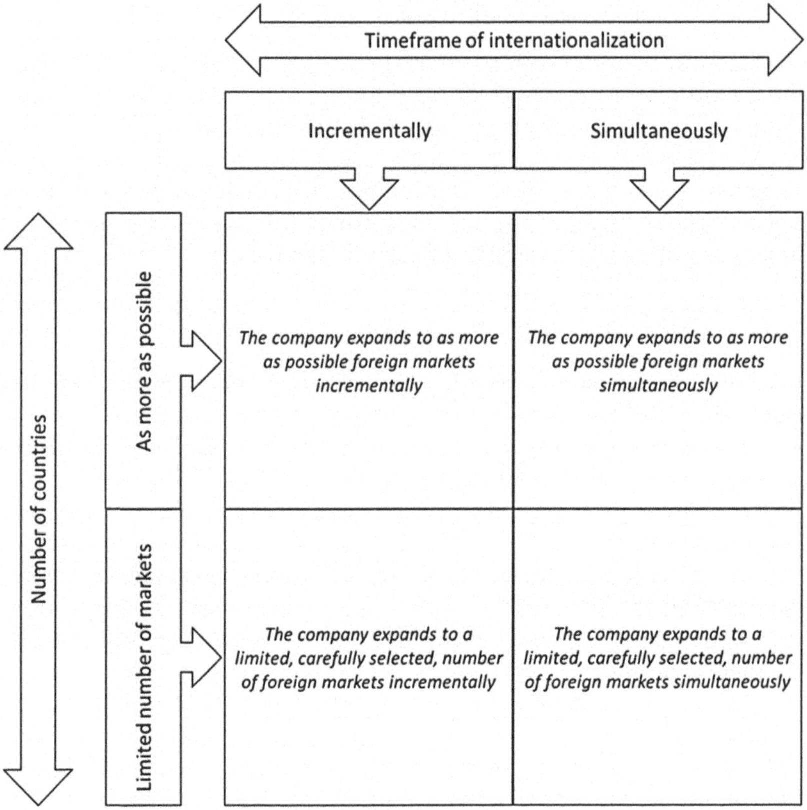

Fig. 13.1 Typology framework

3.2 *Conceptual Model*

Based on the existing literature, the authors conceptualize the expansion strategies, which arise from the above typology, to the following proposed model including antecedents and consequences (Fig. 13.2).

Having combined the two main decisions for international expansion strategy into a coherent framework, it is apparent that their antecedents should also be merged. Following a careful review of the literature, it became evident that the argument of Bell, Crick, and Young (1998) still holds true. Indeed, the nature and the pace of internationalization is conditioned by (a) company-specific factors as well as (b) variables of the

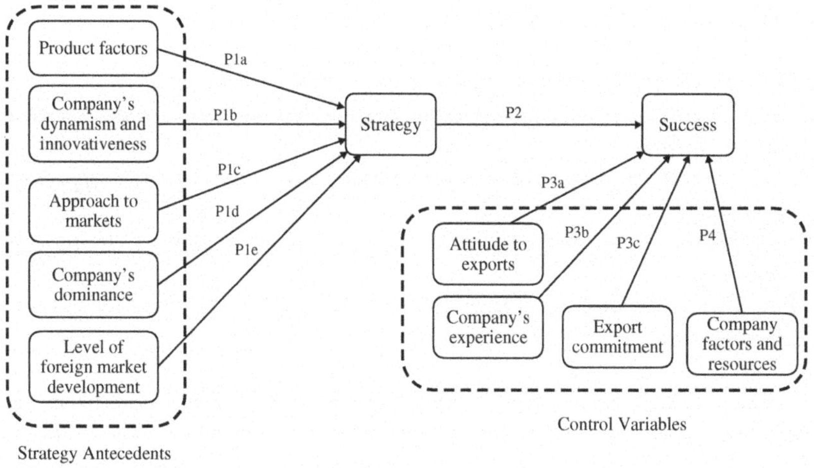

Fig. 13.2 Conceptual model

external, global environment. More specifically, firm characteristics, export marketing efforts, and export-related perception variables were viewed as potentially important discriminating factors between the strategic alternatives (Katsikeas and Leonidou 1996). Katsikea et al. (2005) presented the discriminating variables grouped in factors related to the approach to market, the export organization, the market information processing, and product factors, in order to predict the number of international markets a firm decides to enter. In addition, in a study about the time frame of internationalization, Kalish et al. (1995) showed that firms should either choose rapid expansion or slowly expand, depending on the industry environment in domestic and foreign countries (e.g. demand, growth, number of competitors) and the cost of entering foreign markets (Sleuwaegen and Onkelinx 2014).

Following Leonidou et al.'s (2010) study inducing to investigate simultaneously the various dilemmas export managers are facing, by focusing on issues relating to the market, the product, and the competitive environment, the present study proposes five antecedent constructs that capture all of the proposed variables. In particular, market issues are covered by "Level of foreign market development", product issues by "Product factors" and "Company's Dynamism & Innovativeness", and issues of competition by the construct "Company's Dominance".

Thus, we develop the following prepositions:

P1 a: Market expansion strategy is determined by product factors.
P1 b: Market expansion strategy is determined by company's dynamism and innovativeness.
P1 c: Market expansion strategy is determined by company's approach to markets.
P1 d: Market expansion strategy is determined by company's strength of dominance.
P1 e: Market expansion strategy is determined by level of foreign market development.

In accordance to previous studies (Katsikea et al. 2003; Cieślik et al. 2012), a construct of internationalization success or performance of international activities acts as the main dependent variable, providing evidence on the successful deployment of the selected internationalization strategy. Performance in this instance is conceptualized as a formative construct of two items, that is, (a) degree at which the internationalization path provides results better than anticipated (Crick and Jones 2000) and (b) degree to which the international operations perform better than the domestic ones. These measures of export performance were preferred to the single variable called export intensity (i.e. export sales as a percent of total corporate sales) because of Reid's detailed discussion (Cooper and Kleinschmidt 1985). Therefore, the following proposition is formed:

P2: The adopted strategy is positively associated with the company's export success.

In an effort to clearly distinguish the effect of the adopted strategy on export performance, a number of control variables were introduced in the model. The variables are well established in the literature as antecedents of export success (for extensive reviews, see Aaby and Slater 1989; Zou and Stan 1998; Sousa et al. 2008; Chen et al. 2016), and include the following: firm's experience in global markets (measured as a two-item formative construct, including (a) years of international presence and (b) number of foreign markets covered), firm's involvement in exports (measured as the percentage of revenue from global markets to the total corporate turnover), firm's attitude to exports (measured as a two-item reflective construct, including (a) the view of the foreign markets as a long-standing strategic goal and (b) the view of the foreign markets as a significantly greater challenge to the domestic), and firm's deployed resources (measured as a three-item formative construct, including (a) number of employees in the international department, (b) corporate turnover, and (c) corporate profits.

Therefore, the following prepositions are formed:

P3a: Firm's experience is positively associated with the company's success.
P3b: Firm's involvement in foreign markets is positively associated with the company's success.
P3c: Firm's attitude to exports is positively associated with the company's success.
P3d: Firm's resources are positively associated with the company's success.

4 Discussion

Given the complexity of the decisions managers take regarding the expansion to international markets, this study contribute to the existing knowledge offering theoretical and managerial implications. Especially, this study offers a new typology of international expansion strategies based on the number of foreign markets and the time horizon of further internationalization, simultaneously.

These strategies are determined by a number of factors related to the product, the characteristics of the exporting firm, the international market environment, and so on, as has already been well documented in the existing literature.

Since this study constitutes a novel attempt to (a) develop a complex typology of strategies and (b) relate these strategies with their antecedents and consequences, this work represents a significant contribution to the further development of the international expansion field. Academics and researchers could use this complex typology to their studies in the international marketing field. Moreover, this study has implications for business practitioners. Managers could take under consideration not only the strategies' classification, but also their antecedents and consequences during their expansion decisions for the selection of the most appropriate strategy and, finally, the strategy's implementation.

The typology suggests that a number of factors affect managers' view and approach to the international expansion. Therefore, testing of this typology should be assumed in order to provide the empirical basis for a taxonomical foundation of international strategic expansion. Empirical testing should examine whether product's factors, firm's dynamism and innovativeness, firm's approach to markets, firm's strength of dominance, and level of foreign market development are associated with the selected strategy.

References

Albaum, G., Jesper S., and Edwin D., (2002). *Inter-National Marketing and Export Management*. Wokingham, UK: Addison-Wesley.

Aspelund, A., Madsen, T.K. & Moen, O., (2007). A Review of the Foundation, International Marketing Strategies, and Performance of International New Ventures. *European Journal of Marketing*, 41(11/12), 1423–1448.

Ayal, I. & Zif, J., (1979). Market Expansion Strategies in Multinational Marketing. *Journal of Marketing*, 43 (Spring), 84–94.

Barkema, H.G. and Drogendijk, R., (2007). Internationalising in Small, Incremental or Larger Steps?. *Journal of International Business Studies*, 38(7), pp.1132-1148.

Barkema, H.G. and Vermeulen, F., (1998). International Expansion Through Start-Up or Acquisition: A Learning Perspective. *Academy of Management Journal*, 41(1), pp.7–26.

Bell, J., Crick, D., & Young, S. (1998, April). A holistic perspective on small firm growth and internationalisation. In Academy of International Business Conference, City University Business School.

Cavusgil, S.T. & Zou, S., (1994). Marketing Strategy-Performance Relationship: An Investigation of the Empirical Link in Export Market Ventures. *The Journal of Marketing*, 1-21.

Cellard, S. and Prange, C., (2008). How Do Age and Speed of Internationalization Affect Foreign Growth. *In Academy of Management Conference*, Anaheim.

Chetty, S. & Campbell-Hunt, C., (2004). A Strategic Approach to Internationalization: A Traditional Versus a "Born-Global" Approach. *Journal of International Marketing*, 12(1), 57-81.

Cieślik, J., Kaciak, E. & Welsh, D. H. B., (2012). The Impact of Geographic Diversification on Export Entrepreneurship. Online First, 11 February 2012, 1–24.

Cooper, R. G. & Kleinschmidt, E. J., (1985). The Impact of Export Strategy on Export Sales Performance. *Journal of International Business Studies*, 37–55.

Crick, D. & Jones, M.V., (2000). Small High-Technology Firms and International High-Technology Markets. *Journal of International Marketing*, 8(2), 63–85.

Da Rocha, A., Christensen, C.H. and Eduardo da Cunha, C., (1990). Aggressive and Passive Exporters: A Study in the Brazilian Furniture Industry. *International Marketing Review*, 7(5).

Eriksson, K., Johanson, J., Majkgard, A. & Sharma, D. D., (1997). Experiential Knowledge and Cost in the Internationalization Process. *Journal of International Business Studies*, 337–360.

Fenwick, I. & Amine, L., (1979). Export Performance and Export Policy: Evidence from the UK Clothing Industry. *Journal of the Operational Research Society*, 30 (8), 747–54.

Hammermesh, R.G., Anderson, M.J. & Harris, J.E. (1978). Strategies for Low Market Share Business. *Harvard Business Review*, 56 (May–June), 95–102.

Hirsch, S., Lev, B., (1973). Foreign Marketing Strategies. *Management International Review*, 13, 81–90.

Hollensen, S., (2011). *Global Marketing: A Decision-Oriented Approach* (5th Edition). Prentice Hall.

Jieke Chen, Carlos M.P. Sousa, Xinming He, (2016) The Determinants of Export Performance: A Review of the Literature 2006–2014. *International Marketing Review*, Vol. 33 Issue: 5, pp.626–670.

Johanson, J. & Vahlne, J.E., (1977). The Internationalization Process of the Firm: A Model of Knowledge Development and Increasing Foreign Market Commitment. *Journal of International Business Studies*, 8(1).

Kalish, S., Mahajan, V. & Muller, E., (1995). Waterfall and Sprinkler New-Product Strategies in Competitive Global Markets. *International Journal of Research in Marketing*, 12 (2), 105–119.

Katsikea, E. S., Papavassiliou, N., Theodosiou, M. & Morgan, R. E., (2005). Export Market Expansion Strategies of Direct-Selling Small and Medium-sized Firms: Implications for Export Sales Management Activities. *Journal of International Marketing*, 13(2), 57–92.

Katsikeas, C. S., & Leonidou, L. C., (1996). Export Market Expansion Strategy: Differences Between Market Concentration and Market Spreading. *Journal of Marketing Management*, 12(1–3), 113–134.

Keegan, W. and Green, M. (2000). *Global Marketing*, 2nd ed.. Electronically Reproduced by Permission of Pearson Education, Inc., Upper Saddle River, New Jersey.

Knight, G. A. & Cavusgil, S. T., (2004). Innovation, Organizational Capabilities, and the Born-Global Firm. *Journal of International Business Studies*, 35(2), 124–141.

Knight, G., Madsen, T.K. & Servais, P., (2004). An Inquiry into Born-Global Firms in Europe and the USA. *International Marketing Review*, 21 (6), 645–665.

Kuivalainen, O., Saarenketo, S. and Puumalainen, K., (2012). Start-Up Patterns of Internationalization: A Framework and its Application in the Context of Knowledge-Intensive SMEs. *European Management Journal*, 30(4), pp.372–385.

Lages, L.F., Lages, C. & Lages, C.R., (2006). Main Consequences of Prior Export Performance Results: An Exploratory Study of European Exporters. *Journal of Euromarketing*, 15(4), 57–75.

Lee, Chong S. & Yoo S. Yang, (1990). Impact of Export Market Expansion Strategy on Export Performance. *International Marketing Review*, 7 (4), 41–51.

Leonidou, L.C., Katsikeas, C.S. & Samiee, S., (2002). Marketing Strategy Determinants of Export Performance: A Meta-Analysis. *Journal of Business Research*, 55(1), 51–67.

Leonidou, L. C., Katsikeas, C. S., & Coudounaris, D. N., (2010). Five Decades of Business Research into Exporting: A Bibliographic Analysis. *Journal of International Management*, 16(1), 78–91.

Lu, J.W. & Beamish, P.W., (2006). SME Internationalization and Performance: Growth vs. Profitability. *Journal of International Enterprise*, 4(1),27–48.

Madsen, T.K. & Servais, P., (1997). The Internationalization of Born Globals: An Evolutionary Process. *International Business Review*, 6, 561–583.

March, J.G., (1991). Exploration and Exploitation in Organizational Learning. *Organization Science,* 2(1), pp.71–87.

Morgan-Thomas, A. and Jones, M.V., (2009). Post-Entry Internationalization Dynamics Differences Between SMEs in the Development Speed of their International Sales. *International Small Business Journal*, 27(1), pp.71–97.

Nils-Erik Aaby, Stanley F. Slater, (1989). Management Influences on Export Performance: A Review of the Empirical Literature 1978–1988. *International Marketing Review*, Vol. 6 Issue: 4.

Oviatt, B.M. & McDougall, P.P., (1994). Toward a Theory of International New Ventures. *Journal of International Business Studies*, 25(1), 45–62.

Oviatt, B.M. & McDougall, P.P., (1995). Global Start-Ups: Entrepreneurs on a Worldwide Stage. *Academy of Management Executive*, 9 (2), 30–43.

Pangarkar, N., (2008). Internationalization and Performance of Small and Medium-Sized Enterprises. *Journal of World Business*, 43(4), 475–485.

Piercy, N.F., (1981). Export strategy: Concentration on Key Markets vs Market Spreading. *Journal of International Marketing*, 1(1):56– 67.

Piercy, N.F., (1982). *Export Strategy: Markets and Competition.* George Allen and Irwin, London.

Preece, S. B., Miles, G., & Baetz, M. C., (1999). Explaining the International Intensity and Global Diversity of Early-Stage Technology-Based Firms. *Journal of Business Venturing*, 14(3), 259–281.

Rugman, A.M. and Verbeke, A., (2004). A Perspective on Regional and Global Strategies of Multinational Enterprises. *Journal of International Business Studies*, 35(1), pp.3–18.

Shaoming Zou, Simona Stan, (1998) The Determinants of Export Performance: A Review of the Empirical Literature Between 1987 and 1997. *International Marketing Review*, Vol. 15 Issue: 5, pp.333–356.

Sleuwaegen, L. and Onkelinx, J., (2014). International Commitment, Post-Entry Growth and Survival of International New Ventures. *Journal of Business Venturing*, 29(1), pp.106–120.

Sousa, C. M., Martínez-López, F. J., & Coelho, F. (2008). The Determinants of Export Performance: A Review of the Research in the Literature Between 1998 and 2005. *International Journal of Management Reviews*, 10(4), 343–374.

Stremersch, S., Tellis, G.J., (2004). Understanding and Managing International Growth of New Products. *International Journal of Research in Marketing* 21, 421–438 (Marketing Science, 22(2): 188–208).

Tessler, A. (1977). Alternative Strategies and the Key Market Principle. Paper presented at a conference sponsored by the London Chamber of Commerce and the Institute of Export, Graham and Trotman Ltd.

Tookey, D. (1975). *Export Marketing Decisions*. London: Penguin Venturing, 28 (2), 316–334.

Vissak, T. and Masso, J., (2015). Export Patterns: Typology Development and Application to Estonian Data. *International Business Review*, 24(4), 652–664.

Index[1]

[1] Note: Page numbers followed by 'n' refer to notes.

I. T. Kokores et al. (eds.), *Money, Trade and Finance*,
https://doi.org/10.1007/978-3-030-73219-6

The manufacturer's authorised representative in the EU is Springer Nature Customer Service Centre GmbH, Europaplatz 3, 69115 Heidelberg, Germany. If you have any concerns regarding our products, please contact ProductSafety@springernature.com

Printed and bound by CPI Group (UK) Ltd, Croydon, CR0 4YY
30/09/2026
02225456-0007